CNE 3

Resource Library

Volume 3

Doug Archell
Dorothy Cady
Peter Kuo
Deborah Niedermiller-Chaffins

New Riders Publishing, Indianapolis, IN

CNE 3 Resource Library, Volume Three

By Doug Archell, Dorothy Cady, Peter Kuo, and Deborah Niedermiller-Chaffins

Published by:
New Riders Publishing
201 West 103rd Street
Indianapolis, IN 46290 USA

Printed in the United States of America 1 2 3 4 5 6 7 8 9 0

Library of Congress Cataloging-in-Publication Data

CIP data available upon request

Warning and Disclaimer

This book is designed to provide information about the NetWare network operating system. Every effort has been made to make this book as complete and as accurate as possible, but no warranty or fitness is implied.

The information is provided on an as is basis. The author(s) and New Riders Publishing shall have neither liability nor responsibility to any person or entity with respect to any loss or damages arising from the information contained in this book or from the use of the disks or programs that may accompany it.

Publisher	Don Fowley
Publishing Manager	Emmett Dulaney
Marketing Manager	Mary Foote
Managing Editor	Carla Hall

About the Authors

Doug Archell is President of DJA Systems, a network consulting and publishing company located just east of Toronto, Ontario. With extensive experience in the field working with some of the loargest companies in Canada, his area of expertise is network and user management issues. As a Certified NetWare Administrator, Certified NetWare engineer, and Master Certified NetWare Engineer, Doug has assisted many others with their networking problems through various electronic messaging systems, such as CompuServe NetWire, where he is a SysOp. doug writes regulary for NetWare Connection magazine and has also worked on various book projects, such as *NetWare Unleashed, Using NetWare 3.12 Special Edition, NetWare 4.1 Survival Guide,* and *NetWare 3.12 system Administrators Reference.*

Most recently, Doug is the publisher of a free newsletter called NetNotify, a bi-weekly publication to keep users up-to-date about industry promotions, new patches and fixes being released, and much more. Doug can be contacted via e-mail at 70751.767@compuserver.com or darchell@netcent.com.

Dorothy L. Cady is a freelance writer and Certified Novell Instructor. She has made more than 23 years of experience in the computer industry, in both the public and private secotrs. Her background includes experience as a NetWare network administrator for the Federal Aviation Adminsitration, as a computer specialist for Utah State Tax Commission, and as a systems and prcdures analyst/writer for several small businesses and large U.S. corporations. In addition, her background includes five years with Novell, Inc., during which time she worked on the software documentation testing and/or technical writing teams for Novell's NetWare Lite, Personal neWare, DR DOS 6.0, Novell DOS 7, NeWare 2.2, Netware 3.*x*, NetWare 4, and other Novel products.

Ms. Cady, also holds a CNE (Certified Novell Engineer), a Master CNE, and two CNAs (Certified Novell Administrator—NetWare 3 and Netware 4.) In addition, she is certified to teach community college and university computer science courses for the statae of Arizona, and teaches certified Novell NetWare couses for Training Solutions, an Arizona-based NAEC.

Ms. Cady has written several books for New Riders Publishing, including *Designing and Implementing NetWare 4 Networks, CNA Study Guide, New Riders' Guide to NetWare Certification,* and *Inside Personal NetWare.* In addition, Ms. Cady has coauthored several other New Riders' publications. She is also the author of *Bulletproof Documentation: Creating Quality Through Testing.*

Peter Kuo, Ph.D., is the president of DreamLAN Network Consulting, a Toronto-based firm specializing in connectivity and network management. Peter is the first Canadian Enterprise Certified NetWare Engineer and a Certified Novell Instructor. His areas of expertise include advanced NetWare topics, such as network management, IBM, and Unix connectivity issues. Peter is a SysOp on NetWire (CompuServe), supporting many advanced sections for Novell, such as connectivity, network management, NetWare 4.*x*, and client software. He also is a member of Novell's Professional Developer's Program and was a coauthor of *Inside TCP/IP,* also from New Riders Publishing.

Debra Niedermiller-Chaffins is Training Manager for MicroAge of Southeast Michigan located in Novi, Michigan. Debra has been working since 1988 to help organizations develop automony and self-sufficiency in training future Certified NetWare Engineers operations. She is a Certified NetWare Instructor and a CNE. In addition to teaching, Debra also supports a small client base, which provides her with a background of real-world networking scenarios. She is the author of *Inside Novell NetWare, Special Edition, NetWare Training Guide: Managing NetWare Systems, NetWare Training Guide: Networking Technologies,* and *Inside NetWare Lite,* also published by New Riders Publishing.

Trademark Acknowledgments

Development Editor
John Sleeva

Project Editors
Amy Bezek
Phil Worthington

Copy Editors
Lillian Yates

Technical Editors
Todd Brown
Kurt Schernekau
Lance Skok

Associate Marketing Manager
Tamara Apple

Acquisitions Coordinator
Stacia Mellinger

Publisher's Assistant
Karen Opal

Cover Designer
Karen Ruggles

Cover Production
Aren Howell

Book Designer
Sandra Schroeder

Production Manager
Kelly Dobbs

Production Team Supervisor
Laurie Casey

Graphics Image Specialists
Steven Adams
Dan Harris
Clint Lahnen
Laura Robbins

Production Analysts
Jason Hand
Bobbi Satterfield

Production Team
Kim Cofer
Aleata Howard
Krena Lanham
Erich J. Richter
Scott Tullis
Christine Tyner
Megan Wade
Christy Wagner

Indexer
Chris Wilcox

Contents at a Glance

Table of Contents

QVIVIRA
TOLM.
TOTONTEAC.
MARATA.
CVLIACAN.
ASTATLAN
TERLICHICHIMECI
HISPANIA NOVA
TOPIRA
MECHVACAN
MAR VERMEIO
CHIPELAGO DI
N LAZARO.
MAR DEL SVR, quod
Circulus Æquinoctialis
PACIFICUM
Insulæ Salomonis
GVINEA. Andre
RA AVSTRA
LIS SIVE
MAGELLA
NICA HAC
TENVS IN
COGNITA.
AMERICAE SIVE
NOVI ORBIS, NO
VA DESCRIPTIO.

Part 1

CD Software

Part 1 is the first section in Volume 3 of this three-volume set. It consists of 20 chapters which provide basic information about installing and running the software demonstration, limited-use, and shareware software contained in the 20 related directories on the CD. Each chapter is named for the directory on the CD in which you can find the related software. The 20 chapters included in Part 1 are as follows:

NORVMBEGA
CALICVAS
CAPASCHI
MARATA
CVLIACAN
HISPANIA NOVA
TOVA
CVBA
HISPANIOLA
MAR DEL SVR, quod
PACIFICVM
CHARCAS
PARANA
CHILE
Archipelago del C. deßeado
ICAE SIVE
ORBIS, NO
SCRIPTIO.

1

CHAPTER

AND_TECH

The software provided in the AND_TECH directory on the CD is distributed by A.N.D. Technologies. This version is a 45-day trial version. It includes a software program called PCOUNTER v3.12a. *PCOUNTER* is a page-counting print server for use with Novell NetWare networks. PCOUNTER is available in both an executable and a NetWare Loadable Module (NLM) version.

For more information about A.N.D. Technologies' software, or to obtain a fully registered version of PCOUNTER, contact A.N.D. at the following address:

A.N.D. Technologies
P.O. Box 64811
Los Angeles, CA 90064
(213) 782-6923

You also can contact them at the following electronic addresses:

ANDTECH@NETCOM.COM
CompuServe: 71011,3570

Note

Much of the information contained in this chapter is adapted from the online documentation that A.N.D. Technologies provides with this trial version of PCOUNTER. Their original online documentation consists of almost 100 pages. The version in this chapter is a more limited recital of the product's features and functionality.

If you want to read the entire online documentation produced by A.N.D. Technologies, read the following two files found in the AND_TECH\PCOUNTER directory on the CD:

PCOUNTER.TXT
UPDATE.TXT

The executable version of PCOUNTER (PCOUNTER.EXE) is designed to replace PSERVER.EXE, which ships with NetWare. Novell's PSERVER utility converts a newer PC that otherwise can be used as a workstation into a dedicated print server. A.N.D. Technologies' PCOUNTER software, however, enables you to make use of the older PCs, such as the AT, as well as newer PCs because it can run in non-dedicated mode. By running PCOUNTER.EXE on older PCs, you can use the PC as both a network print server and a workstation (also called a non-dedicated print server).

The PCOUNTER NLM utility is loaded on a NetWare file server. The NLM version of PCOUNTER has the same capabilities as the EXE version. The file server with PCOUNTER.NLM loaded still can function as a NetWare file server.

Besides PCOUNTER, two additional programs are provided to help you configure and manage your PCOUNTER environment. They are PCONTROL and ACCOUNT. *PCONTROL* is a menu-driven utility used for print server, printer, and queue configuration; user/group account balance management; and remote control of PCOUNTER servers. *ACCOUNT* is a command-line utility which allows users to view information about their account balances.

This chapter discusses the following utilities:

- ✔ PCOUNTER
- ✔ PCONTROL
- ✔ ACCOUNT

Using these three utilities, you can set up and configure network printing, as well as track and charge for printing use.

Introducing PCOUNTER

As noted previously, PCOUNTER is software that adapts a PC or NetWare file server into a print server. It provides much of the same functionality as Novell's PSERVER software.

The following are the main features PCOUNTER provides:

- ✔ Functions as a print server, even replacing Novell's PSERVER software.
- ✔ Counts pages on PostScript and LaserJet (PCL) printers, LaserJet4s, and Deskjets.
- ✔ Maintains user account balances using the Novell accounting feature
- ✔ Keeps a log file of all print activity
- ✔ Supports HP LaserJet4 and JetDirect
- ✔ Converts text to PostScript (automatically) when needed
- ✔ Supports the extended character set
- ✔ Provides banner pages that contain extensive information about print jobs, including the page count and account balance
- ✔ Supports printer and queue management from the PCOUNTER console
- ✔ Grants remote control of the print server
- ✔ Places jobs on automatic hold, allowing held jobs to be deleted if needed
- ✔ Rejects incorrect print job types and incorrect paper sizes
- ✔ Provides a built-in screen blanker
- ✔ Reboots the print server automatically if the file server goes down (executable version only)

In addition, you can use PCOUNTER to provide parallel printing support using direct port access, and serial printing with baud rates up to 115 KB using the executable version. PCOUNTER also can communicate directly with network printers using the TCP/IP protocol. In addition, it provides the capability to spool jobs to Unix hosts using the LPR protocol.

Starting the PCOUNTER 45-Day Trial

To use PCOUNTER, start it the first time to begin the 45-day trial period. To start PCOUNTER the first time, follow these steps:

1. Type **PCONTROL**, and press Enter. The PControl menu opens (see fig. 1.1).

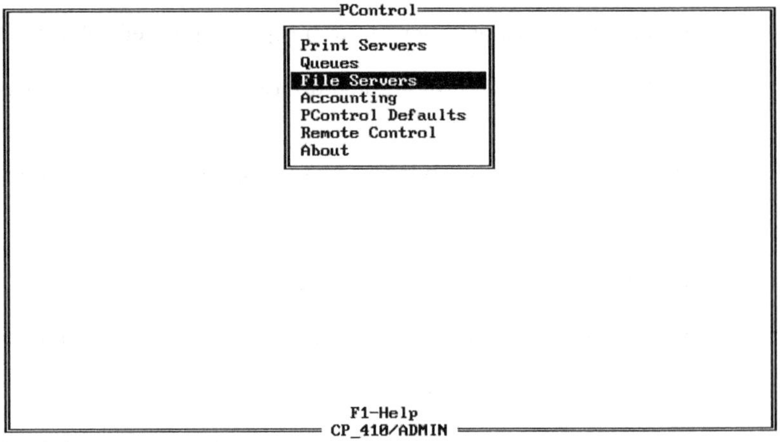

Figure 1.1
The PControl menu.

Note All configuration parameters that are relevant to PCOUNTER are set up using PCONTROL. The use of NetWare's PCONSOLE is not necessary, except for queue management.

PCONTROL creates the directory SYS:SYSTEM\PCOUNTER if it does not already exist. The PCOUNTER server is given read, write, and create access in this directory, which is used to log files and read header and footer files.

2. Choose File Servers from the PControl menu. A list of available file servers opens (see fig. 1.2).

3. Select (highlight) the file server with which you want to register PCOUNTER, then press F8. The Register *file_server* screen opens (see fig. 1.3).

4. Press Enter to begin the registration process. When the registration is complete, the `Registered for 45 day trial period!` message appears in the Register *file_server* screen (see fig. 1.3).

5. Register each file server on which you will run PCOUNTER. To register additional file servers, press Esc when the first file server registration is complete. Then, choose another server from the file server list, and press Enter to complete its registration.

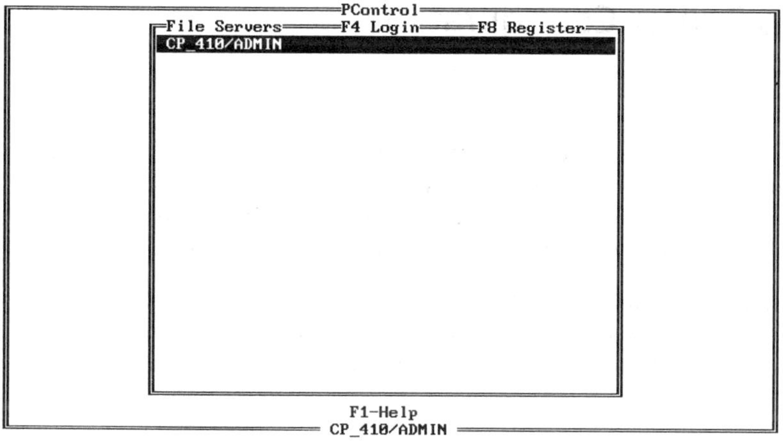

Figure 1.2
PControl's list of available file servers.

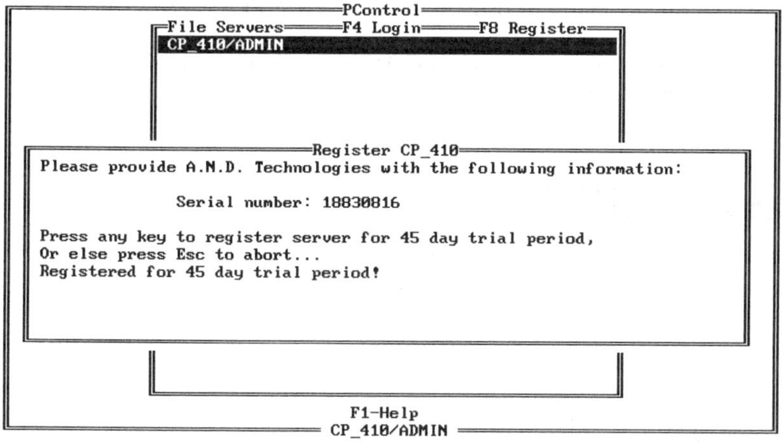

Figure 1.3
The Register *file_server* screen.

Note When registering file servers with PCOUNTER, and otherwise configuring printing using PCOUNTER, keep in mind the following PCOUNTER limitations:

- ✔ Each PCOUNTER print server can log in to a maximum of eight file servers.
- ✔ PCOUNTER print servers can print on up to 32 printers.
- ✔ Each printer can service up to 16 queues.
- ✔ A printer name can be no longer than 14 characters.

When the 45-day trial period expires, accounting functions are disabled, and PCOUNTER can run for only two additional hours.

Setting Up Printer Configurations

After you register PCOUNTER with the file server, you must set up your printer configurations.

Printer configurations (found in PCONTROL, Print Servers, Printer list) serve to tell PCOUNTER how to handle and communicate with each printer, such as the printer port. The *printer port* connects the PCOUNTER server to the printer. A printer configuration also includes the queues that are serviced by that printer.

Queue configurations determine how PCOUNTER handles each print job serviced in that queue. Many options are specific to PCOUNTER, whereas others, such as Job notify, Banners, Form feed, and so on, provide extensions to Novell's printing services.

Like configuring NetWare print servers, when you configure a PCOUNTER print server you must include at least one printer configuration, which must then include at least one configured queue. Without proper setup, PCOUNTER cannot run.

To set the PCOUNTER configuration, use the PCONTROL utility. You must have Supervisor rights to use PCONTROL.

Introducing PCONTROL

You use PCONTROL to configure PCOUNTER. Before you can use PCONTROL to configure PCOUNTER, you must configure a print server, a printer, and a print queue.

Configuring a Print Server

To configure a print server, complete the following steps:

1. Start the PCONTROL utility by typing **PCONTROL**, and pressing Enter. The PControl screen opens.

2. Choose Print Servers to open a list of print servers.

3. Choose a print server. A list of configuration options for the chosen print server appears (see fig. 1.4).

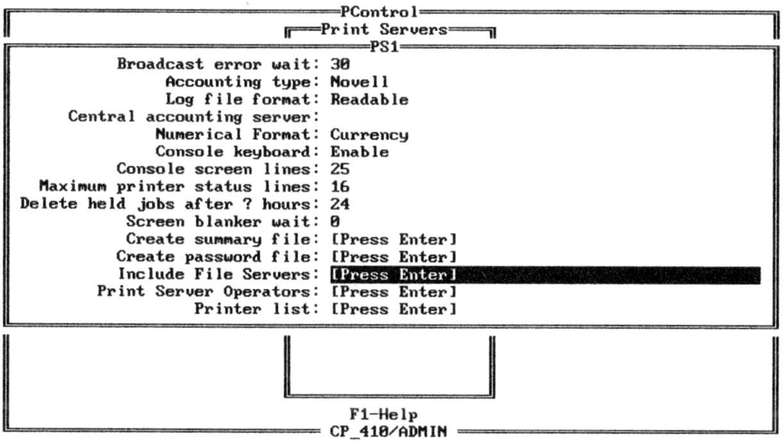

Figure 1.4
Print server configuration options.

4. Choose Include File Servers from the list of configuration options when the network has more than one file server. The Included and Not Included lists appear (see fig. 1.5).

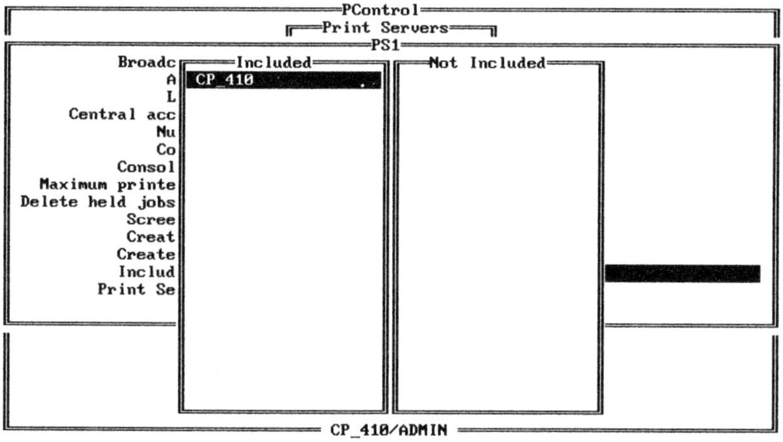

Figure 1.5
Lists of included and not included file servers.

5. Choose a file server from the Not Included list to add it to the Included list, then press Esc to return to the file server configuration screen.

Configuring a Printer

To configure a printer, complete the following steps immediately after you complete step 5 of configuring a print server:

1. Choose Printer list from the list of configuration options. The Printers list appears.

2. Press Ins to issue the `Enter new Printer:` prompt (see fig. 1.6). Type the name of the printer and press Enter to display the printer list.

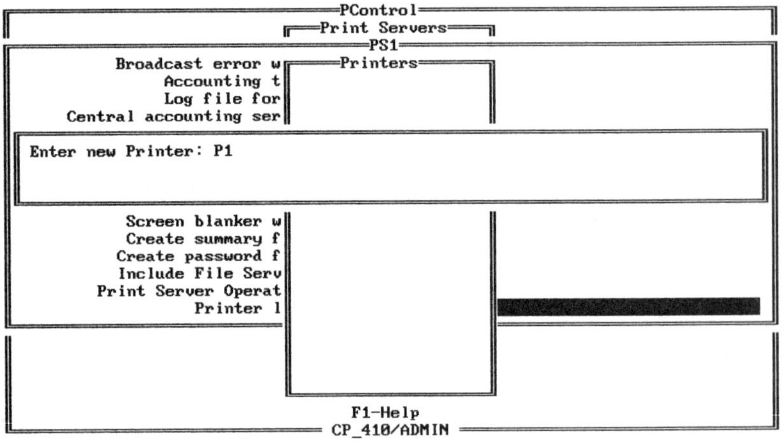

Figure 1.6 Type the name of the printer and press Enter to display the list.

3. Choose a printer from the printer list to open the printer's configuration menu (see fig. 1.7).

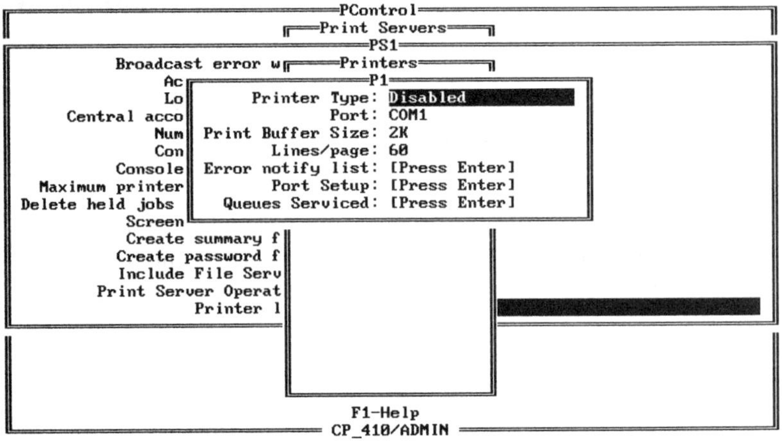

Figure 1.7 The printer configuration menu.

4. Choose Printer Type to open a list of printers from which to choose, then choose the type of printer being used, such as PostScript or LaserJet4.

5. Choose Port to specify the port that connects the print server to the printer. Figure 1.8 shows the online (F1) help screen you can open to see your options. If using a print queue, choose Queue, then select a queue.

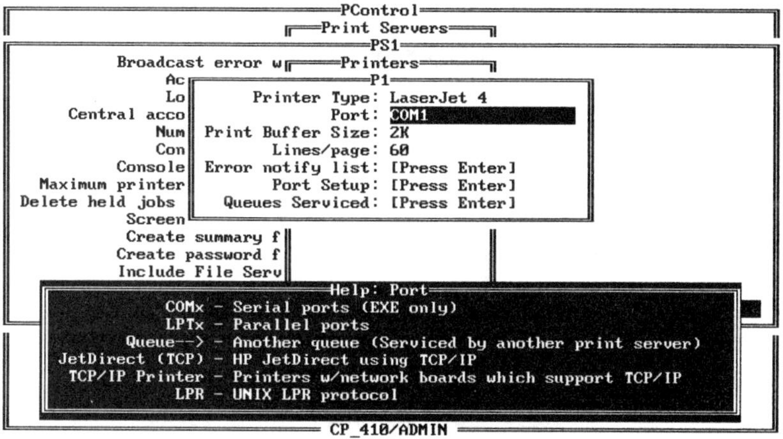

Figure 1.8
The online help screen for the Port option.

6. Press Esc to return to the printer configuration menu.

7. Choose Queues Serviced from the menu, then choose all queues you want this printer to service.

8. Press Esc until you return to the PControl menu.

Configuring a Print Queue

After you complete step 8 of the "Configuring a Printer" section, complete the following steps to configure a print queue:

1. Choose Queues from the PControl menu. The Queues list appears.

2. Create a print queue by pressing Ins and providing a queue name and location when prompted (see fig. 1.9).

3. Choose the print queue from the Queues list. The print queue configuration screen opens (see fig. 1.10).

4. Choose Queue users. The Queue Users/Not Queue Users lists appear.

5. Add one or more users to the list of Queue Users by choosing them from the list of Not Queue Users.

Note You also can modify any other configuration items if their defaults do not reflect your needs, or accept all of the defaults.

6. After you finish adding users, press Esc three times to return to the PControl menu. Then exit PControl.

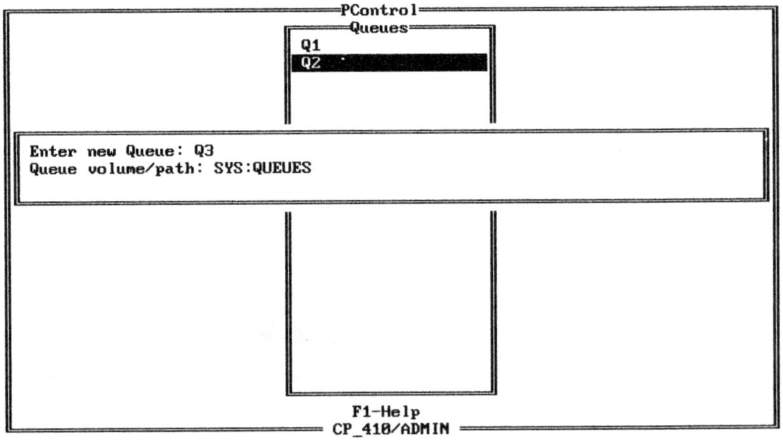

Figure 1.9 Print queue name and location prompt.

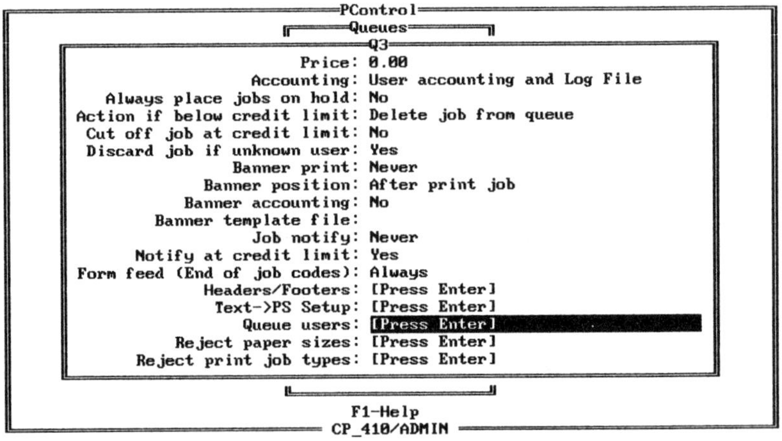

Figure 1.10 The print queue configuration screen.

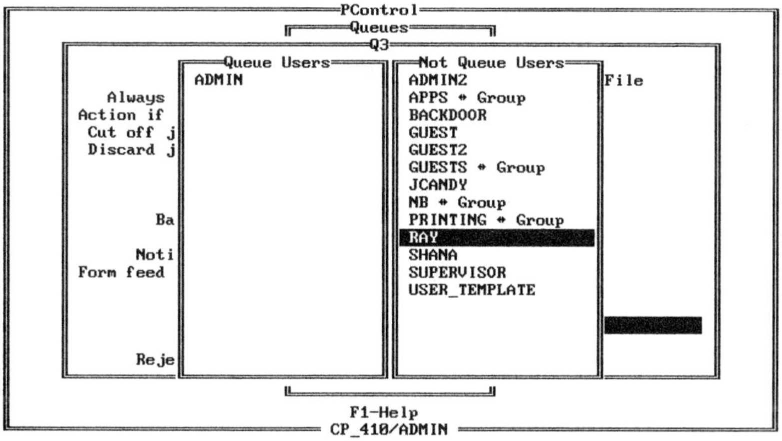

Figure 1.11
The Queue Users and Not Queue Users lists.

Loading the Print Server

To load the print server, type the following at the file server console, replacing *print_server_name* with the name of the assigned print server, and press Enter:

LOAD SYS:SYSTEM\PCOUNTER\PCOUNTER ***print_server_name***

To load the print server at the workstation, change the default drive to the location of the PCOUNTER.EXE file, then type **PCOUNTER** ***print_server_name***, replacing ***print_server_name*** with the name of the print server, and press Enter.

Now set any applications you are running to use the print queue you set up. You then should be able to print.

Introducing Accounting

User account balances are maintained using the Novell accounting feature. To use Novell's accounting feature, you must enable it using SYSCON/NWADMIN.

If you currently are using accounting for tracking connect time or disk usage, and the account balances are not in currency units, then user account balances will not appear to be consistent if you also use PCOUNTER. Please check to make sure none of these features are enabled on your file server before implementing PCOUNTER in this fashion.

You also have to choose the numerical format, and consider the following guidelines:

- ✔ **Pages.** One accounting unit equals one page.
- ✔ **Currency.** Accounting is kept in terms of local currency. The type and format of the local currency are determined from DOS information in CONFIG.SYS (*note*: U.S. users need not set anything in CONFIG.SYS).
- ✔ **Cost.** The cost for each print job is defined in the queue's configuration. If you are collecting money for printing, and you want to deduct the cost of each print job from a user's account balance, then use positive prices. Only use negative prices to keep a running total of print activity in account balances.

The PCOUNTER server keeps a running log of all print activity in the text file called SYS:SYSTEM\PCOUNTER\PCOUNTER.LOG. Multiple PCOUNTER servers write to a single PCOUNTER.LOG file and share header/footer files. PCOUNTER automatically flags PCOUNTER.LOG as shareable. PCOUNTER.LOG can be written in either of two formats: readable or ASCII delimited.

If PCOUNTER.LOG is Readable, then it contains limited information, but is easy to read, and therefore is best for showing users their print activities. If PCOUNTER.LOG is ASCII Delimited, then it contains all information about the print job. You can then import it into a spreadsheet or database program for further analysis. The ASCII Delimited version is not easy to read, but is beneficial for keeping more detailed information, such as total print activity for each printer.

After you install accounting on your file server, each user should have an account balance and a credit limit. You can use PCONTROL and ACCOUNT to modify user account balances and credit limits. In addition, PCONTROL may be used for groups. PCONTROL and ACCOUNT optionally can keep records in PCOUNTER.LOG.

NetWare creates a file called SYS:SYSTEM\NET$ACCT.DAT when you use accounting. This file contains binary records of all accounting transactions on the file server, as well as logins and so on. This file should be deleted periodically; in time, it can grow to a rather large size.

ACCOUNT is a DOS command-line accounting tool designed for quick accounting access to user accounts. To run this utility from the DOS prompt, issue the ACCOUNT command using one of the following formats, and press Enter:

- **ACCOUNT [*DEPOSIT* | *BALANCE* | *LIMIT*] [[*FileServerName/*]*UserName*] [*Amount*]**

  DEPOSIT: Used to add an amount to a user's account balance

  BALANCE: Used to set a user's account balance

  LIMIT: Used to define a user's minimum account balance

- **ACCOUNT CHARGE [[*FileServerName/*]*UserName*] [*Amount*] [*ChargeReason*]**

  CHARGE: Used to reduce a user's account balance

- **ACCOUNT BALANCE [*FileServerName/*]**

  BALANCE: Used to view one's own account balance

- **ACCOUNT CONFIG**

  This command is used to set PCOUNTER.LOG and formatting defaults for accounting. ACCOUNT.CFG is written into the same directory as ACCOUNT.EXE, and must be kept in the same directory as ACCOUNT.EXE.

WBALANCE

If your users have access to Microsoft Windows, they can use the WBALANCE Windows utility to view their account balances. WBALANCE defaults to the primary login file server (often the Preferred Server in NET.CFG), and displays the currency amount using two-decimal digits. You can change these values by placing the following command-line options in Program Manager, File, Properties:

- *d* = *n*, where *n* = the number of decimal digits. If Numerical format = Pages, use *d* = 0. The default is *d* = 2.

- *s* = *FileServerName*, where *FileServerName* is a file server other than the primary login file server.

To run WBALANCE, choose **R**un from the **F**ile menu. When the Run dialog box opens, type the exact path and name of the utility, then choose OK. Otherwise, use the **B**rowse option to locate the executable program for this utility, which is called *WBALANCE.EXE*.

The WBALANCE utility shows users their current account balance (see fig. 1.12).

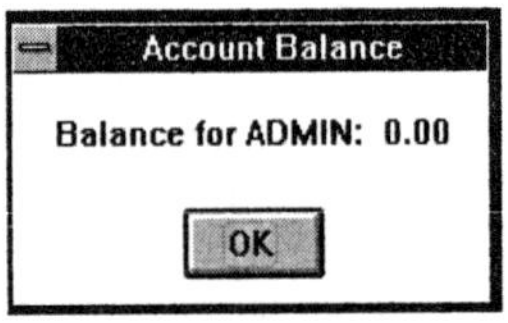

Figure 1.12
User Admin's account balance.

WCLIENT

Another Windows-based accounting utility is called *WCLIENT*. This utility prints accounting information for the user.

To run WCLIENT, choose **R**un from the **F**ile menu. When the Run window opens, type the exact path and name of the utility, then choose OK. Otherwise, use the **B**rowse option to locate the executable program for this utility. The executable program file for this utility is called *WCLIENT.EXE*.

Running WCLIENT displays the Print Accounting dialog box, as shown in figure 1.13.

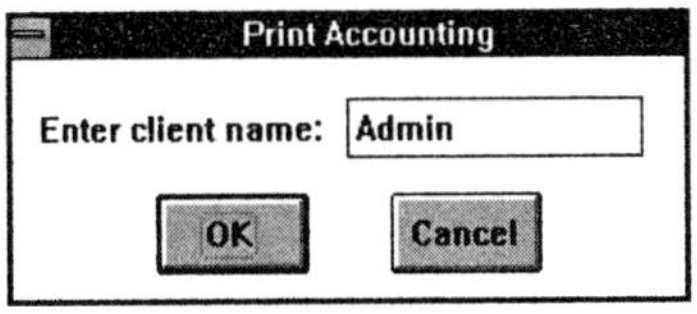

Figure 1.13
The Print Accounting dialog box for client Admin.

CHILAGA
NORVMBEGA
FRANCIA
MARATA
CVLIACAN
CAPASCHI
CALICVAS
TERLICHICHIMECHI
HISPANIA NOVA
TOVA
LA FLORIDA
CVBA
HISPANIOLA
MAR DEL SVR, quod
PACIFICUM
CHARCAS
CHILI
PATAGONES vel REGIO GIGANTVM
Archipelago del C. desseado
ICAE SIVE
ORBIS, NO
ESCRIPTIO.

2

CHAPTER

BLULANCE

The BLULANCE directory on the CD contains software for a product called LT Auditor v4.0+. *LT Auditor* is network-activity monitoring and reporting software. Its purpose is to give the network administrator an overview of what is happening on the network. LT Auditor enables you to monitor users' activities on the network, such as which files they are accessing, how much time they are spending in a file or running an application, and who deleted or renamed a file.

LT Auditor includes the capability to set filters and run reports against the database of information it tracks, which enables you to find only the information you need, without having to wade through all the information collected in the database.

Before you can use LT Auditor, you must install and configure it. In addition, you need to understand how to set filters, run reports, and use the LT Auditor utilities to maintain your auditing environment and information. To help you accomplish the basics of working with LT Auditor, this chapter discusses the following topics:

- ✔ Installing, setting up, and configuring LT Auditor
- ✔ Creating and modifying filters
- ✔ Preparing and printing reports
- ✔ Using LT Auditor utilities

Note Much of the information furnished in this chapter is adapted from the online help and written documentation provided by Blue Lance. This chapter, however, condenses the company's documentation. The intention is to provide you enough information to successfully try LT Auditor, so you can decide for yourself whether you want to purchase the product. In addition, the chapter is designed for ease of reading, following, and implementing its instructions. If you choose to purchase this product, however, you will find that Blue Lance's documentation is relatively easy to follow.

Installing and Configuring LT Auditor

To use LT Auditor, you must first install it, then configure it. The following sections explain the basic installation and configuration processes.

Installing LT Auditor

To install LT Auditor, change your PC's CD-ROM drive to the BLULANCE\LTAUDITR\V4.2 directory, or add the exact path to your workstation's DOS path command. You can then install LT Auditor v4.2. After you install v4.2, run the update utility to update LT Auditor to include any additional software changes made by the manufacturer after the original release of this software. To update LT Auditor, run UPDATE.EXE from the DOS prompt. To run UPDATE.EXE, type **UPDATE *file_server_name***, replacing ***file_server_name*** with the name of the file server on which you installed LT Auditor.

Installing LT Auditor v4.0

To install LT Auditor v4.0, complete the following steps:

1. Start Windows, then choose Run from the File menu.
2. Type the drive letter and exact path to the directory in which the LT Auditor INSTALL.EXE program is located, or use the Browse button and search until you find it.
3. When the Command Line in the Run dialog box shows the executable installation file, choose OK. The LT Auditor Installation Utility welcome screen opens.
4. Press Enter to continue. A list of the available file servers appears (see fig. 2.1).

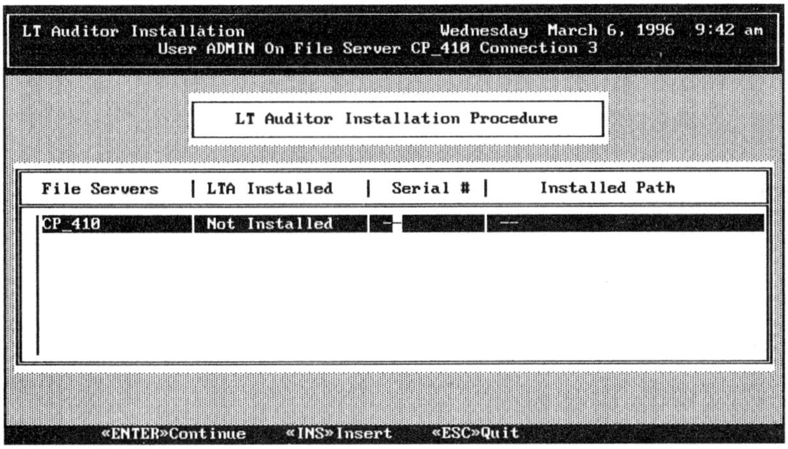

Figure 2.1
The list of available file servers for LT Auditor.

5. Select (highlight) the file server onto which you want to install LT Auditor, then press Enter to view a list of volumes. (Note that you must have Supervisor rights on the file server you choose.)

6. Choose the volume onto which you want to install LT Auditor.

7. Type the path to the directory on the chosen volume onto which you want to install LT Auditor, then press Enter, or simply press Enter to use the default.

8. When prompted, choose Yes to audit all users. If you choose No, you can later configure filters to refine your audit choices.

9. When prompted, choose the print queue to be used when printing LT Auditor reports.

10. When prompted, choose the date format to use on printed reports. Choose AMERICAN, for example, to use the month/day/year (mm/dd/yy) format (see fig. 2.2).

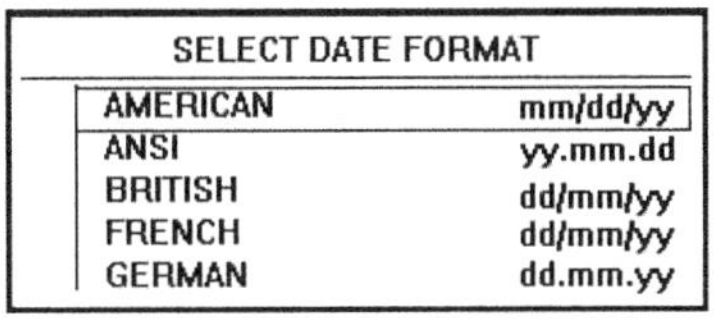

Figure 2.2
The SELECT DATE FORMAT list.

11. When the next screen opens, choose Yes to view a list of user accounts. Save all user accounts by pressing Esc, or mark only some user accounts. To mark user accounts, highlight the user's name and press F5. Repeat this procedure for each user whose account you want to mark. Then press Enter to save the marked user accounts.

12. Read the five steps listed in the Installing and Configuring LT Auditor screen, then press Esc to exit the installation program.

Setting Up LT Auditor

To set up LT Auditor, you must complete two primary steps. The first is to load the LT Auditor NetWare Loadable Module (NLM) at the file server. To load this NLM, type **LOAD LTAPLUS** at the file server console and press Enter, and the auditing process commences.

The second primary step is to install the Hardware Auditor on each workstation. To install the Hardware Auditor, complete the following steps:

1. Log in to the network as Supervisor or equivalent.

2. Type **SYSCON** at the DOS prompt and press Enter, to open the SYSCON Available Topics menu (see fig. 2.3).

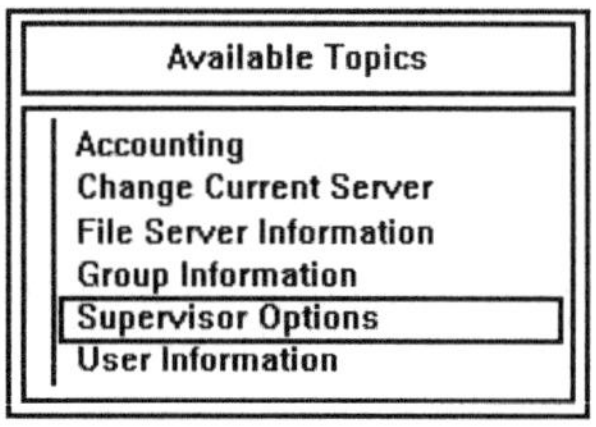

Figure 2.3 The SYSCON Available Topics menu.

3. Choose Supervisor Options to open the Supervisor Options menu (see fig. 2.4).

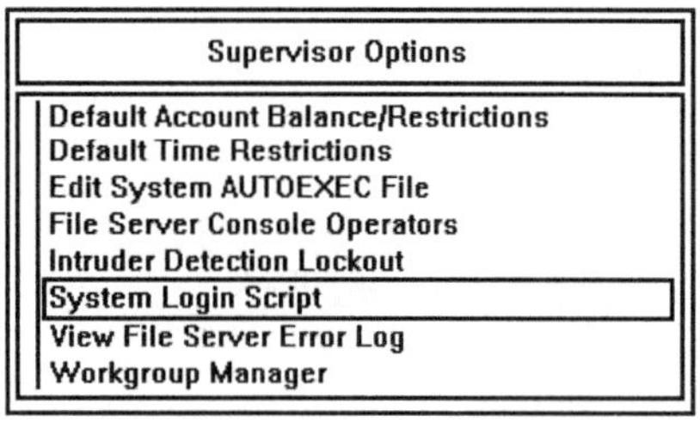

Figure 2.4 The SYSCON Supervisor Options menu.

4. Choose System Login Script to open a blank or a pre-existing system login script.

5. Place the following line into the system login script:

   #file_server_name\volume:lt_path\HWA.EXE

   Replace *file_server_name* with the name of the file server that contains the LT Auditor software; *volume* with the volume that contains the LT Auditor software; and *lt_path* with the directory that contains the LT Auditor software.

6. Save the changes and press Esc until prompted to exit SYSCON, then choose Yes.

Note If you prefer, you can add the ***#file_server_name\volume:lt_path*** **HWA.EXE** line to individual user login scripts rather than the system login script, or run HWA.EXE from each workstation. You also can create a batch file to run HWA.EXE.

After you install LT Auditor, you can refine it by setting specific configuration information.

Configuring LT Auditor

You can configure various items associated with LT Auditor. You can determine who can run LT Auditor, for example, set a date format, and choose a print queue to use for printing reports. In addition, you can configure LT Auditor for the following:

- ✔ **Alarms.** To choose which users are notified when hardware changes occur
- ✔ **System parameters.** To set configuration and bindery auditing parameters
- ✔ **Node information.** To record a list of all stations and the users working on them

The installation program includes choosing which users can use LT Auditor, setting a date format, and specifying a printing queue. You can use the LT Auditor utility (LTA.EXE) to change these configurations later. This section, however, explains only how to work with alarms, system parameters, and node information.

To set or modify any LT Auditor configuration information, start the LT Auditor utility by typing **LTA** at a workstation DOS prompt and pressing Enter. This screen is preceded by an Intro screen; simply press Enter to move past this screen. The LT Auditor Main Menu opens (see fig. 2.5). From the MAIN MENU, select System Configuration to open the System Configuration menu, then complete the steps outlined in the following sections for each configuration change.

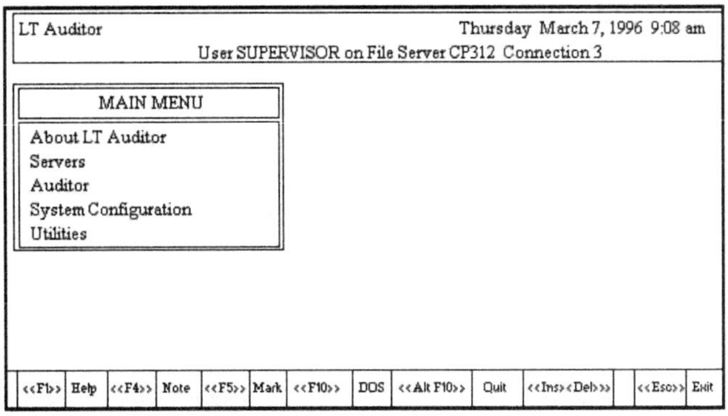

Figure 2.5 The LT Auditor MAIN MENU.

Setting Alarm Configurations

To set alarm configurations, complete the following steps:

1. Choose Alarm Configuration to open a list of alarm conditions (see fig. 2.6).

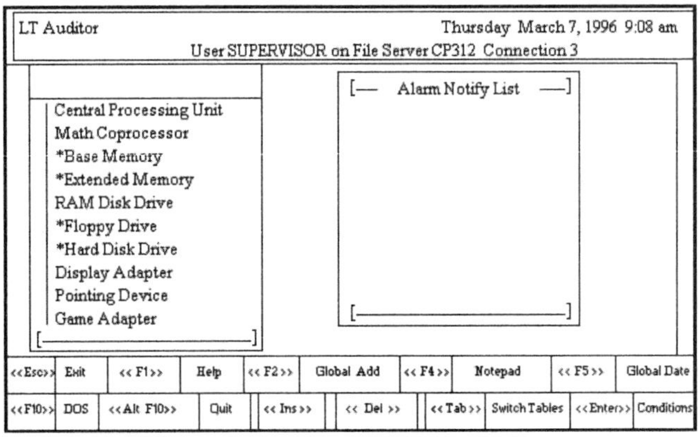

Figure 2.6 The Alarm Notify List.

2. Select (highlight) the alarm condition for which you want to specify a list of users to be notified, then press Insert to open the Network Users list.

3. From the Network Users list, choose which users are to be notified. To choose users, highlight each user's name, then press F5. This action marks the users' names and adds them to the Alarm Notify List shown in figure 2.6.

4. Repeat this process for each hardware item for which you want to add users to an alarm notify list, then escape out when finished.

Setting System Parameters

To set system parameters, complete the following steps:

1. Choose Set System Parameters from the System Configuration menu to open the Configuration Parameters window.

2. Use the up- and down-arrow keys to highlight any of the fields in the Configuration Parameters window.

3. Set any of the following fields to YES to have the related function performed, or to NO to prevent the function from being performed, or modify the value as appropriate:

   - ✔ Auto Archive
   - ✔ File Limit Size (MB)
   - ✔ Display/Size Limit
   - ✔ Environment Diags
   - ✔ Meter Q Hold Time (MIN)
   - ✔ Hide NLM Screen
   - ✔ Auto Delete Freq. (Min)
   - ✔ Disallow LT Auditor NLM Broadcast To Work Stations

4. Set the File Limit Size (MB) field to the maximum size the audit information file is allowed to reach, if applicable. The size ranges from 1 to 5 MB.

5. Specify, in minutes, the Meter Q Hold Time, which is the length of time the applications being metered are to be held in the Meter Q for the user.

6. Set the Auto Delete Freq., which is the length of time (in minutes) between each purging of the active audit files.

Reviewing Node Information

To review node information, complete the following steps:

1. Choose Node Information from the System Configuration menu.

2. Press F3 to open the next screen.

3. Press Ins, then in the areas provided, specify which User Name, Node Address, Alias Name, and Node location you want to include in the reports. You also can choose a node, then edit related node information.

4. To save your changes, press Esc, then choose Yes at the `Save Node Information` prompt.

Creating and Modifying Filters

You can create several types of filters. The following list contains the types of filters you can create:

- ✔ File filters
- ✔ LAN filters
- ✔ Bindery filters
- ✔ Auto Delete/Purge filters
- ✔ Metering filters

The process for creating filters is basically the same regardless of the type of filter. To create filters, choose System Configuration from the LT Auditor Main Menu to open the System Configuration menu. Then choose Filters from the System Configuration menu to view the Filters list. Next, choose File, Bindery, or LAN from the Filters list.

The balance of the procedure you follow depends on which item you choose from the Filters list. If you choose File, for example, you have two options: System and User. From these two options, you can choose to create a filter that applies to all users (System) or one that applies only to specific users (User).

Any elements that are already configured are then displayed. If you then press Ins, you can see a list of commands from which to choose.

To complete the configuration, choose the options to be included in the filter. The options available for a System filter are Command, Path, Include, Exclude, Operations, Trap, and Alert. Choose options and make changes as needed to customize the filter.

To navigate the options, use the following keys:

- ✔ **Arrow keys.** Use to move through the options
- ✔ **Delete.** Use to delete the selected operation
- ✔ **Ins.** Use to insert the selected operation

- ✔ **Enter.** Use to exit and save your selections
- ✔ **Esc.** Use to exit without saving your selections

The best way to become familiar with each of these types of filters and filter options is to experiment with them. As the filters are applied to the capture of data, little harm can be done by simply experimenting with each filter and reviewing the results.

Preparing and Printing Reports

You can use reports to view, print, save, and process the audit information that LT Auditor records. To work with reports, choose Auditor Reports from the Main Menu, then complete the following steps:

1. To set up a report configuration and generate a file auditor report, select one of the options from the Reports menu:
   - ✔ File
   - ✔ Bindery
   - ✔ LAN Access
   - ✔ Metering
   - ✔ Hardware
   - ✔ Miscellaneous

   Note File, Bindery, and LAN Access are very similar in functionality, which is why these three are grouped together in the following steps. The other three options (Metering, Hardware, and Miscellaneous) have greater differences and therefore are kept separate in the following steps.

   If you choose File, Bindery, or LAN Access, the Report By menu opens.

   If you choose Metering or Hardware, the Report For menu opens.

   If you choose Miscellaneous, the Misc. Audit Report menu opens.

2. If you chose File, Bindery, or LAN Access, choose either Group or User from the Report By menu. Choosing either of these two options opens the appropriate Audit Report menu (File, Bindery, or LAN).

If you choose Metering, choose Normal Activity, Exceptions, or Concurrent Usage from the Report For menu. Regardless of which option you choose, the Metering Audit Report menu opens (see fig. 2.7).

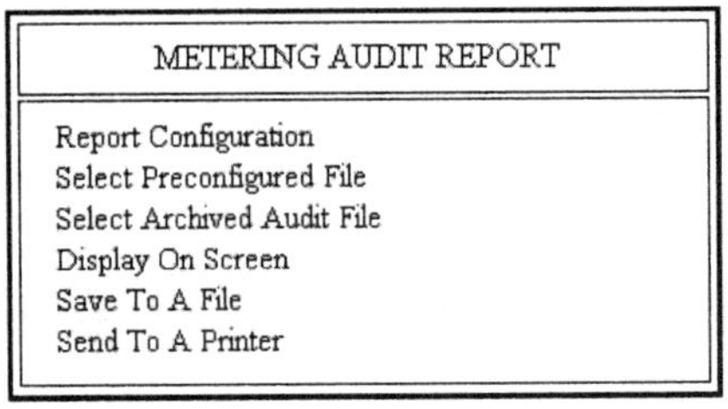

Figure 2.7
The Metering Audit Report menu.

If you choose Hardware, choose either Current Configuration or History Configuration from the Report For menu to open the Hardware Audit Report menu.

3. From the Audit Report menu (regardless of which option you initially chose—File, Bindery, LAN Access, Metering, Hardware, or Miscellaneous), now choose one of the six available options: Report Configuration, Select Preconfigured File, Select Archived Audit File, Display On Screen, Save To A File, and Send To A Printer (refer to figure 2.7).

How you proceed from this point depends on which Audit Report menu option you choose. Each option opens a report configuration screen, and you can specify the report's parameters using this screen. Some of the parameter options of the various screens differ slightly, however. For the most part, the report configuration screen enables you to set at least the beginning and ending dates and times for the report, whether to display the configuration, and whether to save the report.

To complete the process of configuring and printing reports, you might have to provide some additional information. This possibility also depends on which options you chose from each of the preceding menus. If you choose Select Preconfigured File from the Hardware Audit Report menu, for example, you must then provide the file name of the preconfigured file when you are prompted, or press Ins to view a list of files from which to choose.

After you complete the configuration information, press Esc and return to the related Audit Report menu, from which you can choose to do one of the following:

- ✔ View the report on-screen by choosing Display On Screen
- ✔ Save the report information to a file by choosing Save To A File and providing a file name and path
- ✔ Send the report directly to the printer by choosing Send To A Printer

You can then continue to press Escape until you are prompted to exit this utility.

Using LT Auditor Utilities

LT Auditor provides utilities that enable you to perform a variety of tasks. The available utilities let you check files and directories and repair errors, purge and save active audit files, specify when audit files should be automatically purged, and view the auditor console on your workstation.

You access each of these utilities from the LT Auditor Main Menu. To run these utilities, choose Utilities from the Main Menu to open the Utilities menu. The next choice you make depends on what you want to accomplish. For example, you might want to automatically run an environment diagnostics or purge the audit files. These two options, as well as the other options, are discussed.

Running Environment Diagnostics

To run environment diagnostics, choose Environment Diagnostics from the utilities menu. The program automatically runs the diagnostics and keeps you posted on the status of the diagnostics process. Generally, a `Successful` message is posted next to each item checked. Examples of items being checked might include Subdirectory Structure, LT Auditor Data Files, LT Auditor File Attributes, Trustee Paths, and so on. After the diagnostics are complete, press Esc to exit the diagnostics utility.

Purging Active Audit Files

To purge active audit files, complete the following steps:

1. Choose Purge Active Audit Files from the Utilities menu, and press Enter. The Select File to Purge screen opens.

2. Choose a file to purge. The Purge Options menu opens.

3. Choose either Copy Before Purge or Purge. Choosing Copy Before Purge saves a copy of the audit data in the active audit file before it purges the audit file. If you choose this option, you are prompted to provide a path and file name into which to copy the audit data.

4. After making your choice and when prompted, choose Yes to purge the selected file.

If you save audit files before purging them, you can later load the audit files into the Reports *module* (the portion of this software program which is responsible for collating and generating reports) to view or print the audit data.

Auditor Console

Choosing Auditor Console from the Utilities menu enables you to view on your workstation's monitor the same display that appears on the LT Auditor Console. You then can choose from the six menu options shown in figure 2.8.

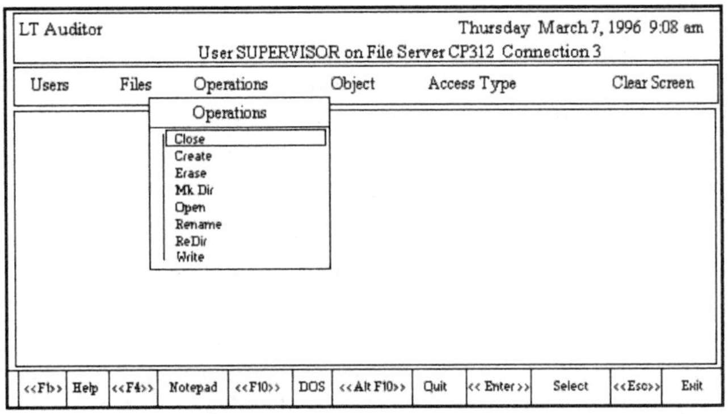

Figure 2.8 The LT Auditor Console menu options, with the Operations menu open.

- ✔ **Users.** Choose Users to open a list of users from which you can choose in order to view information about one or more users. To see information about one user, select that user and then press Enter. To see information about more than one user, first use the F5 key to mark each user's name.
- ✔ **Files.** Choose Files to see which files are in the directory. The default wild card *.* appears, but you can change it to specify any combination of characters. r*.*, for example, displays all files whose name begins with the letter *r*. After you specify which files you want to view, those files are displayed on the console.
- ✔ **Operations.** Choose Operations to open a list of operations which can be performed on or to files or directories. You can choose one operation, or mark multiple operations using the F5 key. The available operations are Close, Create, Erase, Mk Dir, Open, Rename, ReDir, and Write (refer to figure 2.8).
- ✔ **Object.** Choose Object to open the Objects menu, from which you can choose any of the available objects: Blue Lance, File Server, Other, Print Queue, Print Server, User, and User Group.
- ✔ **Access Type.** Choose Access Type to open the Access Type menu. From this menu, you can choose Bindery Access, File Access, or LAN Access.
- ✔ **Clear Screen.** Choose Clear Screen to clear the Auditor Console screen.

CHILAGA
FRANCIA
NORVMBEGA
MOCOSA
AVACAL
APALCHEN
CALICVAS
CAPASCHI
TEAC
MARATA
CVLIACAN
TERLICHICHI MECHI
HISPANIA NOVA
TOVA
XALISCO
TOPIRA
MEXICO
CVBA
HISPANIOLA
MAR DEL SVR, quod
Circulus Aequinoctialis
240
250
260
270
280
290
et PACIFICVM
CHARCAS
PARANA
CHILI
PATAGONES, vel REGIO GIGANTVM
Archipelago del C. delleado
CAE SIVE
ORBIS, NO
SCRIPTIO.

3

CHAPTER

CITADEL

Citadel Computer Systems, Inc., provides software called NetOFF System IV. *NetOFF* is network security software, which can perform the following functions:

- ✔ Blank the screen and lock the workstation's keyboard and mouse after a period of inactivity
- ✔ Automatically log a user off the network after a period of inactivity, or at any preset time
- ✔ Identify open programs and files, and save open files before automatically logging a user off the network

Note Much of the information in this chapter is adapted from the printed and online information provided with NetOFF System IV.

NetOFF is designed for use on a network with multiple workstations. NetOFF System IV is licensed per workstation, in increments of 20 workstations, with a minimum of 100 licenses per network file server. The copy of NetOFF provided on the CD is for demonstration purposes.

If you want information about NetOFF System IV v4.52 beyond what this chapter provides, or want information about purchasing this product, you can contact Citadel Computer Systems, Inc., at the following address:

Citadel Computer Systems, Inc.
2950 North Loop West, Suite 1080
Houston, TX 77092

Citadel's phone numbers are as follows:

Technical Support: (713) 686-6400
U.S. Sales: (800) 962-0701
FAX: (713) 686-6495

You also can reach Citadel through e-mail on the Internet at the following address:

contact@citadel.com

Installing NetOFF

To install NetOFF from the CD, change your default drive to the following path on the CD:

CITADEL\NETOFF

Next, copy the contents of this directory and its subdirectories into a location on the workstation's hard disk in which all files can be accessed.

Warning Ensure that you copy all files into a single directory, not into multiple directories, or the software will not be able to find the files that it expects to find on the second disk.

If you do not already have Windows running, start Windows and then choose Run from the File menu. Either type the exact path to where you copied the files from the NETOFF directory followed by a slash and the word **INSTALL**, or use the Windows

Browse option to locate INSTALL.EXE in the specified path. After INSTALL starts, complete the following steps:

1. When prompted, agree to the licensing terms by choosing OK.
2. Specify the directory in which you want to install NetOFF, then choose OK to view a list of components to be installed.
3. Choose the components you want to install, then choose OK. By default, three components are installed: NetOFF for DOS, NetOFF for Windows, a nd NetOFF Administrator.
4. When prompted to insert Disk 2, choose OK to continue.
5. When the installation is complete, a NetOFF group and two associated icons are created: NetOFF for Windows and NetOFF Administrator.

The NetOFF Administrator must be installed on at least one file server, but does not have to be installed on any additional file servers.

Warning In some instances, after you install NetOFF, you might not be able to delete the executable file. Be sure, therefore, to install it when and where you want it.

After you install NetOFF, you need to create NetOFF profiles and configure NetOFF.

Creating NetOFF Profiles

To create a profile, first choose the NetOFF Administrator icon from the Windows NetOFF group, to open the NetOFF Group Administrator dialog box (see fig. 3.1).

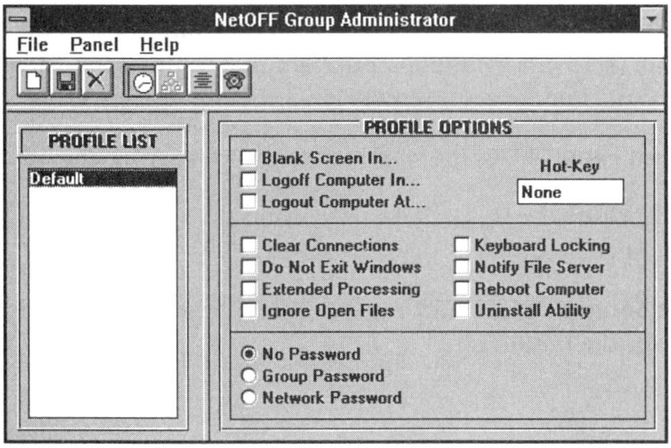

Figure 3.1
The NetOFF Group Administrator dialog box.

Now, choose New Group from the File menu. Mark the profile options you want to set for this group. Choose Blank Screen In, for example, to cause the workstation's screen to become blank after a preset amount of time, then specify the amount of time in hours and minutes (hh:mm).

You can set as many options as you want, providing no one option conflicts with another. You can choose No Password, Group Password, or Network Password, for example, but you cannot choose any two or three of these options.

You set group profile options in three categories. Those three categories are not titled, but can generically be called workstation options, connection/file server options, and password options.

The following are the workstation options:

- ✔ **Blank Screen In.** Causes the screen to become blank after a preset amount of time, and allows you to specify that time up to 99 hours and 99 minutes.
- ✔ **Logoff Computer In.** Logs the workstation out of the server after a preset amount of time has elapsed since the workstation last accessed the server. You also can specify the amount of time.
- ✔ **Logout Computer At.** Logs the workstation out of the server at a specific time.
- ✔ **Hot-Key.** Enables you to set a key sequence the user can use to enable the screen saver at any time.

The following are the connection/file server options:

- ✔ **Clear Connections.** Clears users' connections to the file server.
- ✔ **Do Not Exit Windows.** Leaves Windows open even if the user's connection is cleared.
- ✔ **Extended Processing.** Prevents screen blanking and elapsed-time logoff when the workstation is running a program that requires an extended processing time, but does not require periodic input from the user.
- ✔ **Ignore Open Files.** Closes the workstation without saving any open files.
- ✔ **Keyboard Locking.** Locks the keyboard when the specified amount of idle time, or the specified time of day, is reached.
- ✔ **Notify File Server.** Writes information to the file server's log whenever it logs a user off the network.

- **Reboot Computer.** Reboots the user's workstation logging off the user.
- **Uninstall Ability.** Enables the user to deactivate and uninstall NetOFF for DOS.

The following are the password options:

- **No Password.** Enables a user to unlock the screen without a password.
- **Group Password.** Enables you to set a password for a specific group of users, such as administrators, so they can unlock each other's workstations.
- **Network Password.** Requires users to provide their network passwords to unlock their workstations.

After you create and configure a NetOFF group, save the configuration by choosing Save Group from the File menu and providing a group name when prompted.

Adding Users to a Profile

After you create a profile, you can add users to that profile. To add users to a profile, first select the profile from the Profile List in the NetOFF Group Administrator dialog box, then complete the following steps:

1. From the Panel menu, choose Novell User List (see fig. 3.2). The Novell User List appears, which contains the Users Not Included and the Users Included lists (see fig. 3.3).

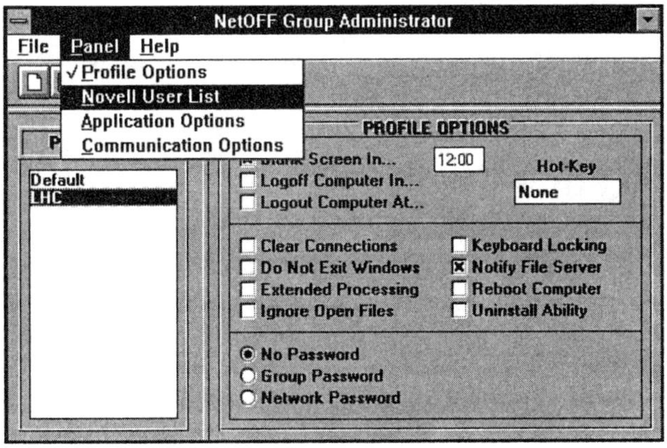

Figure 3.2
The Panel menu.

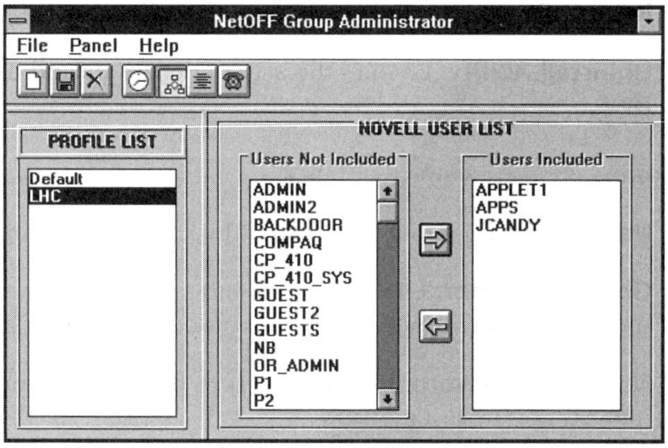

Figure 3.3
The Users Not Included and Users Included lists.

2. Select the users and groups you want to add to the profile from the Users Not Included list. To select users, place the mouse pointer on the user or group and click the right mouse button.

3. Press the right arrow button to move the selected users and groups from the Users Not Included list to the Users Included list.

After you create profiles for groups and add users to them, you are finished creating NetOFF profiles. You can now configure other NetOFF options, such as application programs.

Configuring NetOFF

To configure NetOFF, you determine how applications and communications are to be handled, and set configurations accordingly.

Setting Application Configuration

By setting application configuration, you can specify which files are saved and closed before the user is logged out. To set application configuration, choose Application Options from the Panel menu to open the Application Options window. Choose the double file-folder icon to open a list of applications that you can configure. The Application Manager dialog box opens (see fig. 3.4).

From the Application Manager dialog box, select an application. Next, choose Edit to open the edit window. You then can edit configuration information associated with the application (see fig. 3.5).

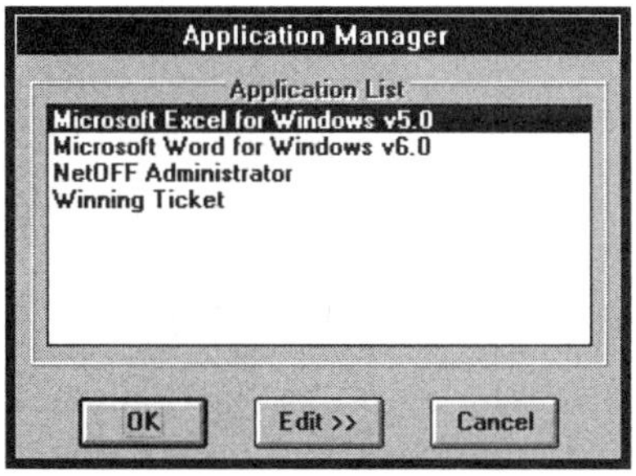

Figure 3.4
The Application Manager dialog box.

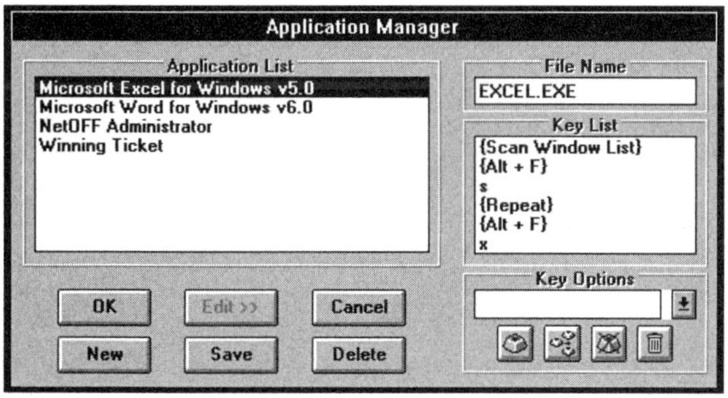

Figure 3.5
The Application Manager edit window.

From the edit window, you can edit the Key List, add other applications and edit their key lists, or delete applications from the list. The *key list* contains the series of keystrokes the user completes to save an application's file and exit the application. Correctly entering the keystrokes is important for the save-and-close-before-logout feature to function properly.

You can edit the key list of any application currently in the list. In addition, you can delete applications, add other applications, or modify the key list for any application.

To delete an application from the list, choose Delete. Choose OK when prompted `Delete Application` *`application_name`*.

To add an application, choose New. When prompted, provide a description of the application (see fig. 3.6), then choose OK.

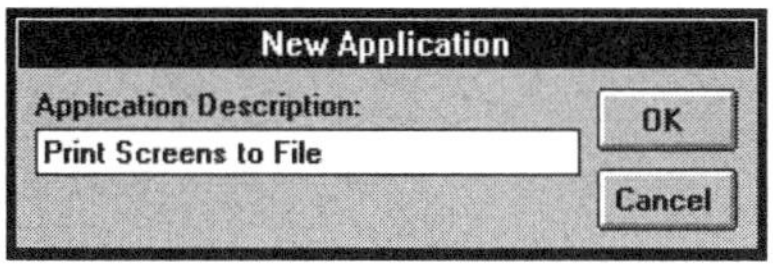

Figure 3.6
The Application Description prompt.

To modify an application's key list, choose the Key Options arrow to expand the Key Options box, then choose the keys one at a time. After you enter the key options, choose the button to the far left (the one that looks like a key on a keyboard) to add the new key options to the key list.

Setting Communication Configuration

You also can set communication configuration. Choose Communication Options from the Panel menu to open the Communication Options window. Next, mark the Enable Communications Check box (see fig. 3.7).

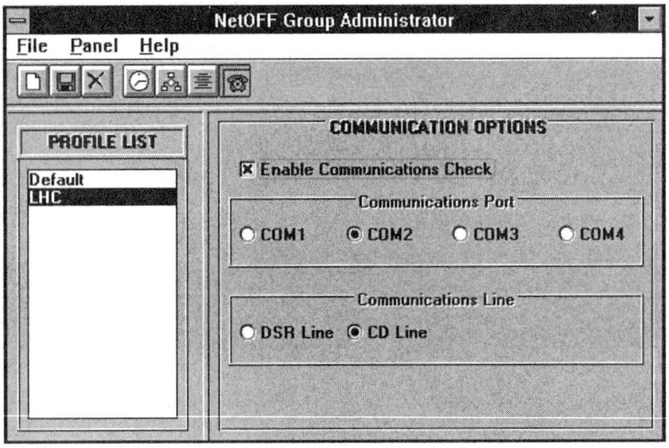

Figure 3.7
The Communication Options window.

You now can specify which communications port to use (COM1, COM2, COM3, or COM4).

You also can specify which communications line to use (DSR or CD). Choosing DSR (Data Set Ready) tells NetOFF to monitor any workstation traffic on the chosen communications port. Choosing CD (Carrier Detect) directs NetOFF to monitor the communications port to determine whether it is online and active, or offline. As long as the port (modem) is online and active, NetOFF treats the connection as if it were an active workstation.

Other CITADEL NetWare Utilities on the CD

The CD also includes other CITADEL utilities. Each of these utilities are NLMs, and thus must be loaded at the NetWare file server using the LOAD *NLM_name* command, replacing *NLM_name* with the name of the NLM.

These NLMs are found in the CITADEL\NWUTIL directory under other subdirectories:

- ✔ **NetClear.** NetClear periodically scans the network for workstations that are taking up valuable connections, but for which no user is actually logged in. NetClear releases (clears) the connection, thus making it available to other workstations.

- ✔ **NetCONSOLE.** NetCONSOLE automatically handles routine activities or tasks that otherwise require input at the server. If you need to unload one or more NLMs before running a backup, for example, you can use NetCONSOLE to handle those activities for you. When you set your backups to function after hours, NetCONSOLE can perform any tasks that you otherwise would have to be present to handle yourself.

- ✔ **NetPURGE.** NetPURGE scans the network for files that meet certain criteria you can specify, and then logs, backs up, or deletes those files as required.

- ✔ **NetQ.** NetQ enables a network supervisor or user to view or modify information about print jobs in print queues.

- ✔ **NetWATCH.** NetWATCH scans the file server for unowned files, changes their ownership to SUPERVISOR, and keeps a log file of all actions taken by the program. The log file can be presented to you in hard copy or on-screen.

CHILAGA
NORVMBEGA
FRANCIA
TEAC.
MARATA.
CVLIACAN.
AVACAL
CALICVAS.
CAPASCHI.
TERLICHICHIMECHI.
HISPANIA NOVA
TOVA
CVBA
HISPANIOLA
MAR DEL SVR, quod
Circulus Æquinoctialis
PACIFICVM
CHARCAS
CHILI
PATAGONES vel REGIO GIGANTVM
ICAE SIVE
ORBIS, NO
SCRIPTIO.
Archipelago del C. delleado

4

CHAPTER

COMAUTSY

The COMAUTSY directory contains a shareware program (DOS *and* Windows versions included) that helps you prepare for the NetWare 3 CNE tests. The program provides a series of flash cards that both test your current knowledge and help you remember the information you need to know about NetWare 3 to pass the CNE tests.

This software (Flashcards) is free for a 30-day trial period. If after 30 days you want to purchase the software, contact:

Thomas Neuman
Computer Automation Systems
2280 Old Orchard Drive
Marietta, GA 30068
(404) 565-6187

This chapter explains how to use the DOS and Windows versions of Flashcards.

Installing and Using the DOS Version of Flashcards

The DOS version of Flashcards is stored as a zipped file on the CD in the COMAUTSY\FLSHCRDS\DOS directory. The FLASHDOS.EXE program unzips the stored files to your default drive. You must, therefore, set your default drive to the exact path to which you want to store the Flashcards files. To run FLASHDOS.EXE, type **FLASHDOS** at the DOS prompt, and press Enter. The files are then unzipped and stored in the default directory.

You start the DOS version of Flashcards by typing **FL** and pressing Enter. An opening screen appears that provides information about the authors of the program and how to contact Computer Automation Systems. When you press Enter at this screen, you are prompted to provide a user name (see fig. 4.1).

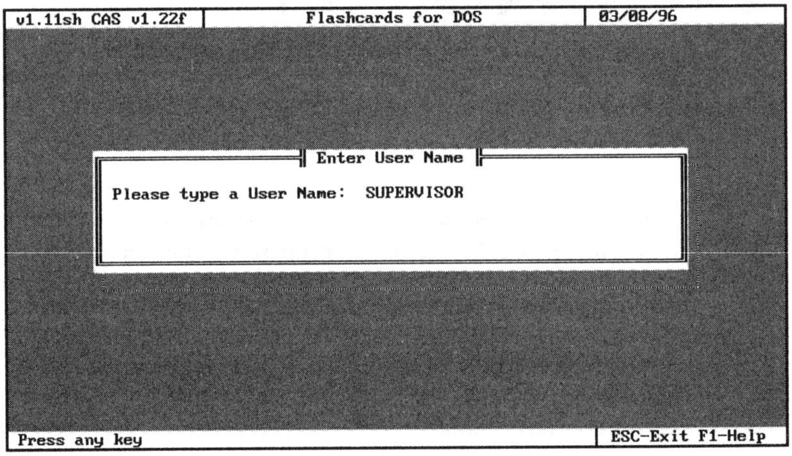

Figure 4.1
The user name prompt.

Type a user name and press Enter. Verify the user name is correct by choosing Yes when prompted. The Flashcards for DOS Main Menu opens (see fig. 4.2).

The Main Menu provides five options from which you can choose:

- ✔ Choose database
- ✔ Choose category
- ✔ Run Flashcards
- ✔ View User information
- ✔ Quit

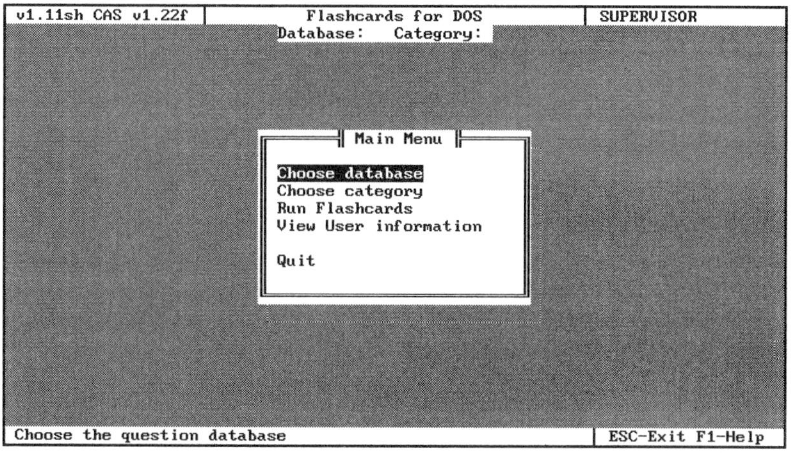

Figure 4.2 The Flashcards for DOS Main Menu.

The fifth option, Quit, closes the Flashcards for DOS utility. Each of the other four options are explained in the following sections.

Choose Database

The *Choose database* option enables you to select which database to use. When the list of database files (DBF) opens, choose one. Only one file is available, however: NW31XADM.DBF (see fig. 4.3).

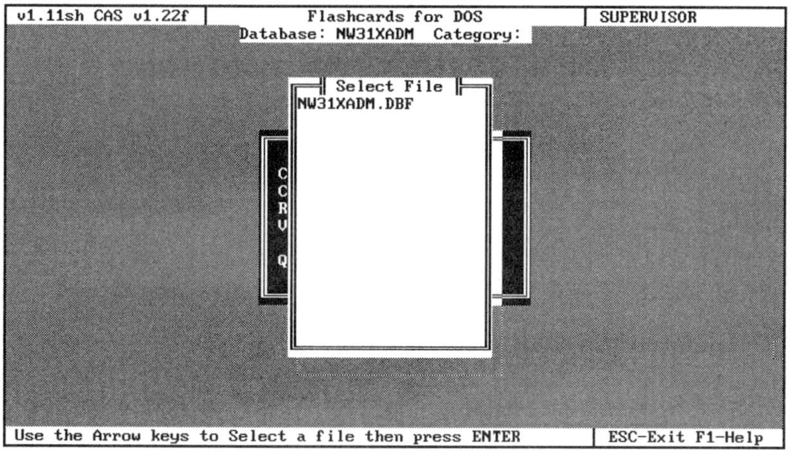

Figure 4.3 The list of database files.

After you choose a database you want to run, Flashcards returns you to the Main Menu.

Choose Category

The *Choose category* option enables you to select the category of information for which flash cards are presented (see fig. 4.4). You can choose from 15 categories of information. Some of these categories, however, have subcategories, amounting to a grand total of 27 categories. In addition, two introductory categories are included: Information about this database and Online Help. The following list contains the 27 categories and subcategories from which you can choose:

- ✔ Connecting to the Network
- ✔ Using NetWare 3.12 Resources
- ✔ Planning Network File Systems
- ✔ Accessing Network File Systems
- ✔ Managing Network File Systems (2)
- ✔ Login Security - Initial Access
- ✔ Login Security - Bindery
- ✔ NCP Packet Signature
- ✔ Directory and file rights
- ✔ Trustees and inheritance
- ✔ Access rights and effective rights
- ✔ File attributes
- ✔ Automating the user environment
- ✔ Login scripts
- ✔ Login script variables
- ✔ User menus
- ✔ Managing the NetWare server
- ✔ Network printing environment
- ✔ NetWare print server
- ✔ NetWare print job redirection
- ✔ Managing print jobs

- ✔ Customizing print jobs
- ✔ System fault tolerance
- ✔ Storage Management Services
- ✔ Implementing electronic mail
- ✔ Network applications

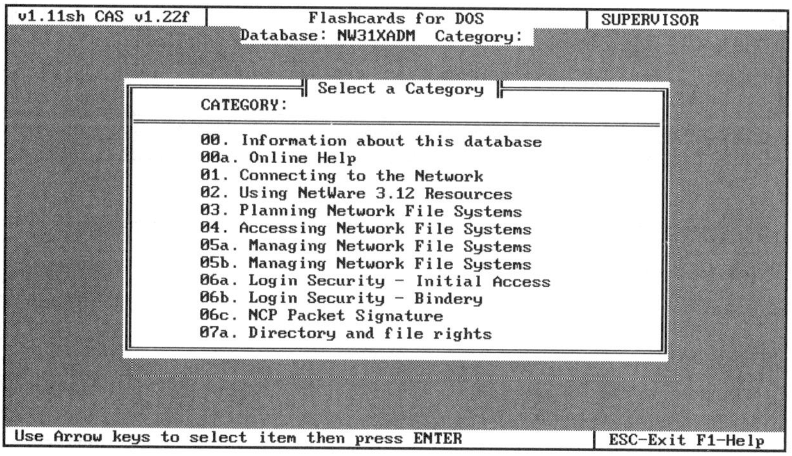

Figure 4.4
The Flashcards CATEGORY menu.

Run Flashcards

After you choose a database and a test category, choose Run Flashcards to begin testing. If you do not choose a database before you choose Run Flashcards, the Database menu opens, forcing you to make a choice. If you do not choose a category of information to test, the first category is automatically selected when you choose Run Flashcards. If you make your choice of database and choose a category, choosing Run Flashcards presents you with your first question. If you choose the Connecting to the Network category, for example, the screen shown in figure 4.5 opens.

When you see a test question, type your answer into the Your answer area, then press Tab. If your answer is correct, Flashcards presents the next test question. If not, the correct answer appears in the Expected answer area, as shown in figure 4.6.

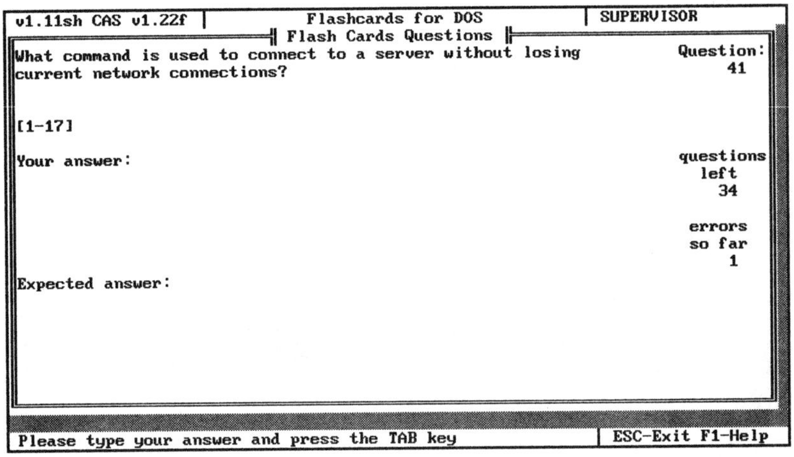

Figure 4.5 The first test question for the Connecting to the Network category.

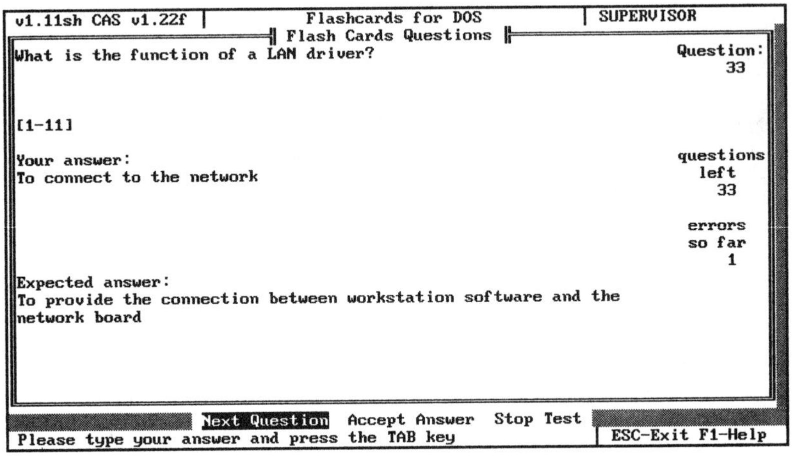

Figure 4.6 A test question with user response and correct response.

You can stop the presentation of test questions at any time by pressing Esc, then choosing Stop Test from the list of options that appear across the bottom of the screen (see fig. 4.7).

After you complete the test or choose to stop the test, you can retest on the questions you miss. To choose whether to retest, choose Yes or No at the prompt (see fig. 4.8).

If you answer all the questions correctly, the `Congratulations, you had no errors` message appears. Press Enter to choose OK and exit Flashcards.

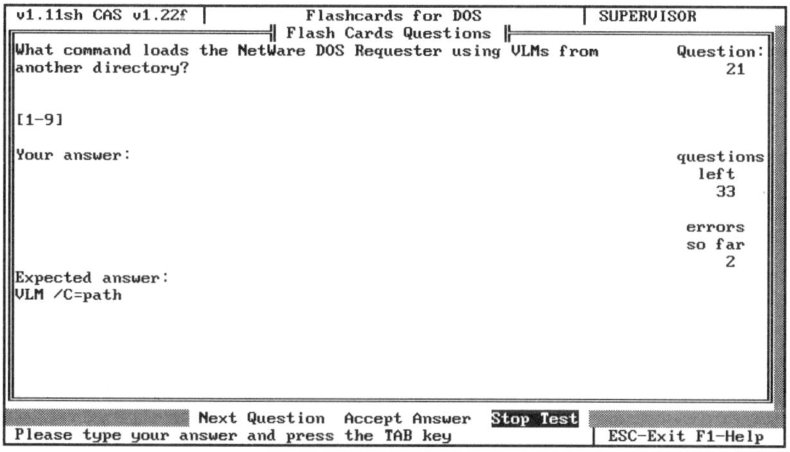

Figure 4.7
A test with options displayed across the bottom of the screen.

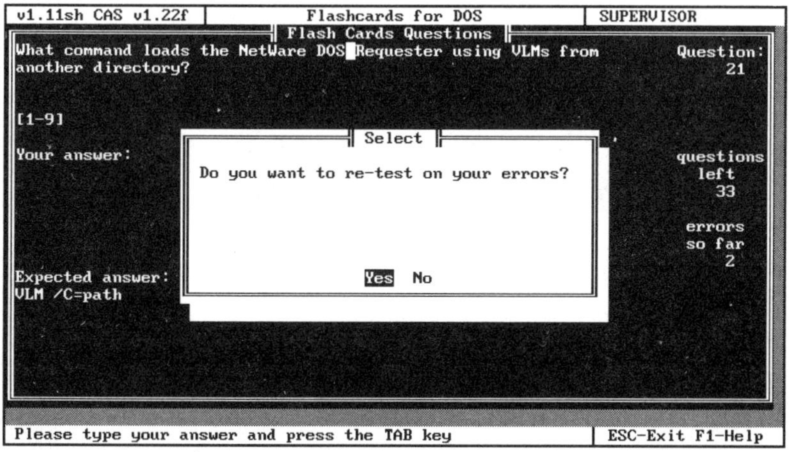

Figure 4.8
The prompt to retest on missed questions.

View User Information

Choosing View User information from the Main Menu opens the User History Information screen, revealing a list of users and their associated test databases (see fig. 4.9).

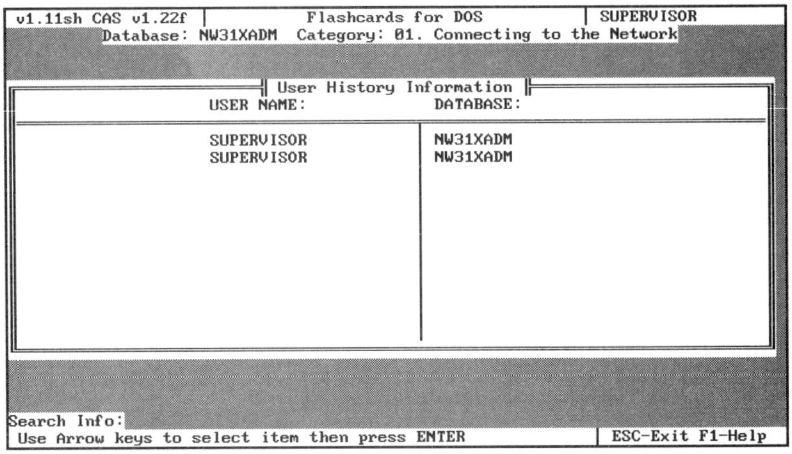

Figure 4.9
The Flashcards User History Information screen.

To see information about a user's testing history, choose that user from the user list. The Add/Change User History Information screen opens (see fig. 4.10).

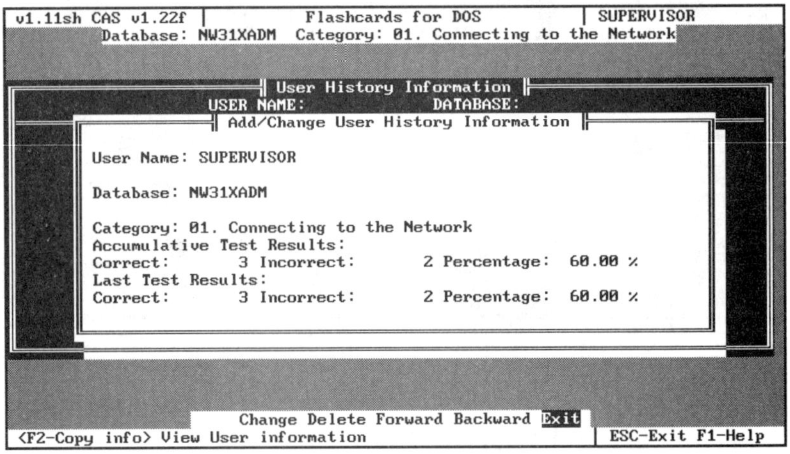

Figure 4.10
The Add/Change User History Information screen.

From this screen, you can perform any of the following tasks by choosing the associated option located at the bottom of the Add/Change User History Information screen:

- ✔ **Change.** To change a specific field of information, highlight the field and then choose Change.
- ✔ **Delete.** To delete a user's test, choose the test to delete, then choose Delete. Answer Yes when Flashcards prompts `Are you sure you want to DELETE this information?`

- **Forward.** To page forward through the information pages for each category of test the user took, choose Forward.
- **Backward.** To page backward through the information pages for each category of test the user took, choose Backward.
- **Exit.** To close the Add/Change User History Information screen, choose Exit.

After you close the Add/Change User History Information screen, press Esc to exit to the Main Menu. Choose Quit from the Main Menu to close the Flashcards for DOS utility.

Installing and Using the Windows Version of Flashcards

The Flashcards for Windows files are in zipped format on the CD. Follow the installation prompts which occur when following the installation instructions outlined below in order to automatically unzip the files. If you receive an error message that indicates the files cannot be unzipped, be certain your default drive is set to a directory to which you have the rights to create files and directories.

Installing Flashcards for Windows

To install the Windows version of Flashcards, complete the following steps from the DOS prompt:

1. Create a directory into which to install Flashcards for Windows.
2. Change your default drive to the directory you created for installing Flashcards for Windows.
3. Change to your CD-ROM drive.
4. Using the DOS CD command, change the path for your CD-ROM drive to COMAUTSY\ FLSHCRDS\WINDOWS.
5. Change your default drive back to the directory you created for installing Flashcards for Windows.
6. Type ***CD_drive*\FLWINPRG**, and press Enter. Replace ***CD_drive*** with the drive letter of your CD drive, which you changed to reflect a direct path to the COMAUTSY\ FLSHCRDS\WINDOWS directory on the CD.

7. Change your default drive to C:\WINDOWS\SYSTEM (or to the drive on which your Windows SYSTEM file is located).

8. Type ***CD_drive*\FLWINPMSC** and press Enter, where ***CD_drive*** represents your CD-drive's drive letter, which you changed to create a direct path to the COMAUTSY\FLSHCRDS\WINDOWS directory. This step installs six DLL files and two VBX files into the WINDOWS\SYSTEM directory.

9. Copy FLWIN.INI into the WINDOWS directory.

10. If you did not load SHARE.EXE before starting Windows, close Windows, load SHARE.EXE, and restart Windows.

After the files are unzipped and placed in the correct directories, you can run the Flashcards for Windows utility.

Running Flashcards for Windows

You must be running Windows before you can start the Flashcards for Windows utility. Choose **R**un from the **F**ile menu, use the **B**rowse option to find the Flashcards for Windows executable program (FLWIN.EXE), and choose OK. Choose OK once more to start Flashcards for Windows and open the DOS/Windows:*User_name* dialog box.

Enter your name when prompted and click on OK. Choose the Database button, then choose NW31XADM.DBF. Press Enter to choose OK to open the NetWare 3.1x administration database of questions and the list of available testing categories. To choose a category, open the list (choose the down arrow), scroll through the list until you find the category you want, such as `07a. Directory and file rights` (as shown in figure 4.11), and then choose that category .

Choose the **T**est button to begin the presentation of questions for the chosen category. Type your response to each question in the Response box, then choose **D**one. Figure 4.12 shows the test question screen, including the **D**one button.

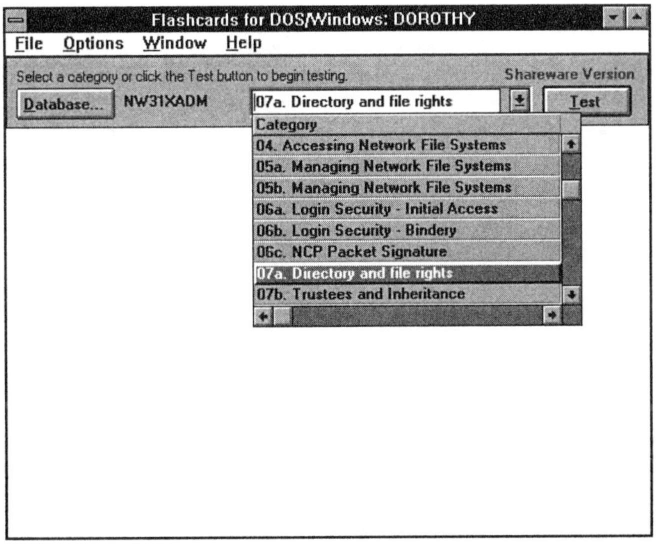

Figure 4.11
The Flashcards for DOS/Windows screen with the list of categories displayed.

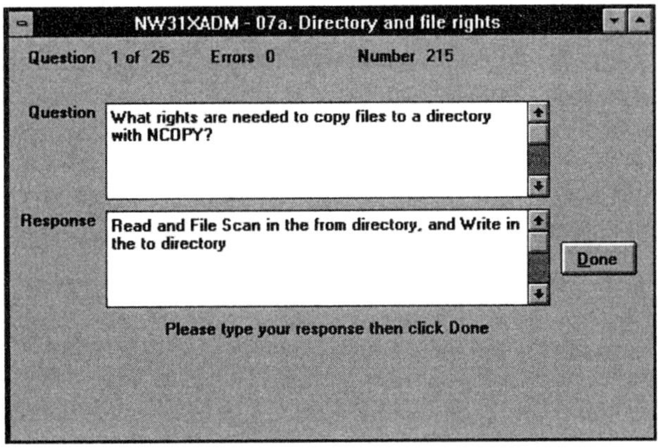

Figure 4.12
The Question window with a question and a user response.

If your answer is correct, Flashcards presents the next question. If your answer is incorrect, Flashcards shows the correct answer in the Answer area (see fig. 4.13).

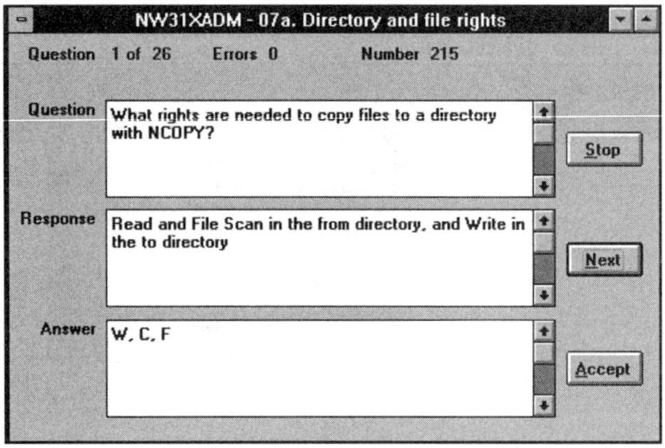

Figure 4.13
A test window showing a question, a response, and a correct answer.

Note

For some questions, the program can have difficulty determining if your answer is perfectly correct. If, for example, an answer requires that you enter only letters that represent rights (such as W, C, F), the program can easily verify whether the answer is correct. If you have to enter a description of something, however, the program marks your answer incorrect if it doesn't exactly match the correct answer. Do not panic, therefore, if your answer is correct, but is marked wrong because it does not exactly match the program's correct answer.

To replace your answer with the correct answer, choose Accept. To move on to the next question, choose Next. Answer all the questions. After you finish the test, Flashcards prompts you to retest the questions you missed; choose Yes or No.

As in the DOS version of Flashcards, you can view and modify user information or delete a user's test in the Windows version. To accomplish any of these related tasks, choose User Information from the Window menu to open the User Test History dialog box (see fig. 4.14). Then choose View Form to open the User Test History detailed information dialog box (see fig. 4.15).

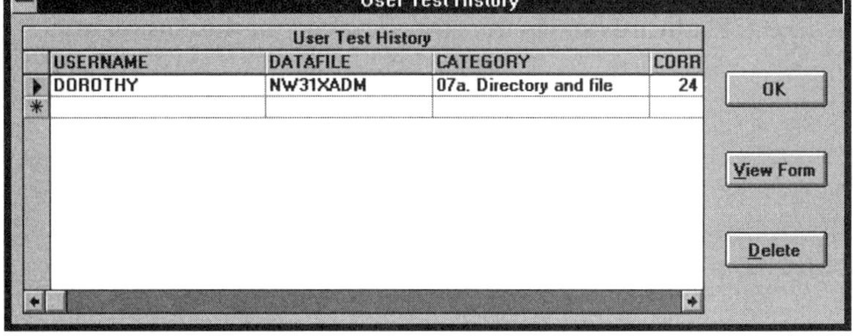

Figure 4.14
The User Test History dialog box.

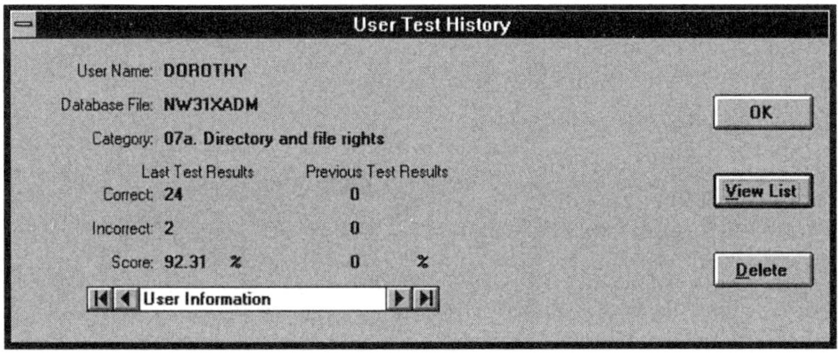

Figure 4.15
The User Test History detailed information dialog box.

With the user's User Test History dialog box open, you can delete any user's test by selecting the test, then choosing **D**elete and choosing Yes at the prompt.

CHILAGA
NORVMBEGA
FRANCIA
MOCOSA
AVACAL
APALCHEN
CALICVAS
CAPASCHI
TEAC
MARATA
CVLIACAN
ASTATLAN
TERLICHICHIMECHI
HISPANIA NOVA
TOPIRA
MEXICO
MECHVACAN
LA FLORIDA
CVBA
IVCATAN
HISPANIOLA
MAR DEL SVR, quod
Circulus Æquinoctialis
240
250
260
270
280
290
et PACIFICVM
CHARCAS
PARANA
CHILI
PATAGONES
REGIO GIGANTVM
CAE SIVE
ORBIS, NO
SCRIPTIO.
Archipelago del C. delleado

5

CHAPTER

COM_TYME

The software programs in the COM_TYME directory on the CD are provided as evaluation copies. You can use them for evaluation purposes. If you want to purchase the software, you can contact the manufacturer at the following address and phone numbers:

Computer Tyme
411 North Sherman, Suite 300
Springfield, MO 65802

(417) 866-1222 Technical Support
(417) 866-1665 BBS/FAX
(800) 548-5353 Sales

This chapter discusses how to install and use the software, beginning with instructions for installing it.

Installing Computer Tyme's Software

If you are on a network, map a drive to an area on the file server where you have sufficient rights for creating directories and files. Next, create a directory into which you can install the software, then change to that directory. Copy the *CD_drive*:\COM_TYME\MARXMENU directory into the new directory. Then, type ***drive*:INSTALL**, replacing ***drive*** with the drive letter mapped to the directory you just created, and press Enter.

During the installation, files are extracted, copied, and so on (see fig. 5.1). Menus are compiled, libraries checked, and topics tested. When this part of the installation process ends, the copyright screen for Computer Tyme's MarxMenu and associated programs, languages, and so on, appears. When this happens, just press Enter to continue the installation.

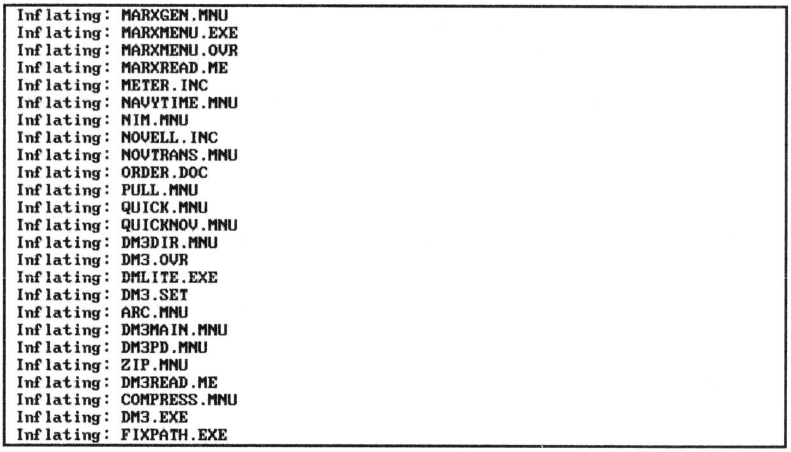

Figure 5.1 Screen displaying unpacking and installing of files.

Several quick screens flash by during the installation process. A warning screen opens to tell you how to use the MARX Menu command. Read this screen, then press Enter to continue. The process ends and clears your screen except for the DOS prompt and a message that reads `All Done!`. You now have successfully installed MarxMenu, and can run any of the related menus by typing **MARX *menu_name***, where *menu_name* is the name of the menu file, and pressing Enter.

Programs

After installing Computer Tyme's software, you can find a wide variety of executable files in the directory you just created. Each file has its own purpose. Each file that you can run from the DOS prompt as a separate executable program is listed and briefly described in this chapter.

To run many of these programs requires only a simple command-line command. To display information about space on volumes and in memory, for example, use the FREE command. To use the FREE command, type **FREE** at the DOS prompt, and press Enter (see fig. 5.2).

```
F:\COM_TYME>free

/? for Help

Total Volume Space: 416,776,192
 Used Volume Space:  88,965,120   21.3%
 Free Volume Space: 327,811,072   78.7%

Deleted File Space: 5,734,400    Not Yet Available: 0

Total DOS Memory: 655,360 bytes
 Free DOS Memory: 456,944 bytes

Total EMS Memory: 1,048,576 bytes
 Free EMS Memory: 1,048,576 bytes

 Total ENV Space: 512 bytes
  Free ENV Space: 251 bytes

F:\COM_TYME>
```

Figure 5.2
Sample output from the FREE utility.

Other files are more complex. Some provide a complete online menu. Typing DM3, for example, opens a file-management menu, such as that shown in figure 5.3.

```
►55RLIB02.TXT 03-08-96   32k      Total ♦ Marked        Totl: 416.8m
 ADDRESS.INC  02-15-95   32k   SizeK:  [   9440 ¦ 0         ]  Free: 327.8m
 ARC.MNU      03-11-90   32k   Files:  [    201 ¦ 0         ]  Sort: Name
 ARC.MRX      03-08-96   32k
 ATTACH.BAT   03-08-96   32k   Path: F:\COM_TYME\*.*
 ATTACH.EXE   08-29-95   96k
 ATTACH.MNU   08-01-95   32k   Size: 2536      Time: 13:05:32
 ATTACH.MRX   03-08-96   32k
 BATEXIT.BAT  03-08-96    0k
 BATZAP.BAT   03-08-96   32k
 BATZAP.EXE   08-29-95   96k
 BATZAP.HLP   04-27-95   32k
 BATZAP.MNU   08-01-95   32k      F1 Full Help  F10 PullDown Menu
 BATZAP.MRX   03-08-96   32k       ? Mini Help  Tab Function Keys
 BBS.INC      04-23-95   64k
 BBSDEF.INC   11-11-94   32k
 BESTNET.EXE  05-31-95   32k
 BINDDUMP.BAT 03-08-96   32k
 BINDDUMP.EXE 08-29-95   64k         <*> Directory Master III <*>
 BINDDUMP.MNU 08-01-95   32k                Computer Tyme
 BINDDUMP.MRX 03-08-96   32k         411 North Sherman Suite 300
 BINDEZ.BAT   03-08-96   32k    Springfield, Mo. 65802 (417) 866-1222
 BINDEZ.EXE   08-29-95   96k     Version 3.15  Release Date 12-02-94
```

Figure 5.3
The DM3 file-management menu.

To run any of these files shown in figure 5.3, type the name of the executable file at the DOS prompt and press Enter. The following files are executable files that function from the DOS prompt and are included in the directory:

- ✔ **ATTACH.EXE.** Similar to the Novell ATTACH command in that you use it to attach to additional file servers.
- ✔ **BATZAP.EXE.** Modifies batch files and other configuration files in text format. You also can use this utility to read system information and conditionally set environment variables and DOS error-level codes used by batch files.
- ✔ **BESTNET.EXE.** Sets an environment variable called NET, which looks at the workstation's DOS version and availability of EMS or XMS memory. You can use this environment variable in a batch file to load your network shell into memory.
- ✔ **BINDDUMP.EXE.** Copies the contents of the NetWare bindery to a printer or file.
- ✔ **BINDEZ.EXE.** Exports bindery information to an INI-type file or imports it from an INI file.
- ✔ **COMSP.EXE.** Increases security by preventing files that shell out to DOS from being able to load COMMAND.COM.
- ✔ **D.EXE.** Views a list of files and directories. D.EXE is the equivalent of the DOS DIR command, but displays information vertically in up to six columns (file name only), adjusting its width automatically to accommodate file-name sizes (see fig. 5.4).

Figure 5.4
Sample output from running D.EXE with the /1 option.

```
VERSION  EXE      12,111    32k   May-31 1995    8:49a  A___
VID      MNU       1,617    32k   May-22 1992    8:49a  A___
VID      MRX         640    32k   Mar-08 1996   12:53p  A___
WATCH    COM       1,081    32k   Oct-18 1993    3:12p  A___
WHEREIS  EXE      13,112    32k   May-31 1995    8:49a  A___
WHOGOWA  EXE      60,160    64k   Aug-29 1995   10:28a  A___
WHOGOWA  MNU       4,561    32k   Aug-01 1995   10:59a  A___
WHOGOWA  MRX       1,536    32k   Mar-08 1996   12:53p  A___
WHOHAS   BAT          58    32k   Mar-08 1996   12:59p  A___
WHOHAS   EXE      60,928    64k   Aug-29 1995   10:28a  A___
WHOHAS   MNU       5,112    32k   Aug-01 1995   10:59a  A___
WHOHAS   MRX       2,048    32k   Mar-08 1996   12:53p  A___
WINSUP   INC       3,598    32k   Apr-16 1994    2:50p  A___
WORM     INC       5,348    32k   Jul-11 1994    2:41p  A___
XMETER   EXE      13,142    32k   May-31 1995    8:49a  A___
YESNO    MNU       3,011    32k   Nov-28 1989    8:00a  A___
YESNO    MRX       1,024    32k   Mar-08 1996   12:53p  A___
ZDEL     EXE       8,244    32k   May-31 1995    8:49a  A___
ZIP      MNU         978    32k   Jan-27 1993    2:39p  A___
ZIP      MRX         384    32k   Mar-08 1996   12:53p  A___

 Free: 328M  Used: 89.0M  Tot: 417M  Files: 201  Using: 9440k  Block: 32k

F:\COM_TYME>
```

- ✔ **DEVICE.EXE.** Produces a report that contains driver name, amount of memory used, and interrupt factors for each driver loaded into memory.
- ✔ **DISABLE.EXE.** Temporarily disables or re-enables a TSR in memory. DISABLE.EXE can be used if you are also using WATCH.EXE.
- ✔ **DM3.EXE.** Manages files.
- ✔ **DMLITE.EXE.** Manages files, but does not have as much functionality as DM3.
- ✔ **DOLIST.EXE.** Functions like the DOS Shell, but with the editing power of a word processor, and enables you to execute commands on a list of files.
- ✔ **FIND.EXE.** A replacement utility for the DOS FIND program.
- ✔ **FIXPATH.EXE.** Corrects your workstation's DOS PATH statement to include only directories that are currently available, thus helping prevent future DOS errors that might occur after logging off a network.
- ✔ **FORK.EXE.** Used with the DOS piping command (symbolized with the | key) to view the contents of a file which is being piped, if you chose to save the piped information to a file.
- ✔ **FREE.EXE.** Displays information about volume, file, and memory space.
- ✔ **GRPTYME.EXE.** Adds, deletes, and modifies Windows Group (GRP) files.
- ✔ **INIDIF.EXE.** Compares two INI files and then creates a third INI file that contains the differences between the two files.
- ✔ **INITYME.EXE.** Manages INI files.
- ✔ **INMEM.EXE.** Finds TSRs, device drivers, and batch files running in workstation memory.
- ✔ **KBD.EXE.** Typically used in batch files to control keyboard functions such as turning caps lock on/off, turning scroll lock on/off, and so on.
- ✔ **LOGOFF.EXE.** Used as a replacement for Novell's LOGOUT command, enabling you to eliminate any references to drive mappings on the network at the same time you log out of the network.
- ✔ **MAPMEM.EXE.** Views which memory-resident programs are installed, and how much memory they are using (see fig. 5.5).

Figure 5.5 Sample output from the MAPMEM utility.

```
F:\COM_TYME>mapmem
MAPMEM 3.5, Copyright 1993 TurboPower Software

Psp  Cnt    Size Name        Command Line         Hooked Vectors
---- --- ------- ----------- -------------------- ----------------------------------
       3  34,864 DOS
0887   1      96 LOADHI      n/a
08AB   1  32,080 MSCDEX      n/a                  E0
1094   1   5,472 VLM         n/a
11EB   2   1,600                                  2F
1253   4   3,296 win386      n/a                  1C 28 4B 67
1318   3   3,376 COMMAND                          23 24
13EF   2 105,968 SNAP        c:\books\3reslib...  05 08 10 13 15 21 25 26 30 E3
                                                  E6 F7
       1     272 ---free---
2DD2   1  10,416                                  22 3F
D478   2     320 (COMMAND)
3071   2 457,216 ---free---
         655,344 ---total--

F:\COM_TYME>
```

- ✔ **MARKNET.EXE.** Saves a picture of the workstation's status to a file so that the picture can be restored later.

- ✔ **ME.EXE.** Manipulates files, including their contents.

- ✔ **MORE.EXE.** Takes the place of the DOS MORE command.

- ✔ **MOREHAND.EXE.** Placed in front of other commands you run, it allows the commands to automatically give themselves more file handles if needed, providing you have already allocated additional file handles. To allocate additional file handles, FILES=99 must be placed in the computer's CONFIG.SYS file. If you have to modify the CONFIG.SYS file to include this line, your computer must be rebooted before using the MOREHAND.EXE command.

- ✔ **MOVE.EXE.** Moves files to other directories, subdirectories, or renames them.

- ✔ **MXPRN.EXE.** Creates MARXMENU.DOC and TOOLBOX.DOC during installation.

- ✔ **PATCH.EXE.** Patches files in ASCII or text format.

- ✔ **PD.EXE.** Changes directories quickly regardless of where you are within the directory structure.

- ✔ **PIPEDIR.EXE.** Used for piping directory and file listings into other programs, deleting files, removing directories, and finding and cataloging files.

- ✔ **RAMMAP.EXE.** Displays what programs are in memory, and where possible, frees any unused and wasted memory space.

- ✔ **RELEASE.EXE.** Removes memory-resident programs and restores interrupt vectors to the state in which they existed prior to installing MARK.

- ✔ **RELNET.EXE.** Removes memory-resident programs, particularly NetWare networking shells.

- ✔ **SHELLZAP.EXE.** Loads the DOS shell and changes COMSPEC variables to prevent problems that may occur when using diskless workstations.

- ✔ **SIEVE.EXE.** Tests processor speed to determine the kind of performance your PC can deliver (see fig. 5.6).

```
F:\COM_TYME>sieve

Byte Magazine Sieve Benchmark * Freeware
Prime Number Test * Version 2.1

By Marc Perkel * Computer Tyme * (417) 866-1222

  This test is the most accurate test as to the performance
that you will ACTUALLY GET out of your computer as far as
PROCESSOR SPEED is concerned. The results of this speed test
correspond to 25 real programs that I have run. The results
of this test are much more real than Norton SI.

  If you are using a V20, V30, 80186, 80286, or 80386 and
are running CADD or very MATH INTENSIVE software, you may
do a little better (maybe 10%) than this program indicates.

  Other factors affecting computing performance include
HARD DISK SPEED and use of a MATH CHIP if you are using
software that talks to math chips.

The processor speed of this computer is 220.9
times faster than the IBM PC/XT.

F:\COM_TYME>
```

Figure 5.6
Sample output from the SIEVE.EXE program.

- ✔ **SMITE.EXE.** Disconnects users, and also can serve to determine which users are connected before specifying which ones to disconnect.

- ✔ **SORT.EXE.** Takes the place of the standard DOS SORT command, because it can sort larger files.

- ✔ **SUBLOGIN.EXE.** Used mostly for software development to establish a quick login to a file server, including providing a needed password.

- ✔ **TRUSTEZ.EXE.** Copies directory trustee information into a file or loads it from a file.

- ✔ **USERLIST.EXE.** Used in place of Novell's USERLIST program, and also can be used on NetWare 4 networks (see fig. 5.7).

Figure 5.7 Sample output from USERLIST.EXE on a NetWare 4.1 file server.

```
F:\COM_TYME>userlist

Computer Tyme USERLIST * Copyright 1993-94 by Marc Perkel
All Rights Reserved * Version 1.02 * Release Date: 11-25-94

User Information for Server CP_410
Connection  User Name         Login Time
----------  --------------    --------------------
     1      CP_410.BUSINESS   03-08-1996  7:40 am
     2    * ADMIN             03-08-1996 10:41 am
     3      PS1               03-08-1996  7:40 am
     4      PS1               03-08-1996  7:40 am

F:\COM_TYME>
```

- ✔ **VERSION.EXE.** Fakes a DOS version number so that you can avoid the error message indicating a file is using the wrong version number.
- ✔ **WHEREIS.EXE.** Locates files, and the resulting information (list of where the files can be found) can be piped into a file.
- ✔ **WHOGOWA.EXE.** Views a list of open files by connection number.
- ✔ **WHOHAS.EXE.** Discovers which users have a given file open.
- ✔ **XMETER.EXE.** Views how many users have a given file open, restricts the number of users who can open a file, and otherwise manages the number of users who access a file so that you can ensure your application usage is within licensed limits.
- ✔ **ZDEL.EXE.** Deletes files from the current directory and from lower directories.

The best way to learn to use these programs is to experiment with them. Run them on your own computer, using switches and options as provided by each program. If you need more information, you can run most of these programs with the /? option after them to obtain online help which will explain, among other things, what switches and options are available for the program. The menu-based programs have a help option in their menus.

CHILAGA
FRANCIA
NORVMBEGA
MOCOSA
AVACAL
APALCHEN
CALICVAS
CAPASCHI
TEAC.
MARATA.
CVLIACAN
ASTATLAN
TERLICHICHIMECHI
HISPANIA NOVA
TOVA
TOPIRA
MEXICO
CVBA
HISPANIOLA
C. Camaron
La Bermuda
MAR DEL SVR, quod
Circulus Æquinoctialis
240
250
260
270
280
290
1. Tarama
2. Xauxa
3. Aguaxe
4. Pacalcama
CHILE
CHARCAS
PARANA
Archipelago del C. delleado
ICAE SIVE
ORBIS, NO
SCRIPTIO.

6

CHAPTER

CYBERPAS

The CYBERPAS directory contains the CNEQUIZR Novell test-preparation software (Windows version). The version of CNEQUIZR on the CD includes 19 tests covering the following 12 topics:

- ✔ Microcomputers
- ✔ Service and Support
- ✔ Networking Technologies
- ✔ NetWare 2.2 Administration and Installation/Configuration
- ✔ NetWare 3.12 Administration and Installation/Configuration
- ✔ NetWare 4.*x* Administration and Installation/Configuration
- ✔ Unix Prerequisites and UnixWare Administration
- ✔ NetWare 3.11 to 4.0 Update
- ✔ NetWare TCP/IP

- ✔ NetWare Connect
- ✔ NetWare NFS
- ✔ LAN Workplace for DOS

CNEQUIZR also includes a tutorial that explains how to use the Micro House Technical Library to find answers to test questions. In addition, information about the CNE program is included (choose the Survival icon). Also included are online help (choose the Help icon) and the capability to uninstall the CNEQUIZR for Windows program.

The CD contains a shareware version of CNEQUIZR. To register a copy with Cyber Pass, Inc., you can contact them at the following address or phone numbers:

Cyber Pass, Inc.
417 Bay Street, Suite 3
Ottawa, ON CANADA K1R 6A5

(800) 255-3763
(613) 237-4991
(613) 230-5279 (FAX)

You must register the software to have access to all the questions in the CNEQUIZR database. In the unregistered version of CNEQUIZR on the CD, you can access only a portion of the questions in the database.

Installing the CNEQUIZR Software

To install the CNEQUIZR software from the CD, map a drive on the file server to a directory in which you want to install the software, or use the DOS CD command to change your C drive to a specific directory. Next, copy the software from the CD to the directory or run the installation process from the CD to the directory in which you want to install it.

Note You cannot have other Windows applications open while you set up this software; the setup program accesses Windows files that might be open. If you receive a message that indicates a file cannot be used, exit the setup program, close other Windows applications, then restart the setup process.

Next, type **SETUP** and press Enter to start the installation process. When the Welcome screen opens, choose OK to install the Monster Collection of CNEQUIZR for Windows. The software then searches for any outdated files (previous versions of this software). If it discovers any outdated files, it prompts you to replace those files. Choose Yes to replace an outdated file with a newer version. Otherwise, choose No. You can stop the setup process by choosing OK at the Cancel prompt, which is continually displayed during the setup process.

After the search and replace for updated files completes, you are prompted to choose the destination directory (see fig. 6.1). Choose the directory into which you want to place the software, then choose OK.

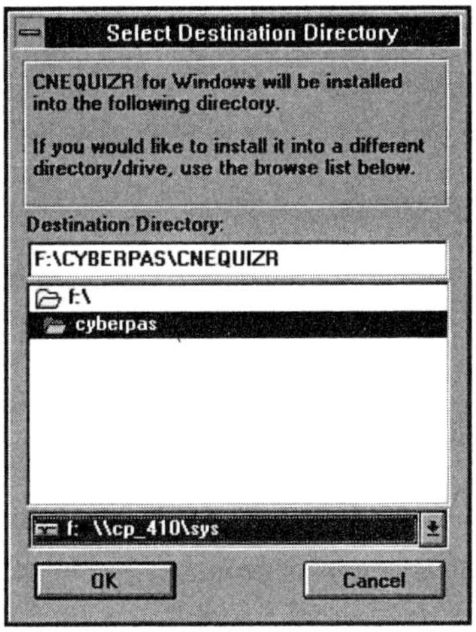

Figure 6.1
The CNEQUIZR setup destination directory prompt.

The setup process then prompts you to determine whether you want it to make backup copies of any files it finds that have the same name as a file it needs to install, before it overwrites the files. Choose Yes or No, or you can stop the setup process at this point by choosing OK. If you choose Yes, you must provide the path for a directory in which you want to store the backup versions.

After these steps are complete, the software installs the files. During installation of the software files, an Installing screen is displayed.

When prompted, select the Program Manager icon group into which you want to place the icons. The default is an icon group named CNEQUIZR for Windows (see fig. 6.2). You can choose another group that already exists or rename the new group. After you select the group, choose OK.

All icons and related software should now be installed. When prompted `Installation Complete`, choose OK.

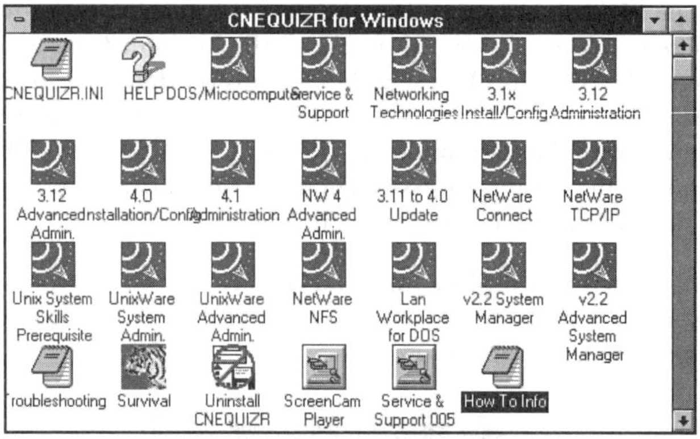

Figure 6.2
The CNEQUIZR for Windows icon group.

Running the Tutorial and Other Non-Test Options

The tutorial included with the Cyber Pass software explains how to use the Micro House Technical Library to find answers to test questions. This tutorial walks you through the process of opening the Micro House Technical Library from within a test question. To run the tutorial, choose the Service and Support 005 icon. During the tutorial, pop-up boxes appear that contain information about using the Micro House Technical Library to find answers to test questions (see fig. 6.3).

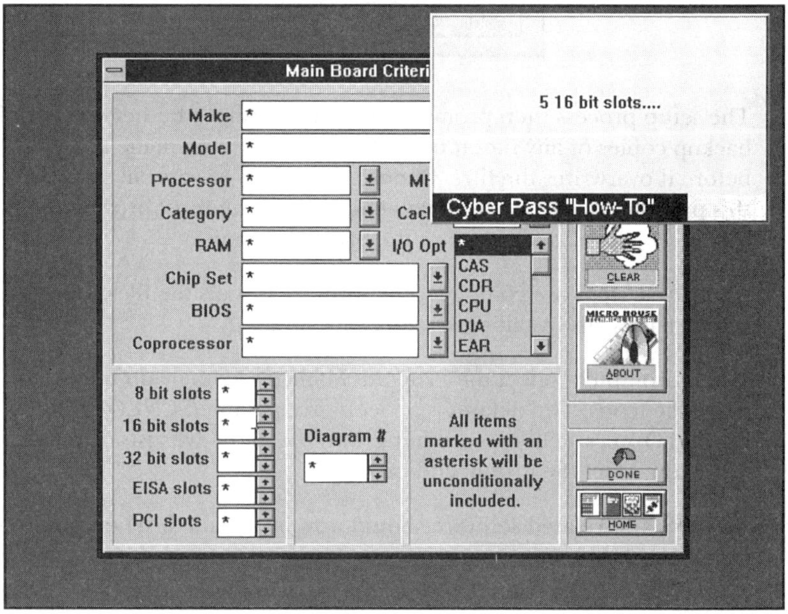

Figure 6.3
A sample screen from the Micro House Technical Library tutorial.

ScreenCam Player

The ScreenCam Player presents a series of screens that show a process, in much the same way you play a movie on VHS. To run the ScreenCam Player, choose the ScreenCam Player icon to open the ScreenCam dialog box (see fig. 6.4). Next, choose Open, then choose which SCN file to play. The only SCN file that comes with the CD version of Cyber Pass is the one for the tutorial. To run that SCN file, choose Play.

Figure 6.4
The ScreenCam dialog box.

Survival

The Survival program provides information about the CNE program itself to help you understand the program and the process. When you choose the Survival icon, a table of contents screen opens from which you can choose any particular section by clicking on the section's title. Click on the A Sample Lesson option under Part 2 - Stalking the Elusive Pray, for example, to read a sample lesson (see fig. 6.5).

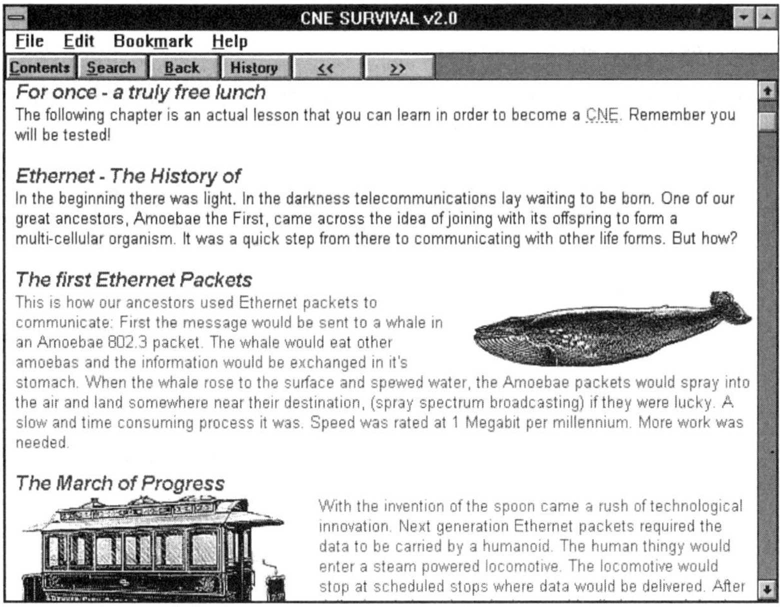

Figure 6.5
A page from the sample lesson.

Running the Tests

Each test in the CNEQUIZR for Windows group functions in the same manner. To run a test, first choose the icon related to the test from the CNEQUIZR for Windows icon group, then answer the questions. To run the NetWare 3.12 Administration test, for example, choose the 3.12 Administration icon. If prompted, provide your user name, and choose OK (see fig. 6.6).

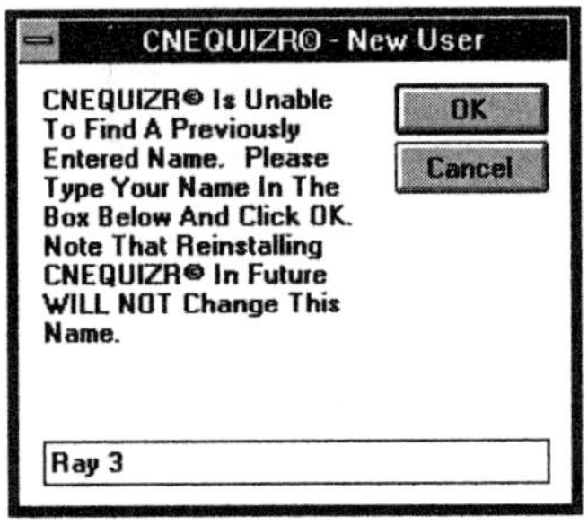

Figure 6.6
The prompt to provide a user name for the test.

Note

If you have not yet registered the software, the Are You Ready To Register? dialog box opens (see fig. 6.7), prompting you to do so. If you register the software, you gain access to all questions in the database; otherwise, your access is limited.

To register the software, choose YES, Register, then follow the steps listed on the registration screen.

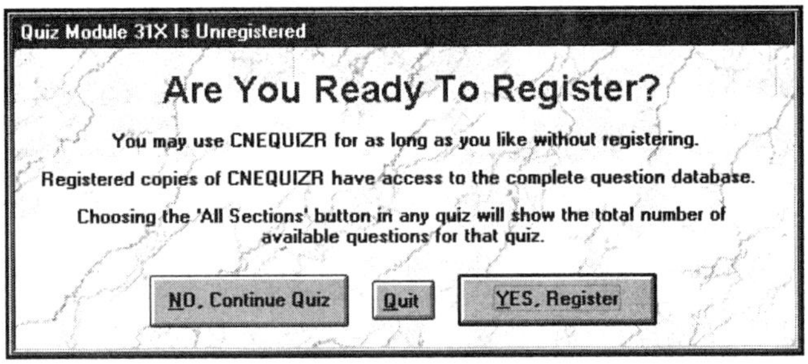

Figure 6.7
The Are You Ready To Register? dialog box.

If you prefer to sample the software rather than register for the time being, choose NO, Continue Quiz. You also can choose Quit to stop the program.

After you choose to continue the quiz, the introductory screen appears (accompanied by music if your system is configured to play it). Next, you see a screen similar to the one shown in figure 6.8, listing the sections from which you can choose. Choose a section. The screen displays a message box telling you that it is retrieving the test for that section.

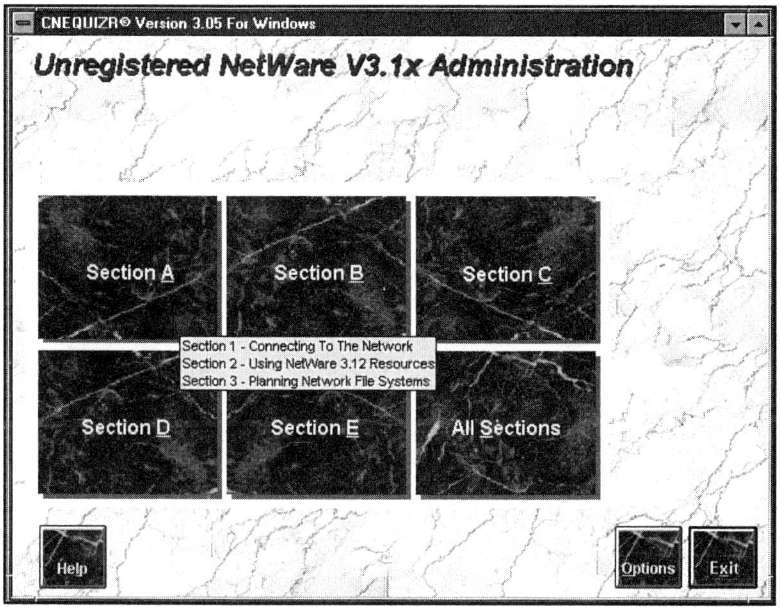

Figure 6.8
The test sections from which you can choose.

A screen appears telling you how many questions are available for the test. The same screen asks you how many of these questions you want to test on (see fig. 6.9). After you specify the number of questions you want to test on, choose OK to continue.

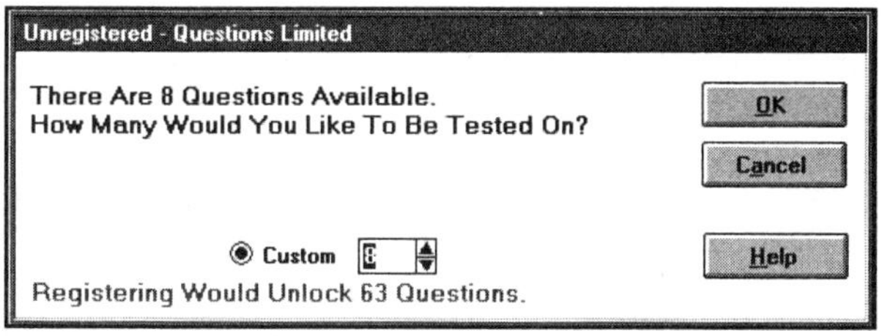

Figure 6.9
The screen from which to choose the number of test questions.

Note

If you have not registered, the screen shown in figure 6.9 also tells you how many locked questions are in the database from which you can choose if you register.

The first test question opens (figure 6.10 shows a sample test question). Choose the best answer, then choose Next to score your answer.

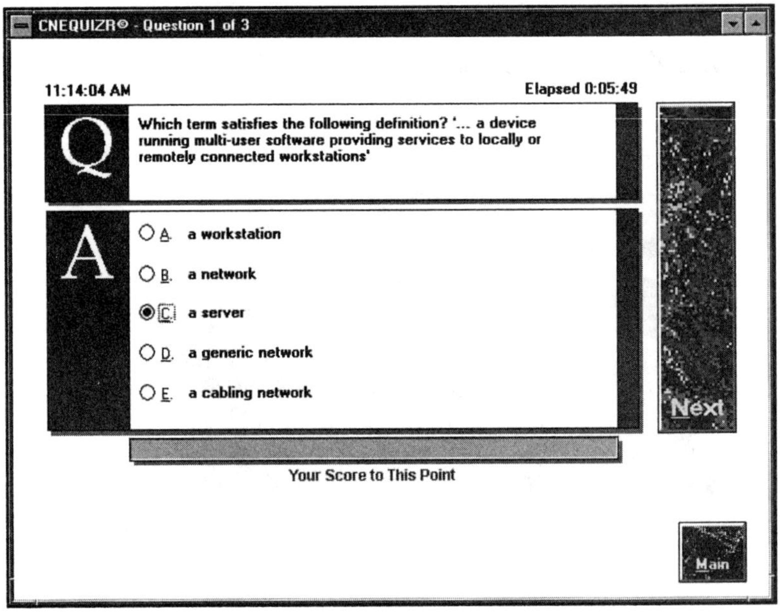

Figure 6.10 A sample test question.

A Results screen appears, telling you whether your answer is correct or incorrect. The Results screen also tells you where to find more information about the topics for which you incorrectly answered the related questions. You then can choose to go to the next question, view more information about the question, or print the question. To view more information about the question, choose the More Info button. The correct answer appears, along with a brief explanation of the answer. Figure 6.11 shows the result of choosing More Info when the answer to your question is incorrect.

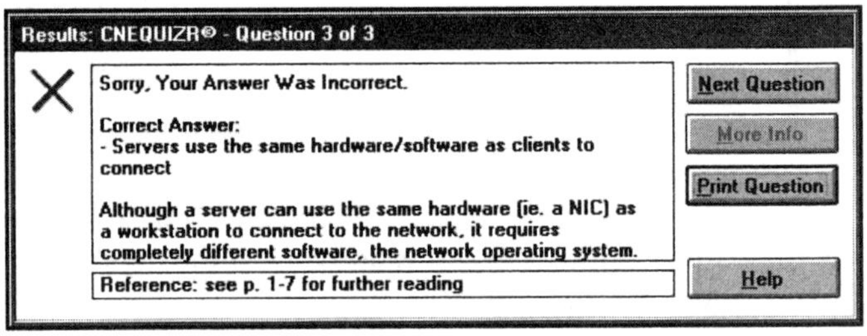

Figure 6.11 The Results screen after choosing the More Info button.

After you finish the test, the Quiz Complete dialog box (see fig. 6.12) shows your results.

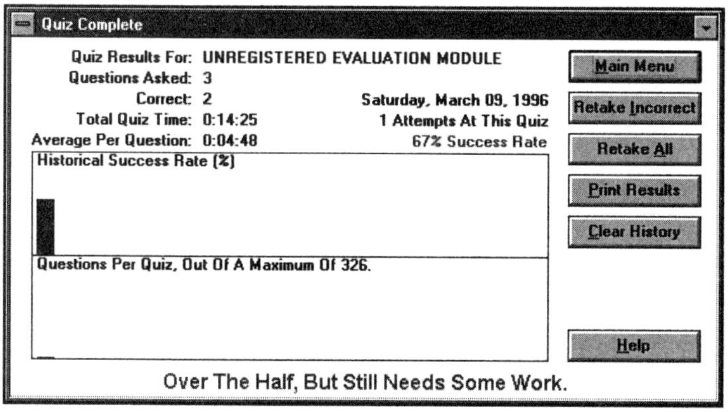

Figure 6.12
The Quiz Complete dialog box.

You can retest on this section, return to the Main Menu, or choose one of the other available options. To finish, choose <u>**M**</u>ain Menu, then choose Quit.

NOVA
CHILAGA
NORVMBEGA
FRANCIA
MOCOSA
AVACAL
APALCHEN
CALICVAS
CAPASCHI
TERLICHICHIMECHI
TOVA
HISPANIA NOVA
TEAC
MARATA
CVLIACAN
ASTATLAN
CVBA
LA FLORIDA
MAR DEL SVR, quod
Circulus Æquinoctialis
240
250
260
270
280
290
In Peru
PACIFICVM
CHARCAS
CHILI
PARANA
PATAGONES, vel REGIO GIGANTVM
FRETVM MAGELLANICVM
Archipelago del C. desleado
CAE SIVE
ORBIS, NO
SCRIPTIO.

7

CHAPTER

FRONTIER

The FRONTIER directory on the CD contains software called CyberJunction, produced by Frontier Technology Corporation. *CyberJunction* provides Novell local area networks (LANs) remote enterprise connectivity and Internet access. CyberJunction spans the gap between the NetWare IPX protocol and the Internet's TCP/IP protocol. In addition, it provides IPX-to-IP bridging through a Windows NT server. The CD includes a one-user version of CyberJunction software.

For more information about this software, you can contact Frontier Technology Corporation at the following addresses, phone numbers, and e-mail addresses:

Frontier Technology Corporation
10201 N. Port Washington Road
Mequon, WI 53092

(414) 241-2565 (Technical Support)
(414) 241-4555 (General Information)

Info@FrontierTech.cCOM or
support@FrontierTech.COM
CompuServe: 70274,2771

Note Much of the information in this chapter is adapted from Frontier Technology Corporation's documentation and the figures in this chapter were taken by capturing screen shots of the functioning software.

Introducing CyberJunction

CyberJunction ships with a set of TCP/IP application programs, including the Internet Browser, MIME Internet Email, Internet News Reader, Telnet terminal emulation, File Transfer Protocol (FTP) Client, Remote Protocols, and other applications. A SuperWeb Server also is available.

To use these applications, they must be installed on each user's workstation. Use your workstation's existing connection software to connect to the CyberJunction file server.

The CyberJunction server is designed to run on a Windows NT machine that already has an existing TCP/IP configuration. This configuration establishes a TCP/IP Winsock. The CyberJunction server communicates with the Windows NT machine through the Winsock. The communication between the CyberJunction server and the Windows NT machine then forms a bridge between the NetWare LAN and the Internet.

Each workstation uses the IJ Client. The *IJ Client* is an IPX-compatible Winsock. Messages are transferred through the IJ Client onto the NetWare LAN, and then onto the CyberJunction server. Users then can run the CyberJunction applications. Installing CyberJunction is not very difficult, and the next section furnishes a step-by-step explanation of how to go about it.

Installing CyberJunction from the CD

To install CyberJunction from the CD, first make a directory into which you have the rights to install the software. Now, complete the following steps to install CyberJunction using the default installation:

1. Start Windows, then choose **R**un from the **F**ile menu to open the Run dialog box.

2. Either type the drive letter of the CD followed by the exact path to the directory containing the CyberJunction INSTALL.EXE program (drive:\frontier\Disk1) into the Run dialog, or use the **B**rowse button to search for and choose that same directory.

3. When the command line in the Run dialog box shows the executable installation file, choose OK.

4. When the CyberJunction License Agreement dialog box opens, read the agreement, then choose Agree to continue. If you do, the Please Choose Default or Custom Installation dialog box opens (see fig. 7.1).

5. Enter a directory name in the Destination Directory text box, or accept

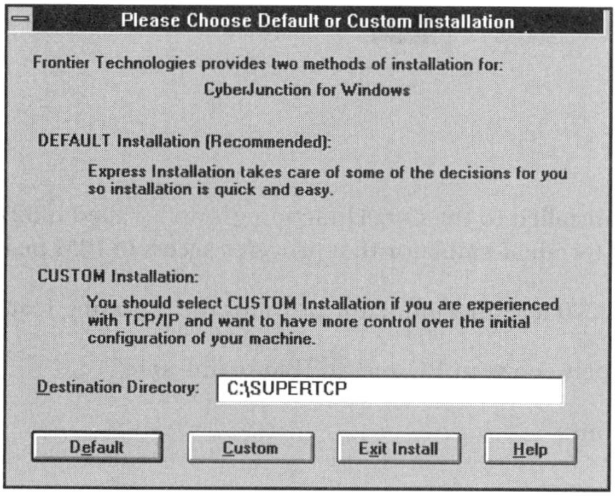

Figure 7.1
The Please Choose Default or Custom Installation dialog box.

C:\SUPERTCP (the default), then choose the Default installation method. The installation program begins to install the files.

6. When the Insert Disk dialog box appears, prompting you to install Disk2, change the Disk1 subdirectory to Disk 2, then choose OK (see fig. 7.2).

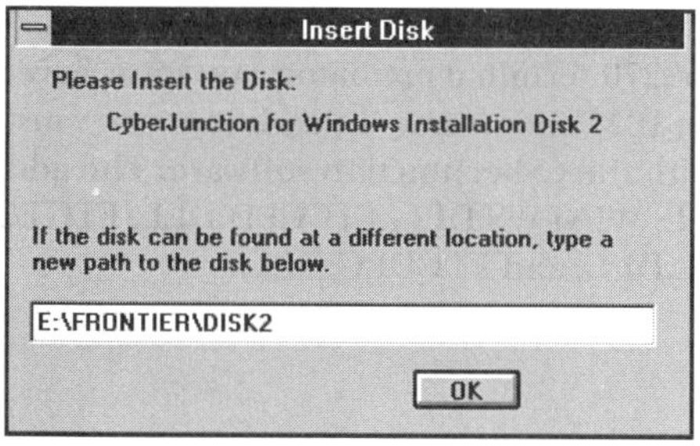

Figure 7.2
The Insert Disk dialog box.

7. The balance of the required files are installed, then the Windows CyberJunction group and associated icons are created (see fig. 7.3).

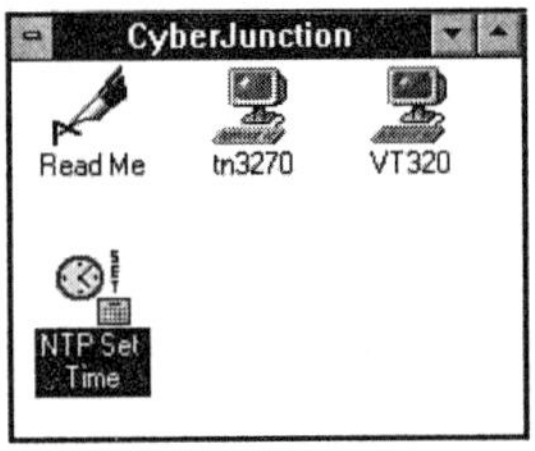

Figure 7.3 The CyberJunction program group.

tn3270

One of the four icons installed to the CyberJunction group is called tn3270; choose it to start a text-oriented terminal emulator that provides access to IBM mainframes.

The CyberJunction tn3270 terminal emulator provides the following features:

- ✔ File transfers between your PC and an IBM mainframe
- ✔ Multiple sessions
- ✔ Session printing
- ✔ Keyboard mapping
- ✔ Font selection
- ✔ Color selection
- ✔ Connection information profiles

To use the CyberJunction tn3270 terminal emulator, you must have a connection to a network that has access to an IBM mainframe. In addition, you must have several DLL files that are not included with the CyberJunction software. The additional DLL files you need are WINSOCK.DLL, WINFWS.DLL, FTCCPD.DLL, FTCTOOL.DLL, FTCKBMAP.DLL, FTCCTRL.DLL, and FTCDLG.DLL.

VT320

Another icon that the INSTALL program installs is the VT320 icon. Choose the VT320 icon to start a text-oriented terminal emulator that provides access to Unix, VMS, and similar hosts.

The CyberJunction VT320 terminal emulator provides the following features:

- ✔ A full-featured Telnet interface that includes scripting and key mapping
- ✔ Profiles to save connection information and simplify host access

You can use the CyberJunction VT320 independently or in conjunction with the Browser. To customize the VT320 terminal emulator, run the Custom installation option.

To use the CyberJunction VT320 terminal emulator, you must have a connection to a network that has a Unix, VMS, or other available host computer. In addition, you must have several DLL files not included as part of the CyberJunction software. The required DLL files are WINSOCK.DLL, WINFWS.DLL, FTCCPD.DLL, FTCTOOL.DLL, FTCKBMAP.DLL, FTCCTRL.DLL, and FTCDLG.DLL.

NTP Set Time

Use the NTP Set Time icon to reset the clock on your system. As with the tn3270 and VT320 programs, DLL files not included with the CyberJunction software are required. Use of the NTP Set Time icon requires the WINSOCK.DLL file, which is not included with the CyberJunction software.

The CyberJunction Read Me File

Following is a printed copy of the CyberJunction Read Me file. This file is relatively useful to the new CyberJunction user, but is difficult to read and follow on the computer screen. Rather than rewrite or create this text new (reinvent the wheel), I have placed the Read Me file in this chapter to make it easier for you to read and understand. To accommodate the requirements of this book's format, formatting changes have been made. In addition, a small error in the numbering of steps was found in the Read Me file and was corrected in this printed copy. In addition, some minor editing changes have been made. Otherwise, no content changes have been made.

CyberJunction for Windows
Release 1.2
README.WRI
October, 1995

Contents

Precedence

For information on the CyberJunction for Windows applications, consult the online Help files after reading this file. If any discrepancies exist between the Help files and this README.WRI file, this file will contain the correct information.

Recommended Procedures/Comments

✔ CyberJunction must be installed on a PC running Windows and NetWare 3.*x* or 4.*x*. We highly recommend running SCANDISK for those running DOS 6.2 and CHKDSK /F for those running DOS prior to 6.2, before installing CyberJunction.

✔ Before installing any software on your system we recommend making a backup of your configuration files (that is, AUTOEXEC.BAT, CONFIG.SYS, WIN.INI and SYSTEM.INI).

✔ The minimum system requirements to run CyberJunction are 4 MB RAM, 386 Microprocessor, Windows 3.1 or Windows for Workgroups 3.11, and DOS 5.0 or higher. To use the high powered applications such as the Browser, the RAM requirements are 8 MB. Required hard drive space is around 8 MB, which includes working space for applications such as Email and the Browser. The size of this working space will depend on your preferences. For example, if you like to e-mail with large attached images, then you will need more disk space.

✔ After completing the installation of CyberJunction, you will be instructed to restart your machine. If you do not do so, you will encounter NETMUX errors.

- ✔ By default, the Browser uses applications provided with CyberJunction. If you desire other applications, you must set your default application accordingly on the Telnet/tn3270 or FTP tabs which can be found under Options, Preferences dialog in the Browser. The applications for VT100 and FTP can be specified.

- ✔ The Browser provides a "Startup" category, which will allow the bookmarks saved there to be launched every time you invoke the Browser. This works in a similar fashion to the Startup Group Box in Windows. If you want to run the Browser off-line, you shouldn't use the Startup category because it automatically brings you online as soon as you start the Browser.

- ✔ When doing an install over a Novell network, it is a good idea to install CyberJunction on your network by using the following method:

  1. Create a directory named junction and copy all five disks to that one single directory. To perform the copy, type **xcopy a:*.* n:\junction*.* /s/v** without the quotation marks at a DOS prompt. The /s copies all of the subdirectories and their structure, and the /v verifies the copy.

  2. Run *u:*\junction\install by choosing File, Run in Windows, or Start, Run in Windows 95, where *u:* is the directory to which you copied the CyberJunction files.

Troubleshooting Suggestions for CyberJunction for Windows Version 1.2

Frontier Technologies tries to ship the best product, however, here are some common troubleshooting suggestions to make the installation and use of CyberJunction easier.

- ✔ During a Gopher search that is returning a long list of resources, we recommend minimizing Gopher windows while the search is going on. This eliminates the need for the application to update the window display as the data is downloaded. The status of the search will be indicated in the Activity Manager and will indicate when the search is done.

- ✔ After accessing a floppy disk, some applications may try to access that drive again during unrelated operations. You can continue to run with a floppy in the drive or restart the application to clear the problem.

- ✔ The Email program, when deleting multiple messages ("Yes to All") from a folder when a view window is open with those messages, may give an "Unable to read message" dialog box. To correct this, simply press Enter or click on OK.

- ✔ The Email program may have problems when attaching files from a removable drive (such as a floppy drive). If you experience a problem, simply copy the file from the floppy drive to your hard disk drive and send the message with the hard drive file attached.
- ✔ The Browser can cause a GPF in some video drivers upon entering. The Windows For Workgroups 3.11 README states:

  > Most VGA-compatible display-adapter cards and main-adapter chips use additional memory to enhance their performance. When Windows is configured for VGA, Windows detects most of these cards and automatically excludes the additional memory.
  >
  > However, if you have an enhanced VGA that Windows does not recognize, you must exclude the additional memory yourself by adding the following line to the [386Enh] section of the SYSTEM.INI file:
  >
  > **emmexclude=C400-C7FF**
  >
  > For more information about modifying the SYSTEM.INI file, see the SYSINI.WRI online document.

  Try this memory exclusion or contact your video driver vendor for updated drivers. In the short term, you can return your system to standard VGA.
- ✔ In the Browser, if you download a Real Audio (.RAM) sound file, pressing the Play button will not work. You must use the Launch button to play the sound (assuming you have already installed the Real Audio sound player).
- ✔ If you hit the Search button on the Browser toolbar (the one with the search lights on it), you will be prompted to put a SuperHighway Access or CyberSearch CD into your CD-ROM drive if you don't already have one there. If you don't have either CD, you can eliminate this dialog box by going to Options, Preferences, Search tab and clicking on Remote.
- ✔ In SuperTCP Setup, if you want to move the cursor back to the scrolling list of icons on the left side, you must press Ctrl+Home. Tabbing will only work within the dialog boxes.
- ✔ Sharing/unsharing of local printers via Microsoft Windows Network, version 3.11, cannot be performed while the NetPrint Client is enabled. If you are having trouble sharing or removing shared local printers from Print Manager via the Windows for Workgroups network driver (Microsoft Windows Network, version 3.11), you will need to remove the Microsoft Windows Network, version 3.11, and then re-install it as the primary network. To do this, perform the following steps:

1. Go to Network group box and run Network Setup.
2. Click on the Networks button and remove the Microsoft Windows Network, version 3.11. Exit Network Setup.
3. Without restarting Windows, re-enable the Microsoft Windows Network, version 3.11, and any secondary networks. Re-install the adapter you were using along with any protocols. Exit Network Setup.
4. Run the SetupTCP application in the CyberJunction group box. In the Interfaces configuration, remove the appropriate interface and then add it back in.
5. Restart your machine.

Performing the preceding actions to share local printers via Windows for Workgroups disables the NetPrint Client. If you had either of these applications enabled prior to performing the above steps you will need to re-enable them from the SetupTCP application if you wish to use them.

Once printers have been shared via the above procedure, you can re-enable the NetPrint Client without affecting the status of printers shared using the above procedure. The above procedure is necessary only when you wish to add another shared printer or remove a shared printer via Windows for Workgroups.

Known Problems with CyberJunction for Windows Version 1.2

As always, Frontier Technologies tries to ship the best product, however, the following list describes those problems that Frontier could not remedy prior to CyberJunction going into production.

- ✔ The R-Utilities program RCP protocol may not use the correct time when the "Preserve File Creation Date/Time" option is selected when copying a file to a remote machine, which results in an incorrect date and time.
- ✔ When printing images from the Browser using certain printers, you may find the images darker than expected. You may also experience margin problems when printing Web pages. If you are running the Browser on a Windows 95 or NT platform, you may also encounter repainting problems.
- ✔ This version of the Browser doesn't support tables or inline JPEG images.
- ✔ The tn3270 application may have problems with XGA video drivers.

- ✔ CyberJunction can run over Windows 95 for the most part. However, the Net Print Client and NTP Set Time do not function at all.
- ✔ R-Utilities sometimes reports errors when reconnecting to remote sites.
- ✔ When downloading a large file using the Browser, a message box will appear saying that your connection to the server has been lost. The file download will have been completed; however, the file is often corrupt.
- ✔ In Finger, when doing an Edit, Copy of a screen buffer to a notepad, you will see approximately 40 blank lines inserted at the beginning of the selection.
- ✔ In Finger and Who Is, when doing an Edit, Select Entire Screen selects more than one screen.
- ✔ You may notice erratic behavior if you have more than approximately six news groups open, have more than 40 messages active or access a large news service. If you view a list of new groups and click on CatchUp without viewing the article list, an error may occur. To avoid problems, view the article list and then click on CatchUp.
- ✔ In tn3270, the Show Map window does not use the right hand scroll bar because it may result in erratic behavior. Also, the button that reads "1" should read "Add."
- ✔ If you attempt to uninstall CyberJunction by doing the following, not all of CyberJunction will be removed from your hard drive:

    1. Reinstalling and selecting all of the installed modules on the right side.
    2. Clicking on the Uninstall button.

8

CHAPTER

INFINITE

The INFINITE directory on the CD contains software by a company called Infinite Technologies, Inc. The software is stored in five subdirectories under the INFINITE directory: CTREMOTE, C2_SMTP, CONNECT2, EXPRESIT, and MACH2. The CTREMOTE directory contains the INSTALL.BAT file, which is the file you use to install the software.

Each of the five directories contains different software, as follows:

- ✔ **C2REMOTE.** A high-performance message switch for traveling users and telecommuters. The program file used to initiate this software is called C2REMOTE.EXE.
- ✔ **C2_SMTP.** An integrated solution for connecting e-mail products. C2_SMTP supports BeyondMail, DaVinci eMAIL, ExpressIT!, and Notework with the Internet and SMTP-based e-mail. The program file used to run this software is called C2SMTP.EXE.

- ✔ **CONNECT2.** A high-performance switch that provides message transport and exchange within and between a variety of e-mail systems. Supported systems include Microsoft Mail, cc:Mail, DaVinci eMAIL, BeyondMail, ExpressIT!, and Notework. The program file used to run this evaluation version of the software is called C2EVAL.EXE.
- ✔ **EXPRESIT.** A full-featured e-mail product for DOS and Windows. ExpressIT! is easy to use and accessible. Run EXSETUP.EXE to setup the software for this program.
- ✔ **MACH2.** A TCP/IP router for LAN administrators who need Internet access. MACH2 is a software-only router that operates from a DOS-based PC, unlike routers that require additional hardware and Unix. Run MACH2R.EXE after installing this software.

This chapter provides a brief introduction to these five products.

Note Some of the information in this chapter is adapted from the documentation provided by the manufacturer.

You can contact Infinite Technologies, the manufacturer of the software in the INFINITE directory, for more information at the following address or phone numbers:

Infinite Technologies, Inc.
11433 Cronridge Drive
Owings Mills, MD 21117

800-678-1097 (800)
410-363-1097 (voice)
410-363-0846 (Fax)

If you want to get on the "updates" mailing list, you can use the following electronic mail addresses, using a subject of SUBSCRIBE:

MHS: Updates@Infinite
CompuServe: MHS:Updates@Infinite
Internet: Updates@Infinite.ihub.com

If you would like to have an index of files and discussion lists available through Infinite Technologies' library service, you can send a message to one of the following electronic addresses, using a subject of INDEX:

MHS: Library@Infinite
CompuServe: MHS:Library@Infinite
Internet: Library@Infinite.ihub.com

Note These and other ways to reach the manufacturer also are explained in the IMPORTAN.T file in the CTREMOTE directory. You can find other IMPORTAN.T files in other INFINITE subdirectories on the CD, as well.

CONNECT2

The CONNECT2 directory contains one file—C2EVAL.EXE. To use CONNECT2, you must install and configure the CONNECT2 software.

Installing CONNECT2

To install the CONNECT2 software, copy the C2EVAL.EXE file from the CD to a directory to which you have create rights. Then, run the C2EVAL.EXE program from Windows by completing the following steps:

1. Start Windows.
2. From the **F**ile menu, choose **R**un to open the Run dialog box.
3. Choose **B**rowse.
4. Find and select the C2EVAL.EXE program on the CD.
5. When the Command Line box displays the C2EVAL.EXE path and file name, choose OK (see fig. 8.1).

C2EVAL.EXE is a self-extracting file. When you run it, it expands and explodes the files it contains, placing them into the specified directory. After running C2EVAL.EXE, you can delete it from the directory to free disk space.

After you run C2EVAL.EXE, you must configure CONNECT2 as the following section directs.

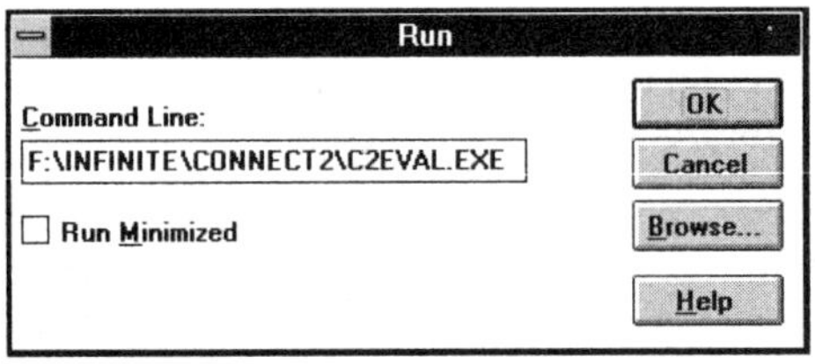

Figure 8.1 The Command Line field in the Run dialog box.

Configuring CONNECT2

To Connect2, change to the directory in which the C2EVAL.EXE program installed the files, and then complete the following steps:

1. Type **C2SETUP** at the prompt and press Enter.
2. When prompted, provide the name of the directory into which you want to place the program's files (see fig. 8.2).

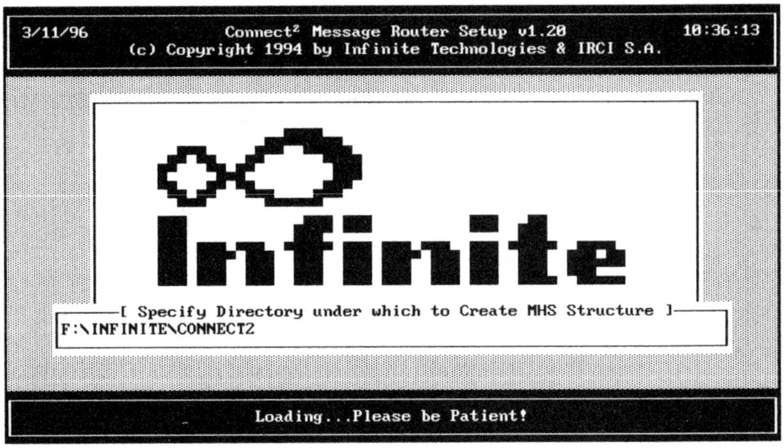

Figure 8.2 The initial Infinite setup screen.

3. When prompted with where to create the MHS directory, type **Y** to answer Yes, accepting the default path.
4. When prompted, provide information about the host, workgroup, hub, and so on (see fig. 8.3). Press F1 for online help, which explains the type of information to provide in each field.
5. Press Ctrl+Enter to accept your changes and open the Host *host_name* in Workgroup *workgroup_name* menu.
6. From the Host *host_name* in Workgroup *workgroup_name* menu, choose the first option: 1. Configure This Host (see fig. 8.4).

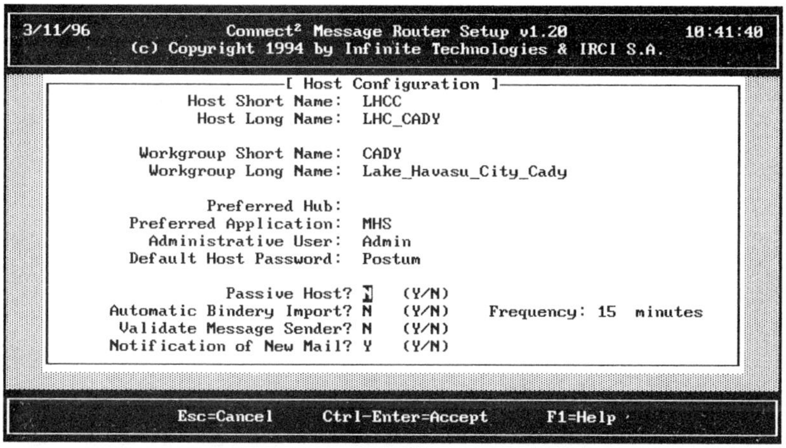

Figure 8.3
The Host Configuration screen.

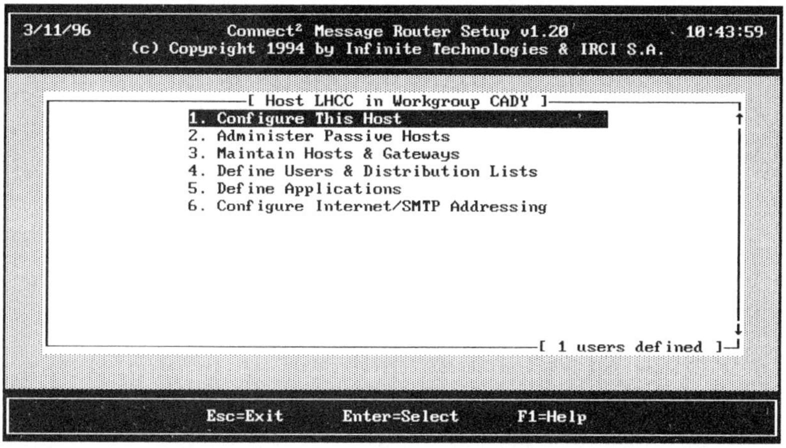

Figure 8.4
The Host *host_name* in Workgroup *workgroup_name* menu.

7. Choose 2. Advanced Host Configuration Options to open the Advanced Configuration Options screen (see fig. 8.5).

8. After you change the settings to your preferences, press Ctrl+Enter to accept your changes.

The preceding steps show you how to configure various aspects of CONNECT2. To configure other CONNECT2 options, complete the following steps.

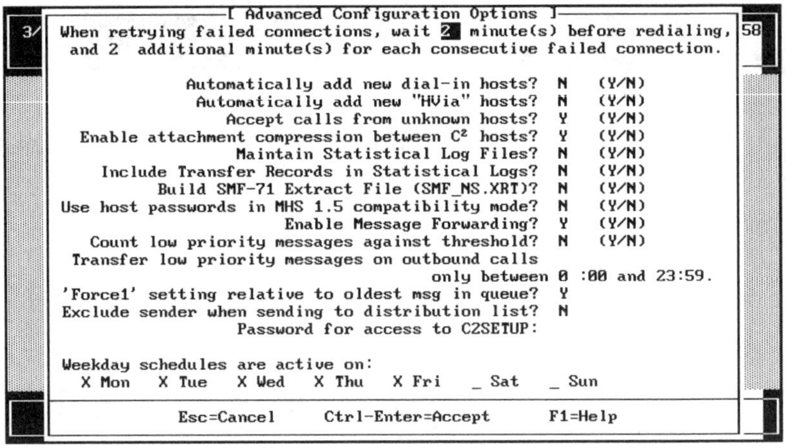

Figure 8.5 The Advanced Configuration Options screen.

From the Host *host_name* in Workgroup *workgroup_name* screen, choose any of the available options. To modify user information, for example, choose 4. Define Users & Distribution Lists. Then, choose 1. Define Local Users, followed by choosing a specific user. The user's configuration screen and menu open (see fig. 8.6) from which you can modify the user's configuration information.

Complete the configuration changes by working through the options on the main setup screen and the resulting screens and menus.

To complete the setup, you must include the following line in the System login script, or issue the equivalent SET command:

DOS SET MV="*path_to_directory*"

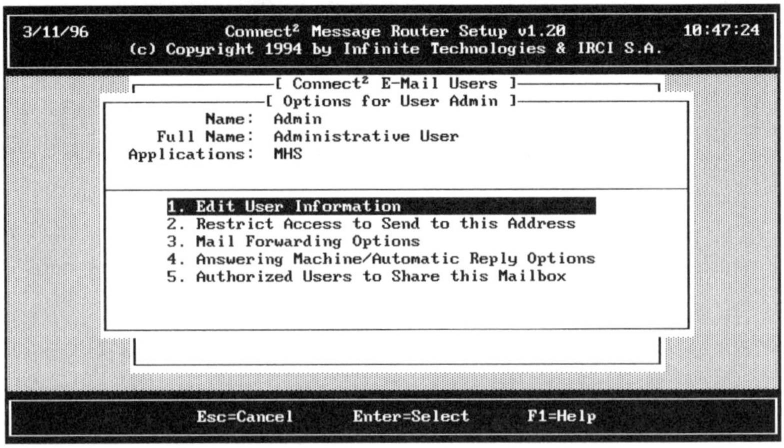

Figure 8.6 Options for user Admin screen.

Replace *path_to_directory* with the exact path to the location in which you place the Command2 software, for example:

DOS SET MV="CP_401\SYS:INFINITE\\CONNECT2"

CTREMOTE

To install CTREMOTE, complete the following steps:

1. Specify a directory to create an MHS structure.

2. From the DOS prompt, change to the INFINITE\C2REMOTE directory on the CD, type **INSTALL** to run the INSTALL.BAT software, and press Enter. The Installation for Connect2 Remote Message Router screen opens.

3. Type **1**, then press Enter to choose to install CONNECT2 Remote.

4. Press Enter to configure CONNECT2 Remote and open the CONNECT2 Remote Setup menu.

5. When the CONNECT2 Remote Setup menu opens, choose one or more options to configure them. Choose the Configure User/Host Information option, for example, to open the Configure User/Host Information screen, shown in figure 8.7.

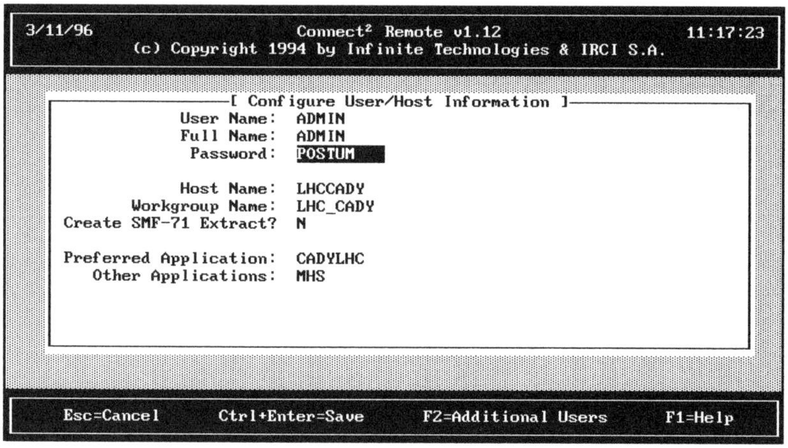

Figure 8.7
The Configure User/Host Information screen.

6. When prompted, exit the configuration menu. A message appears indicating the configuration is complete.

The CD also provides online help for CONNECT2 if you need additional information about installing the product, or the product itself.

C2_SMTP

The following information is taken directly from the text version of the Connect2SMTP documentation on the CD. The documentation has been edited to provide only the most basic of related information and formatted to fit this book. To read the entire text version of the Connect2SMTP documentation, open the C2SMTP.TXT file in the C2_SMTP subdirectory.

A version of the documentation in Microsoft Word for Windows format also is available. To obtain this version, send a message with the subject C2SDOC to Library@Infinite.ihub.com.

Connect2SMTP Introduction

Connect2SMTP provides a completely integrated solution for connecting MHS-based e-mail directly and seamlessly with SMTP-based e-mail. Connect2SMTP runs as a single, uninterrupted program on a dedicated PC. It does not use complex batch files or other programs. Connect2SMTP does not require any routing tables, user name tables, nor alias tables when minimally configured. In addition, monitoring tools are provided.

Connect2SMTP is capable of supporting as many as 100 SMTP mail sessions simultaneously, and it provides the fastest throughput of any PC-based SMTP product. Connect2SMTP natively supports NetWare environments, but also can be used with full capabilities on other network platforms such as LANtastic, LAN Manager, and others.

Connect2SMTP Features

Connect2SMTP includes the following features:

- ✔ Handles inbound and outbound file attachments in both uuencode and MIME formats.
- ✔ Supports both inbound and outbound MIME-formatted messages.
- ✔ Supports a variety of return receipt options.
- ✔ Returns delivery errors in both directions with optional copies to the MHS administrator.
- ✔ Provides separate log file options for errors, as well as for inbound and outbound message traffic.
- ✔ Complies with RFC-821, 822, 1055, 1332, 1334, 1521, 1661, and 1662.

- ✔ Requires minimal administration.
- ✔ Supports MHS 1.1 through 2.0 (SMF-64, SMF-70, and SMF-71).
- ✔ Handles up to 100 inbound or outbound SMTP sessions concurrently.
- ✔ Includes extensive debug tools, such as PING, NSLookup (name serverlookup), and Telnet/25 (telnet to another SMTP host) for troubleshooting.
- ✔ Provides separately configurable scroll back buffers for each loaded module (MHS, SMTP, and so on).
- ✔ Includes the high-performance Mach2 TCP/IP protocol stack that runs directly with Novell ODI drivers or Clarkson Packet Drivers.
- ✔ Functions alternately as a high-performance TCP/IP router between an Internet Service Provider and a local network, and provides other TCP/IP services such as responding to name server queries from local nodes.
- ✔ Passes, if configured to do so, all outbound mail to a nearby Unix host, or extensively uses DNS to directly connect to any host for which it has outbound mail.
- ✔ Provides multi-line asynchronous support for dial-in and dial-out, SLIP, and PPP connections.
- ✔ Provides a scripting language for interactive dial-out SLIP logins, and allows any number of configured users to dial in directly with SLIP or PPP for remote TCP/IP access to the network.

Note The base license supports two asynchronous connections. Licenses to support additional connections are available from Infinite Technologies.

Pre-Installation

Before you begin installing Connect2SMTP, review the minimum system requirements and host configuration information in the following sections.

System Requirements

Before using Connect2SMTP, you must ensure that your system meets the minimum requirements. You must also ensure that your system meets the minimum software requirements. Both hardware and software system requirements for using Connect2SMTP are discussed in this section.

The following are the hardware requirements for Connect2SMTP:

- ✔ IBM PC XT/AT compatible
- ✔ 640 KB conventional memory
- ✔ Network interface card (NIC)
- ✔ Modem (if connecting via a service provider)

The following are the software requirements for Connect2SMTP:

- ✔ Novell NetWare ODI driver or Clarkson Packet Driver for each Network Interface Card
- ✔ Infinite Technologies CONNECT2; or NetWare MHS versions 1.1, 1.5, or 2.0 (SMF-64, SMF-70, and SMF-71)—Connect2SMTP automatically adjusts to the differences and capabilities of each level

Note Please refer to the online documentation for information on additional requirements.

Types of Connectivity

Before you can take advantage of any of the features and information available through the internet, you must be able to establish a connection to the Internet. In general, you can connect to the Internet in two ways.

Small installations, or companies with many geographically dispersed installations, can obtain a dial-up SLIP or PPP account to the Internet from a local service provider. Larger locations might have a functional TCP/IP network capability already in place with the Internet, or with other organizational subnets, through the use of one or more existing TCP/IP routers. The only necessary step is to attach Connect2SMTP to the existing TCP/IP network.

Regardless of which connection method you use, before you can install and configure Connect2SMTP, you need to choose your MHS gateway name. MHS e-mail users might need to use this name when they send mail through Connect2SMTP to an SMTP user.

You also need to obtain a TCP/IP host name from your local domain administrator or service provider. Remote SMTP users use this name when they send mail to your MHS users through Connect2SMTP.

In addition, you need to obtain a dedicated IP address from your local domain administrator or service provider for Connect2SMTP's computer. An *IP address* is a number comprised of four digits separated with dots (sometimes called *dotted notation*) and is the unique identifier on the Internet for your SMTP Gateway.

Note Pre-installation considerations for Each Method of Connection are included in the online documentation. If you need additional information, read the documentation provided on the CD.

Installation and Configuration

This section guides you through installing the MHS for Connect2SMTP product, configuring MHS for Connect2SMTP, configuring Connect2SMTP, and initially testing communications.

Installing Connect2SMTP

Before you begin the installation, you need to know Connect2SMTP's TCP/IP host name, IP address, and MHS gateway name. To install Connect2SMTP, complete the following steps:

1. Copy the Connect2SMTP files.
2. Add a gateway name under MHS.
3. Edit Connect2SMTP's configuration file C2SMTP.INI.
4. Use the REGISTER.EXE program to apply any serial numbers you have purchased, or to start your evaluation period.
5. Modify the NET.CFG file.
6. Make a directory into which to copy the files. You can copy the files to the local hard drive of the PC on which you intend to run the software, or to a network drive.

Note If you install the Connect2SMTP files on the local hard drive, a command-line parameter is available that can log a user into NetWare, so the computer does not need to be logged in before starting Connect2SMTP. If you install the Connect2SMTP files on a network drive, you have to write a login script or batch file to log in to the file server and map drives before you can run Connect2SMTP.

7. Change your default drive to the drive onto which to copy the files, then copy the Connect2SMTP files.

Note This installation procedure assumes you are installing Connect2SMTP with NetWare MHS 1.5 or prior. For instructions on installing Connect2SMTP with NetWare Global MHS, see the section "Native SMTP Syntax" in the online copy of the Technical Reference document. For instructions on installing Connect2SMTP with CONNECT2, see the section "Adding a Gateway Name under CONNECT2" in the online documentation.

After you install the software, you must add the MHS gateway.

Adding the MHS Gateway

When MHS adds a new gateway, it automatically builds a directory structure for the gateway under its mv\MHS\MAIL\GATES subdirectory. To add the MHS gateway, complete the following steps:

1. Start MHS and press Esc within the first few moments. Instead of running the Connectivity Manager, MHS then prompts you to log in.

2. Log in with the MHS administrator's password.

3. Select Directory Manager (under MHS 1.5 this option is called Manage Directories) to open the Directory Manager menu.

4. Select Routes to Workgroups, Hosts, and Gateways.

5. Select Add entry, then choose Define a gateway. The following is a list of recommended settings for using Connect2SMTP with MHS:

   Host Name: SMTP

   Description: Connect2SMTP

   Gateway Version: Enter your level of MHS—64, 70, or 71

   Gateway Commands: Blank

Adding a Gateway Name under CONNECT2

You may either run the C2SETUP.EXE or select System Configuration from the CONNECT2 console menu. To add a gateway name under CONNECT2, complete the following steps:

1. Log in with the CONNECT2 administrator's password, if one is installed.

2. Select Maintain Hosts and Gateways.

3. Press Ins, and enter the following types of information:

   Host Name: SMTP

   Description: Connect2-SMTP

   Gateway Version: 70

   Gateway Commands: blank

The appropriate directory structure for the gateway under Connect2 is built in the mv\MHS\MAIL\GATES subdirectory.

Configuring Connect2SMTP

After you set up Connect2SMTP's gateway entry in MHS, GMHS, or Connect2, you are ready to begin its configuration. A sample, fully commented C2SMTP.INI configuration file is included with Connect2SMTP. If you need more details on any of the options, refer to the online documentation, section "C2SMTP.INI Configuration Settings," which provides a complete description of each option.

C2SMTP.INI is an ASCII text file that you can edit using any standard text editor, such as EDIT.COM or EDLIN.COM.

Using REGISTER.EXE

The *REGISTER* program's primary function involves entering product serial numbers or starting an evaluation period. You also can use it to assign proper NetWare directory rights to the login name under which Connect2SMTP runs. Before you use the REGISTER program, you must create the gateway name under MHS and edit Connect2SMTP's configuration file (C2SMTP.INI).

For NetWare installations, the REGISTER program requires the current login to be a Supervisor or equivalent. To serialize and register the Connect2SMTP software, refer to the online documentation for specific instructions. The process requires that you complete the following general steps:

1. Serialize Connect2SMTP.

2. Grant directory rights to Connect2SMTP.

3. Limit workgroups that can use Connect2SMTP.

4. Modify the NET.CFG file.

   The following is an example NET.CFG file after you add the ETHERNET_II Frame Type:

```
Link Driver NE2000
    PORT 300
    INT 5
    MEM D000
    FRAME ETHERNET_802.3
    FRAME ETHERNET_II
```

5. Perform initial testing and troubleshooting.

6. Start Connect2SMTP.

For more information about Connect2SMTP, refer to the online documentation. You also can subscribe to a Connect2SMTP discussion group that covers Connect2SMTP technical issues and updates. To subscribe, send a message to `C2SMTP@Infinite.ihub.com` with the subject line SUBSCRIBE.

EXPRESIT

If you install ExpressIt! in the Novell Netware Environment without MHS or Connect2, you need to complete the steps in this section. These steps are taken directly from the EXPRESS.DOC file in the INFINITE\EXPRESIT\EXPRESS directory on the CD, with editing and formatting changes. In some cases, the format changes are substantial (the original information was in the form of a checklist), but the content has not been substantially modified. There are several options for installing Expressit!. Look in the EXPRESS.DOC file for other instructions.

The following checklist is designed so that you can mark each completed step when you install ExpressIt! without MHS or Connect2:

1. These procedures assume that you do not currently run Novell's MHS. If you are installing or have already installed MHS, proceed to the next section.

2. Sign on to your file server as SUPERVISOR or a SUPERVISOR equivalent.

3. You need to create the directory structure that MHS normally would create. To do so, execute the FAKEMHS.EXE program.

Note

When you run FAKEMHS, it does the following:

- ✔ Asks you for the drive and directory under which to install the "fake" MHS directory Structure. Specify a drive letter and path.
- ✔ Asks you for the "fake" MHS host name. You are shown the name of your NetWare file server, and in most instances, that's fine. If you would like to use a different name, enter it now. MHS Host Names are limited to eight characters or less.

- ✔ After FAKEMHS creates all files and directories, it displays the MV setting that you need to include in your system login script. Be sure to copy this statement accurately.

  Example:

  DOS SET MV="*FS*/*SYS*:\\"

  FS is the name of your file server and *SYS*: is the name of the NetWare Volume you enter in step 2.

- ✔ ExpressIT! uses the environmental variable MV (Master Volume) to locate the "fake" MHS directories and related files. You must set this variable to use ExpressIT!

You need to make sure that the two settings above are set correctly by logging in to your network after making these changes.

4. Execute EXINSTAL.EXE from the ExpressIT! demo. This program initializes ExpressIT! to your file server.

5. Copy the following ExpressIT! DOS user programs to SYS:PUBLIC (or another appropriate directory) on your file server:

   EXPRESSM.COM
   EXPRESSM.OVR
   EXPRESSM.HLP
   EXPSWAP.OVR
   EXSPELL.EXE
   EXACCESS.EXE
   CHKMHS.COM

   If this is a new installation, you also might want to copy over EXPRESSM.INI.

   An additional file, EXSPELL.DIC, must be present before the spelling checker can function. This file is available separately in a ZIP file, named EXSPEL.ZIP.

6. If you want to use ExpressIT! Windows, copy the following user programs to SYS:PUBLIC (or another appropriate directory) on your file server:

   EXPWINM.EXE
   EXPWINM.HLP

   If you want to use ExpressIT! OS/2, copy the following user programs to SYS:PUBLIC (or other appropriate directory) on your file server:

   EXPOS2.EXE
   EXPOS2.HLP

7. Copy the following ExpressIT! supervisor programs to the MHS\EXE (or other appropriate) directory:

   EXSETUP.EXE
   REGEX.EXE
   EXNICNAM.EXE
   EXMHSNAM.EXE
   EXNOMHS.EXE
   MAILRITE.EXE
   EXCLEAN.EXE

8. To define *all* of your NetWare users to ExpressIT!, you use an ExpressIT! utility called EXSETUP.EXE.

Note

EXSETUP copies the USER NAME and the FULL NAME from your NetWare configuration into your e-mail setup, so be sure to review your NetWare Users and check each user's full name with SYSCON before you run it.

If you need to limit which users to define to ExpressIT!, use the NetWare SYSCON utility and edit the FULL NAME field for each user you don't want to be defined to ExpressIT! so that the first character of the name is a period.

Example:

```
user:      BACKUP
     fullname: .Tape Backup Operator
```

9. Execute EXSETUP, which does the following:

   - ✔ Defines ExpressIT!'s application code of POSTMAST to MHS or the "fake" MHS.
   - ✔ Copies all user information from your NetWare bindery into the e-mail user directory. If you are using MHS, EXSETUP will eliminate the need to manually add users with the MHS Directory Manager.
   - ✔ Converts NetWare users into e-mail user names. If you have user names that are longer than eight characters or names that contain invalid characters, you will be prompted for alternate names.
   - ✔ Converts NetWare groups into public ExpressIT! mailing lists. If group names are over eight characters in length, or contain invalid characters, you will be prompted for an alternate mailing list name.

Note As you add, modify, and delete users from your network, you need to run EXSETUP to keep the e-mail directory and the NetWare bindery synchronized.

10. Continue loading the software by following the steps in the online help, which you can find under the section heading of INSTALLING EXPRESSIT! IN THE NOVELL NETWARE ENVIRONMENT *WITH* CONNECT^2.

MACH2

The MACH2 directory contains a file called MACH2.TXT, which furnishes information about MACH2, including how to install and configure it. The following is adapted from a portion of the MACH2.TXT file's chapter 5, which describes how to install and configure MACH2. For additional information, refer to the MACH2.TXT file in the INFINITE\MACH2 directory on the CD.

Before beginning the installation, be sure you know Mach2's TCP/IP host name and IP address. The steps to install the Mach2 TCP/IP Router are:

1. Copy the Mach2 TCP/IP Router files.
2. Edit Mach2's configuration file MACH2R.INI.
3. Use the REGISTER.EXE program to apply any serial numbers you have purchased, or to start your evaluation period.
4. Modify the NET.CFG file.

There are two ways to install the Mach2 TCP/IP Router. You can install it on the local hard drive of the PC that will run it, or you can install it on a network drive.

The Mach2 TCP/IP Router requires that the workstation acting as a router be logged into a NetWare file server before the router software is started.

You will have to write a login script or batch file to log in to the file server and map any necessary drives before you run the Mach2 TCP/IP Router.

Once you've decided where you'd like to install the Mach2 TCP/IP Router software, make a directory and copy all of its files here. For example, if you choose to install the gateway on a file server, and the drive where the files will reside is drive G:, then:

```
G:\> MD \MACH2

G:\> CD \MACH2

G:\MACH2> XCOPY A:*.*
```

For additional information about installing and using MACH2, refer to the online documentation previously described.

NORVMBEGA
LA FLORIDA
CAPASCHI
MARATA
CVLIACAN
HISPANIA NOVA
TOVA
CVBA
HISPANIOLA
Suala mons
MAR DEL SVR, quod
CHILE
Archipelago del C. delleado
CAE SIVE
ORBIS, NO
SCRIPTIO.

9

CHAPTER

INTRUDEC

The INTRUDEC directory on the CD contains a subdirectory (KANE_SEC) in which the KSA_EVAL.EXE file is located. This file installs the Kane Security Analyst software.

The version of Kane Security Analyst included on the CD is a 30-day evaluation version. You can use it for up to 30 days from installation. After that time, you must contact the company and supply the information and funds requested if you want a permanent version of Kane Security Analyst on your network.

You can contact Intrusion Detection, Inc. for information about or registration of the Kane Security Analyst software at the following address:

Intrusion Detection, Inc.
217 E. 86th St., Suite 213
New York, NY 10025

(212) 349-8900 Voice
(212) 427-9185 Fax

CompuServe: 75162,452

Installing Kane Security Analyst

To use the KSA_EVAL.EXE file to install Kane Security Analyst, complete the following steps:

1. Start Windows, then choose **R**un from the **F**ile menu. Type the path to the KSA_EVAL.EXE file (*CD_drive*:\Intrudec\Kane.sec), or use the **B**rowse button to search for the file, then choose OK to open the Kane Security Analyst Setup menu.

2. Select Install Kane Security Analyst v2.0 EVALUATION, then choose OK to open the Select Files to Install menu (see fig. 9.1).

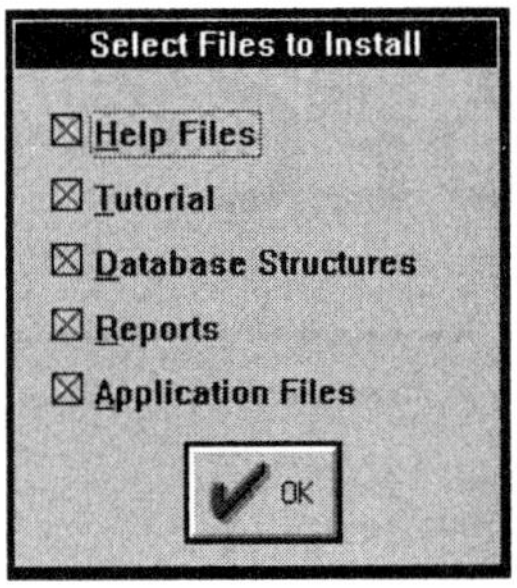

Figure 9.1
The Select Files to Install menu.

3. Mark which files you want to install, then choose OK. By default, all files are installed.

4. When the window that indicates how much space is required to install this software opens, choose No to return to the previous screen and unmark some files to reduce the requirements, or choose Yes.

5. When you choose Yes, you are prompted for the path and directory name into which to install the software. By default, Kane Security Analyst is installed into the directory C:\KSA20. Choose OK to accept the default path, or change the path and then choose OK.

6. When prompted to verify directory creation (assuming the directory did not previously exist), choose Yes.

   The Installing Files screen opens, showing the progress of file installation (see fig. 9.2). If necessary, you can abort the installation process by pressing Esc and following the prompts.

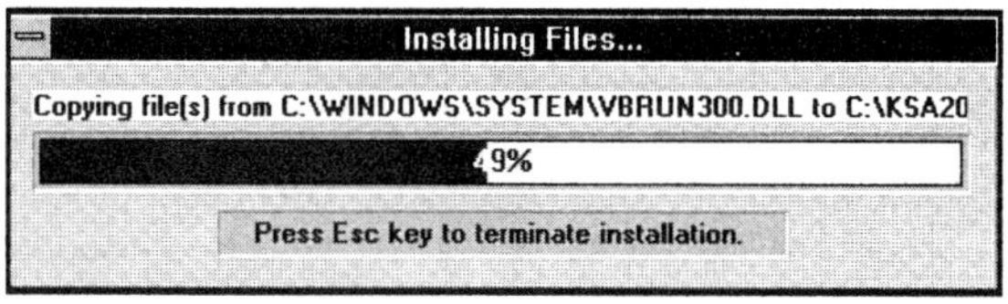

Figure 9.2
Installing files.

7. After the files finish copying, you are prompted to provide your first name. Type your first name and choose OK. When prompted, follow the same procedure to provide your last name, your company's name, and your department. You then are given the opportunity to review the information you just provided and change it if necessary (see fig. 9.3).

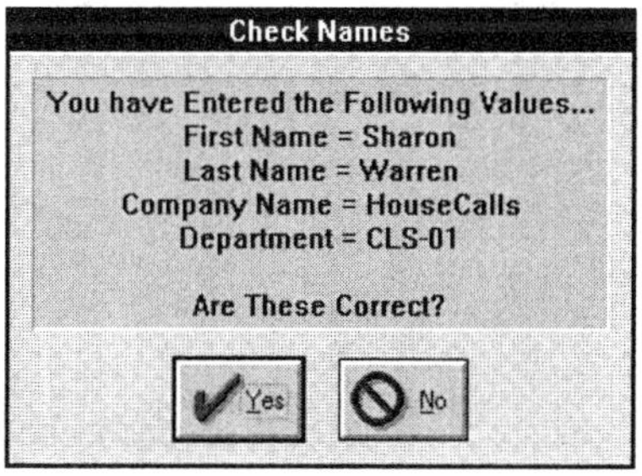

Figure 9.3
The Check Names screen.

8. After you choose Yes to verify the accuracy of the information, the Kane Security group is created, icons are added (see fig. 9.4), additional files are copied, and then you are notified of any changes made to Windows files. When ready, choose OK to continue.

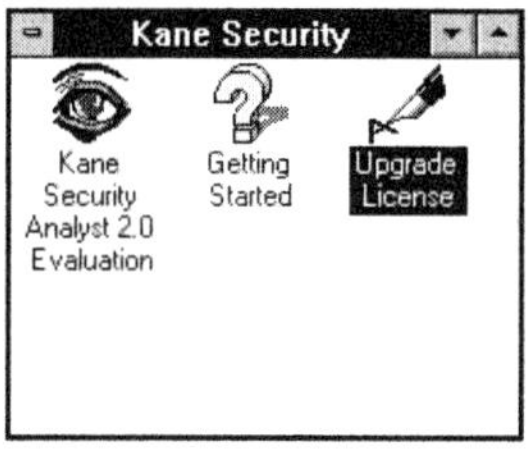

Figure 9.4
The Kane Security group.

9. You are given the option to read the readme file associated with Kane Security. Choose Yes if you want to read the file.

10. The installation is now complete, but you are prompted to restart Windows so the security software can take affect. You can choose Yes or No. If you choose No, however, remember that the security software cannot take effect until the next time you load Windows.

Using Kane Security Analyst v2.0

To use Kane Security Analyst, choose the Kane Security icon from the Kane Security Analyst icon group. The main screen opens (see fig. 9.5) after a brief introduction to the software.

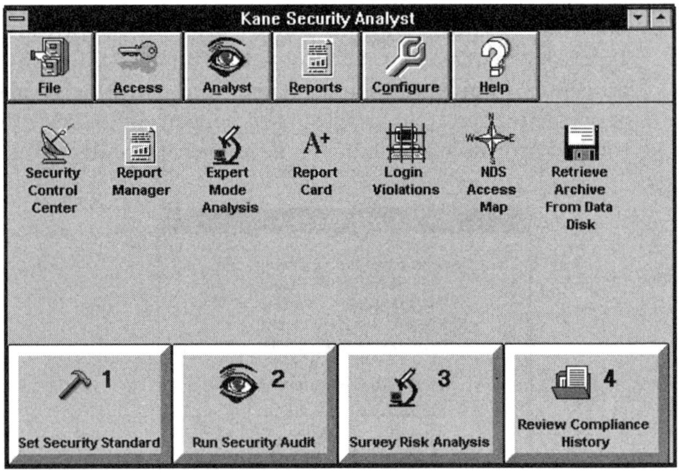

Figure 9.5 The Kane Security Analyst main screen.

From this screen, you can choose a variety of options:

- ✔ **Security Control Center.** Choose this icon to open the Kane Security Control Center screen (see fig. 9.6). This screen displays six security issues in a graphic form. Point to any one of them with the mouse pointer to open a description box, such as that shown in figure 9.6. Choose OK to close the Kane Security Control Center screen.

- ✔ **Report Manager.** Choose Report Manager to open the Report Manager dialog box, which has four options on its menu bar: File, Reports, Window, and Help. Window and Help are standard Windows menu options. The File option is standard to Windows, however the File menu in the Report Manager dialog box contains options specific to the Kane Security Analyst. The most important option, however, is Reports. Open the Reports menu to select the type of report you want to create. Figure 9.7 shows the menu of reports from which you can choose.

- ✔ **Expert Mode Analysis.** Choose the Expert Mode Analysis icon to open the Account Restrictions dialog box (see fig. 9.8). This dialog box contains a detailed analysis of a particular user's account restrictions. To open a different users analysis dialog box, select the user from the list of users in the lower left corner of the screen. From this screen, you also can open the user's Access Control and Password Strength analysis dialog boxes. Choose the related button from the list in the lower right corner of the screen. When finished, choose Close to return to the main screen.

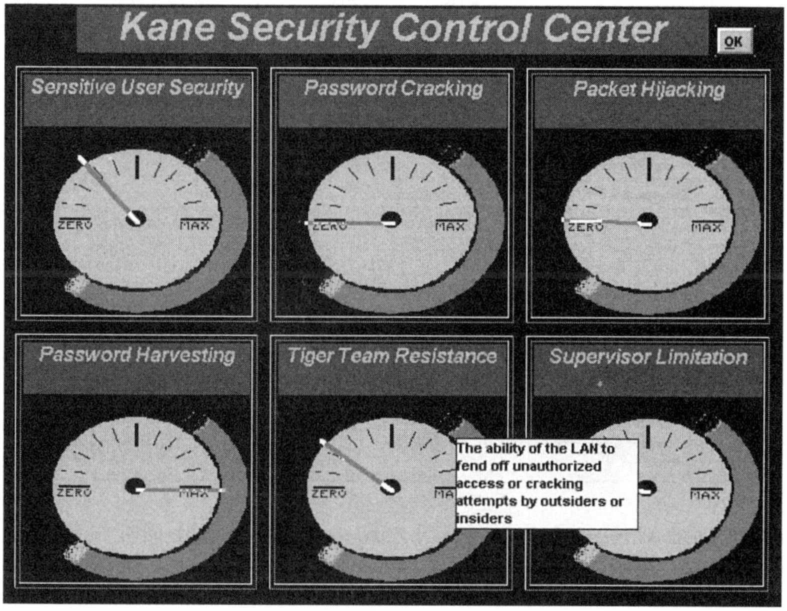

Figure 9.6
The Kane Security Control Center screen.

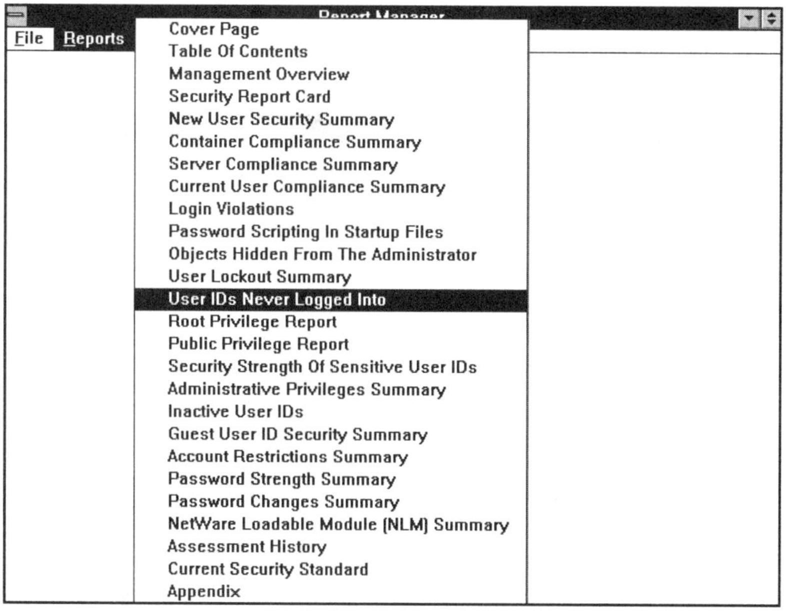

Figure 9.7
The Report Manager Reports menu.

Figure 9.8
The Expert Mode Analysis Account Restrictions dialog box.

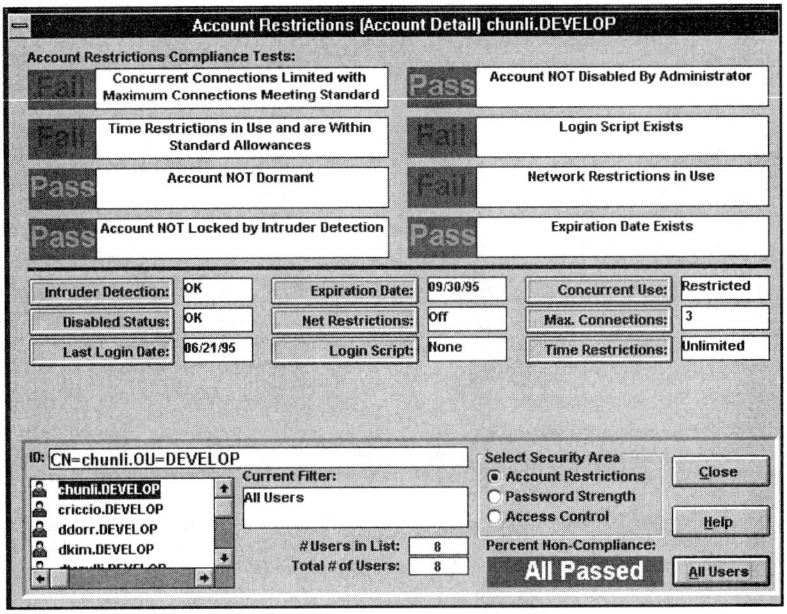

✔ **A+ Report Card.** Choose the A+ Report Card icon to open the Report Card dialog box from which you can run an analysis of various aspects of a specific object and see the results (see fig. 9.9), which include such information as account restrictions, password strength, and so on. From the Report Card dialog box, choose List Risks to see a list of the top risks (see fig. 9.10). To exit the list of risks, choose Close. To exit the Report Card dialog box, choose OK.

Figure 9.9
The Report Card dialog box.

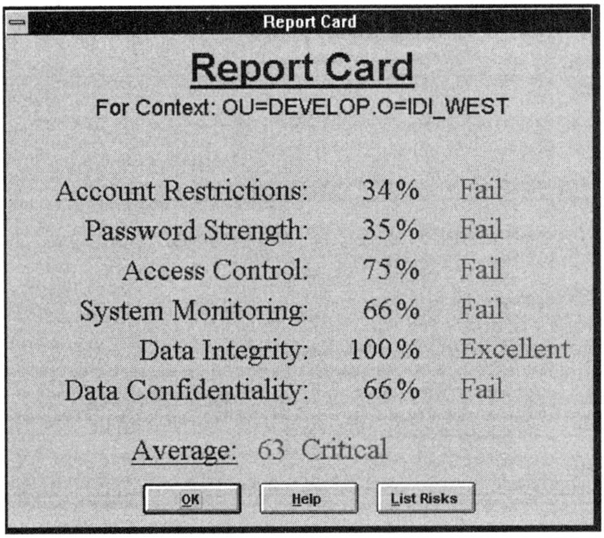

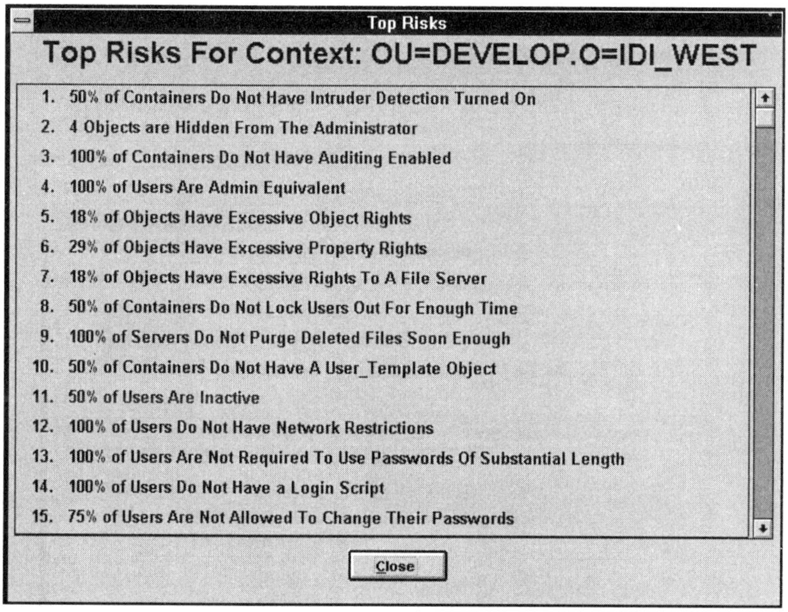

Figure 9.10 The list of top security risks to a particular object.

- ✔ **Login Violations.** Choose Login Violations to open the Login Violations dialog box, which contains a list of users who attempted to log in incorrectly, violating their login restrictions, according to the login time, location, and so on. If no login violations have occurred, the dialog box is blank. Choose Close to close the dialog box.

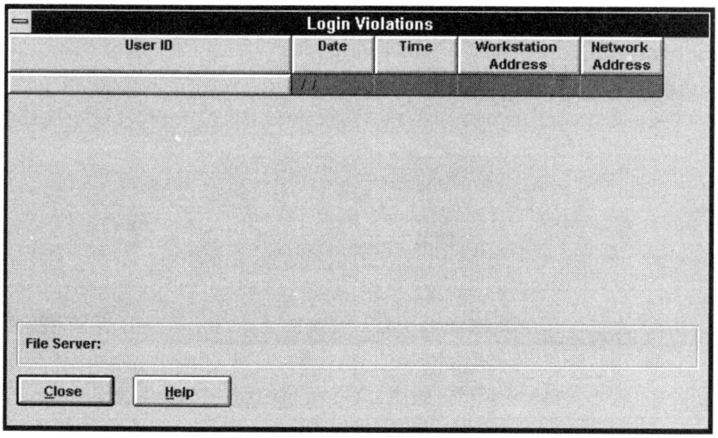

Figure 9.11 The Login Violations dialog box.

- ✔ **NDS Access Map.** Choose NDS Access Map to open the Access Control dialog box, which displays access security information for any chosen NDS object (see fig. 9.12). From this dialog box you can print an accompanying report by choosing Report. Online help also is available by choosing Help. Choose OK to close the dialog box.

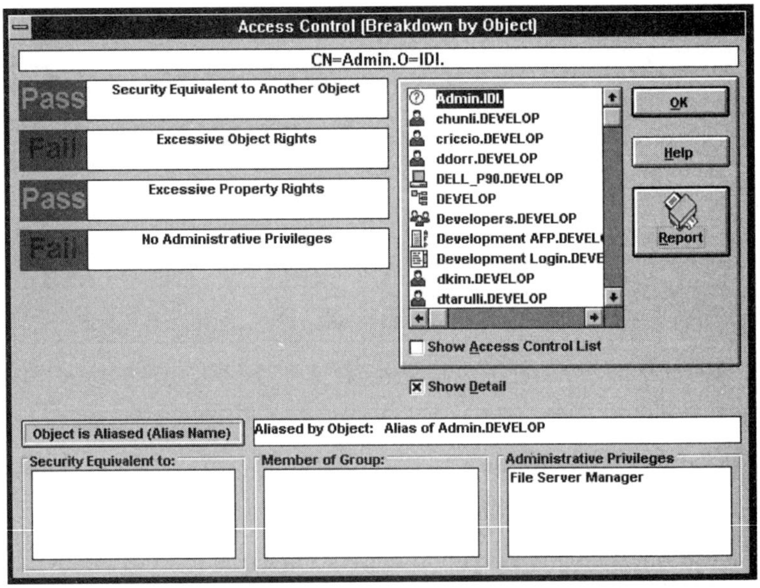

Figure 9.12 The Access Control dialog box for an NDS object.

- ✔ **Retrieve Archive From Data Disk.** Choose the Retrieve Archive From Data Disk icon to open the Retrieve Archive From Data Disk dialog box (see fig. 9.13). Use this dialog box to retrieve archived data. Select the location of the data, then choose Retrieve, and answer Yes when prompted to retrieve the data file. Choose Close to close the Retrieve Archive From Data Disk dialog box.

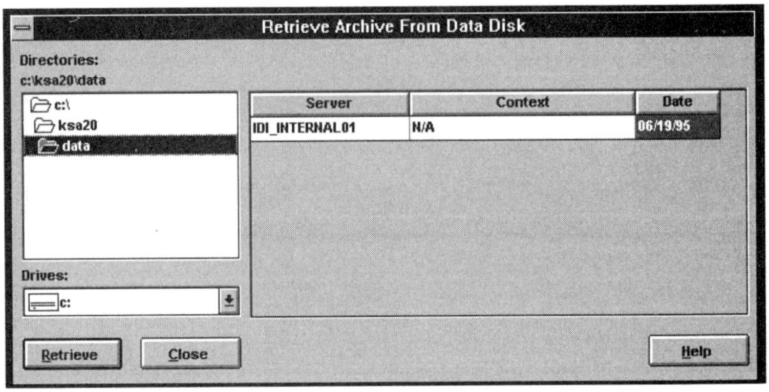

Figure 9.13 The Retrieve Archive From Data Disk dialog box.

The four buttons displayed across the bottom of the Kane Security Analyst screen enable you to view and configure other security information. Choose button 1, Set Security Standard, for example, to open the Set Security Standard dialog box, from which you can change security requirements (see fig. 9.14).

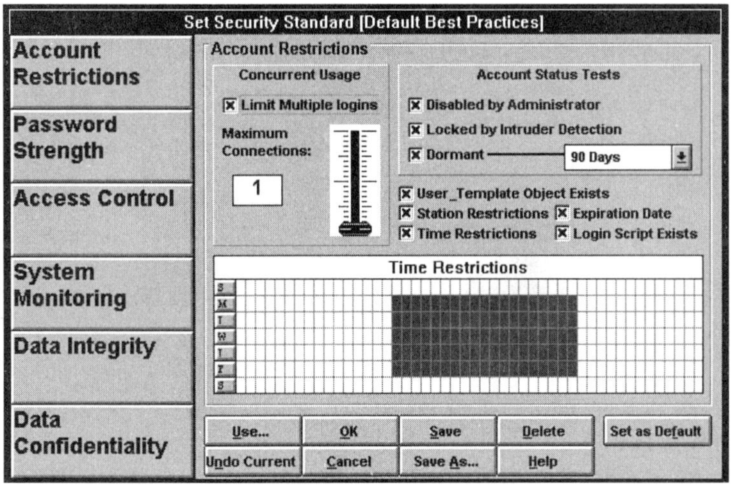

Figure 9.14
The Set Security Standard dialog box.

Modify the options in this dialog box to meet the security standards set by your company. Then choose OK to save settings or Cancel to exit without saving changes.

The following are the other three buttons in the Kane Security Analyst screen, with figures included to show you the screens that open when you click on these buttons:

- Run Security Audit

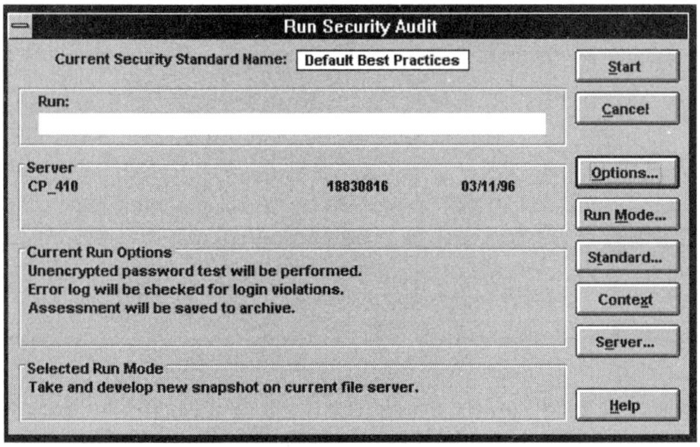

Figure 9.15
The Run Security Audit dialog box.

- ✔ Survey Risk Analysis

Figure 9.16 The Risk Analysis Survey dialog box.

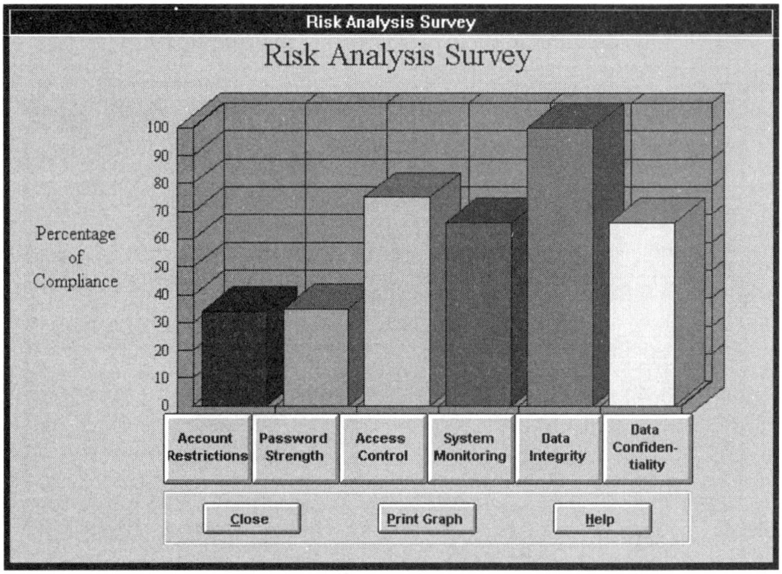

- ✔ Review Compliance History

Figure 9.17 The Security Compliance History Summary dialog box.

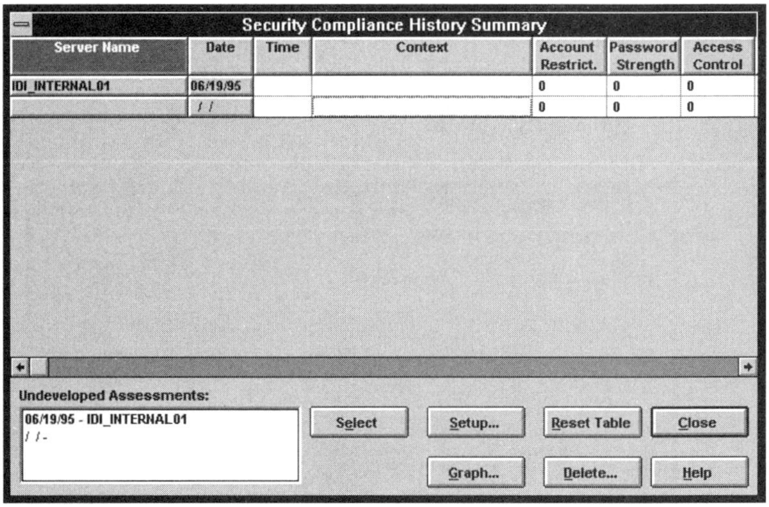

The Kane Security Analyst gives you a wide view of security on your NetWare network. As you might have noticed from the figures in this chapter, Kane Security Analyst also functions on NetWare 4 networks.

CHILAGA
NORVMBEGA
MARATA
CVLIACAN
CALICVAS
CAPASCHI
TERLICHICHIMECHI
LA FLORIDA
HISPANIA NOVA
TOPIRA
MECHVACAN
CVBA
HISPANIOLA
MAR DEL SVR, quod
Circulus Æquinoctialis
PACIFICVM
ICAE SIVE
ORBIS, NO
SCRIPTIO.
CHARCAS
CHILI
PATAGONVM
FRETVM MAGALLANICVM
Archipelago del C. desseado

10

CHAPTER

KLOSTECH

This chapter contains information about the programs included in the KLOSTECH directory on the CD that accompanies the *CNE 3 Resource Library*. Included in the KLOSTECH directory is the PPP ODI driver. Also included are two utilities: PacketView and SerialView. These two utilities are limited (demo-only) versions intended to introduce you to the utilities, and to give you a feel for what they are and how they work so that you can decide whether you would like to purchase them.

This chapter discusses the following KLOS Technologies products:

- ✔ PPP ODI Driver v1.36
- ✔ PacketView v1.18/SerialView v1.18 utilities

If you want to purchase this software, contact KLOS Technologies, Inc., at (603) 424-8300. For additional information about these KLOS Technologies demos, use the DOS TYPE command (including the |MORE ending option) or any DOS text editor to read the TIPS.TXT file (KLOSTECH\PKTVIEW\TIPS.TXT). The entire text file does not warrant full duplication in this chapter, but it might contain a tidbit or two worth your time.

PPP ODI Driver v1.36

PPP ODI is a Novell-compatible, DOS-based, Open Data-link Interface (ODI) software driver that enables PCs to communicate with each other across standard serial ports. PPP ODI supports both the IP and IPX protocols. It also supports Password Authentication Protocol (PAP) and Challenge Handshake Authentication Protocol (CHAP) for security. In addition, PPP ODI supports Van Jacobson compression, for compressing IP headers, and Compression Internetwork Packet eXchange (CIPX) for compressing IPX headers.

To use the PPP ODI driver, first load the appropriate software, depending on which protocol you are using. You can load the PPP ODI driver for use with NetWare IPX, LAN Workplace, and an Ethernet packet driver-based IP stack. After you load the appropriate software, you can communicate with other PCs across standard serial ports.

Loading the PPP ODI Driver for Use with NetWare IPX

The PPP ODI driver functions at the Link Support Layer. Before you can load the PPP ODI driver, therefore, you must load the Novell LSL.COM (Link Support Layer) file. Before you load any related files, however, you must add PPP ODI configuration information to the workstation's NET.CFG file. Figure 10.1 shows a sample NET.CFG file with PPP ODI driver-related configuration information.

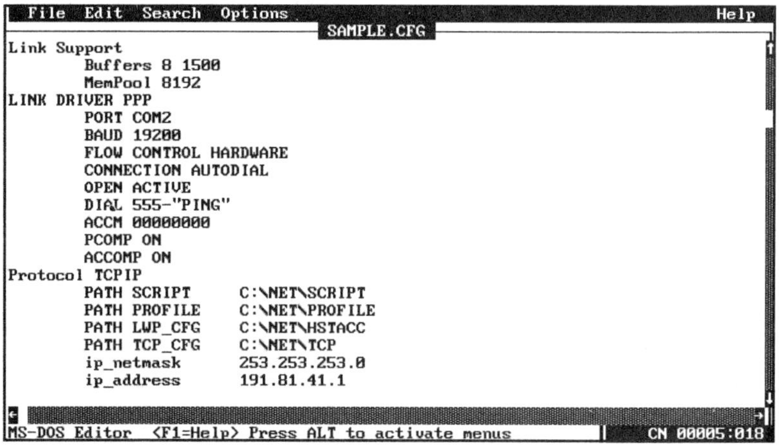

```
 File  Edit  Search  Options                                          Help
                              SAMPLE.CFG
Link Support
        Buffers 8 1500
        MemPool 8192
LINK DRIVER PPP
        PORT COM2
        BAUD 19200
        FLOW CONTROL HARDWARE
        CONNECTION AUTODIAL
        OPEN ACTIVE
        DIAL 555-"PING"
        ACCM 00000000
        PCOMP ON
        ACCOMP ON
Protocol TCPIP
        PATH SCRIPT     C:\NET\SCRIPT
        PATH PROFILE    C:\NET\PROFILE
        PATH LWP_CFG    C:\NET\HSTACC
        PATH TCP_CFG    C:\NET\TCP
        ip_netmask      253.253.253.0
        ip_address      191.81.41.1
MS-DOS Editor  <F1=Help> Press ALT to activate menus          CN 00005:018
```

Figure 10.1 A sample NET.CFG file.

To load the PPP ODI driver so that remote access to a Novell NetWare IPX-based network can be accomplished through a dial-in product, complete the following steps at the workstation used for remote dial-in access:

1. Load the LSL.COM file by placing the LSL command into the workstation's AUTOEXEC.BAT or STARTNET.BAT configuration file and rebooting the PC, or by typing **LSL** at the keyboard and pressing Enter.

2. Load PPP.EXE by placing the command into the AUTOEXEC.BAT or STARTNET.BAT configuration file and rebooting the PC, or by typing **PPP** at the keyboard and pressing Enter.

3. Run the PPPMENU.EXE program to configure PPP and establish a connection. Figure 10.2 shows the PPP Main Menu which opens when you run the PPPMENU.EXE program.

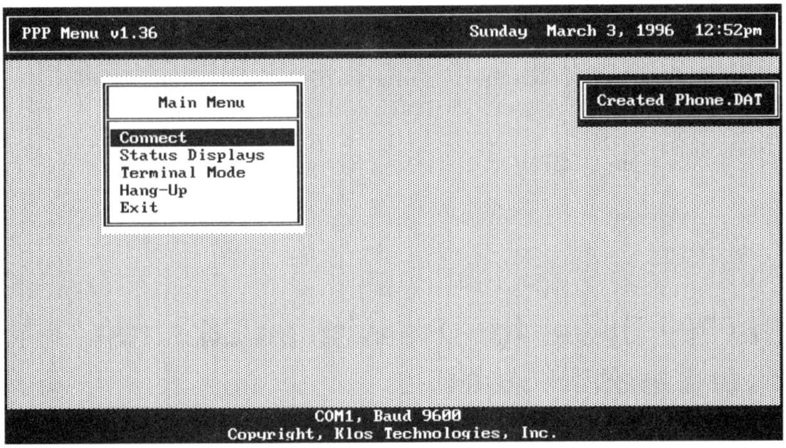

Figure 10.2
The PPP Main Menu.

4. Load the IPXODI.COM file by placing the IPXODI command into the workstation's AUTOEXEC.BAT or STARTNET.BAT configuration file and rebooting the PC, or by typing **IPXODI** at the keyboard and pressing Enter.

5. Load the NetWare Shell (NETX or BNETX) or the NetWare DOS Requester (VLM) by placing the IPXODI command into the workstation's AUTOEXEC.BAT or STARTNET.BAT configuration file and rebooting the PC, or by typing **NETX**, **BNETX**, or **VLM** at the keyboard and pressing Enter.

Note

Information about using the PPPMenu utility to configure PPP is provided in the section "Configuring PPP Using PPPMENU."

You now can log in to your file server using the NetWare LOGIN command.

Loading the PPP ODI Driver for Use with LAN Workplace

To load the PPP ODI driver for use with Novell's LAN WorkPlace products, complete the following steps at the workstation:

1. Load the LSL.COM file by placing the LSL command into the workstation's AUTOEXEC.BAT or STARTNET.BAT configuration file and rebooting the PC, or by typing **LSL** at the keyboard and pressing Enter.

2. Load PPP.EXE by placing the PPP command into the workstation's AUTOEXEC.BAT or STARTNET.BAT configuration file and rebooting the PC, or by typing **PPP** at the keyboard and pressing Enter.

3. Run the PPPMENU.EXE program to configure PPP and establish a connection. To run this program, type **PPPMENU**, and press Enter.

4. Load TCP/IP by typing **TCPIP** and pressing Enter.

You now should be able to run any LAN WorkPlace application, including PING, TNVT220, FTP, and so on.

Loading the PPP Driver for Use with an Ethernet Packet Driver-Based IP Stack

To load the PPP driver for use with an Ethernet packet driver using an IP stack such as PCTCP, Kali, or NCSA telnet, complete the following steps:

1. Load the LSL.COM file by placing the LSL command into the workstation's AUTOEXEC.BAT or STARTNET.BAT configuration file and rebooting the PC, or by typing **LSL** at the keyboard and pressing Enter.

2. Load PPP.EXE by placing the PPP command into the workstation's AUTOEXEC.BAT or STARTNET.BAT configuration file and rebooting the PC, or by typing **PPP** at the keyboard and pressing Enter.

3. Run the PPPMENU.EXE program to configure PPP and establish a connection. To run this program, type **PPPMENU** and press Enter.

4. Load IPSTUB by typing **IPSTUB** and pressing Enter.

You now can load your Ethernet packet driver-based IP stack. To load the stack for the FTP software's PCTCP, for example, load ETHDRV.

Configuring PPP Using PPPMENU

One of the installation steps you must complete before you can load PPP for use with NetWare IPX, LAN WorkPlace, or an Ethernet packet driver-based IP stack is to run PPPMENU and configure PPP. This section explains the basics of PPPMENU.

To open the PPPMENU utility, type **PPPMENU** and press Enter. The PPP Main Menu opens, as shown in figure 10.2. From this menu, you can choose any of five options:

- ✔ Connect
- ✔ Status Displays
- ✔ Terminal Mode
- ✔ Hang-Up
- ✔ Exit

If you choose Connect, the process of connecting from one PC to another PC begins.

If you choose Status Displays, status information appears across the bottom of the screen (see fig. 10.3).

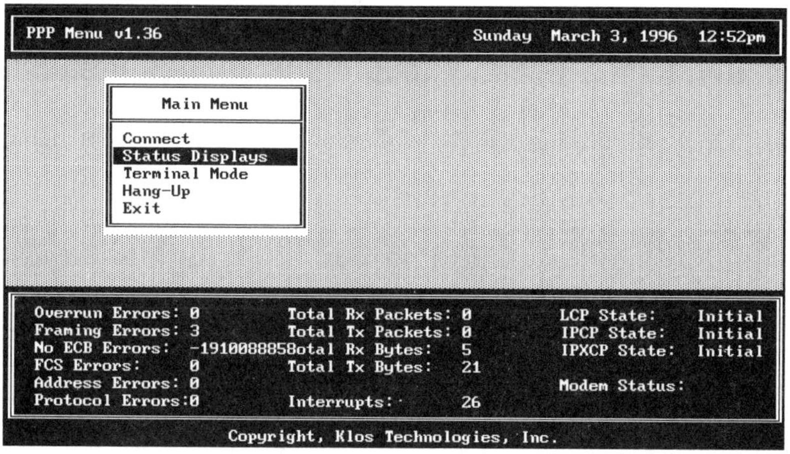

Figure 10.3
The PPP Main Menu screen showing PPP status information.

The status display provides information about errors it detects, such as address and protocol errors. It also displays information about the total number of packets that have been received and sent, and the total number of bytes that have been received and sent. In addition, the status display shows the interrupts, modem status, and the state of LCP, IPCP, and IPXCP where applicable.

Note The demo version of the PPP ODI driver does not provide any online help information. To understand the meaning of some of the status information might require that you already understand such terms as protocol, packets, LCP, and so on.

Choosing Terminal Mode opens the Profile List window, from which you can modify the workstation's current PPP ODI driver profile (see fig. 10.4). To modify the profile, press F1. After you finish modifying the profile, you can press F2 to update the workstation's NET.CFG file.

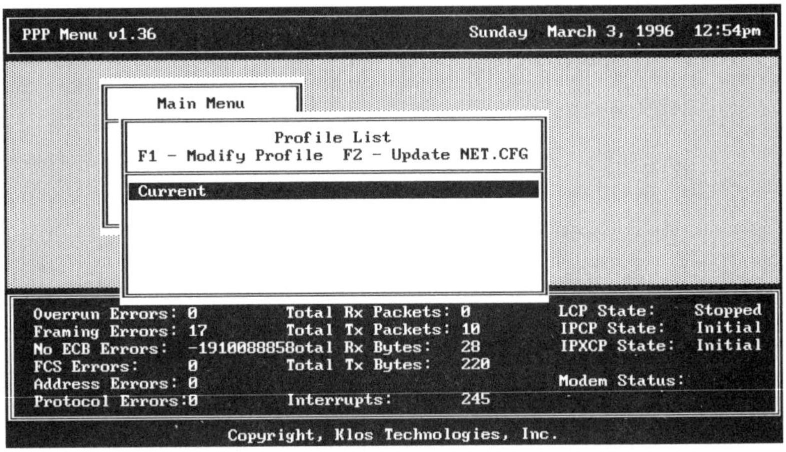

Figure 10.4 The Profile List window.

When you press F1 to modify the current profile, the Configure Menu Current menu opens (see fig. 10.5).

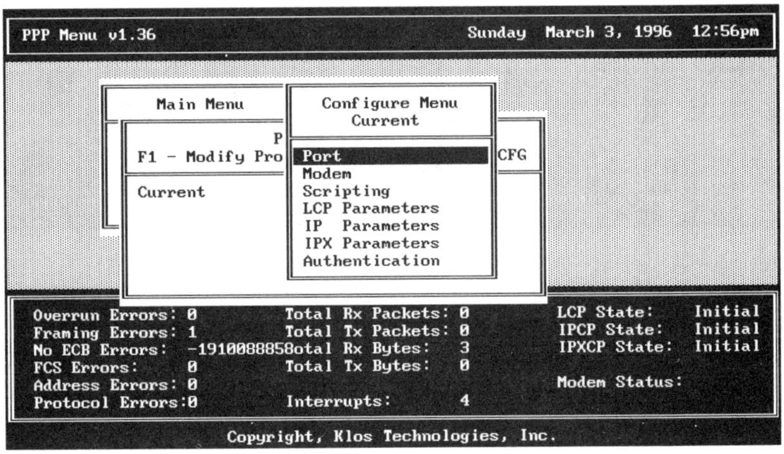

Figure 10.5 The Configure Menu Current menu.

From the Configure Menu Current menu, you can modify information related to the following:

- ✔ **The port.** Choose Port from the Configure Menu Current menu to modify the configuration of the items listed in the Port Menu (see fig. 10.6).

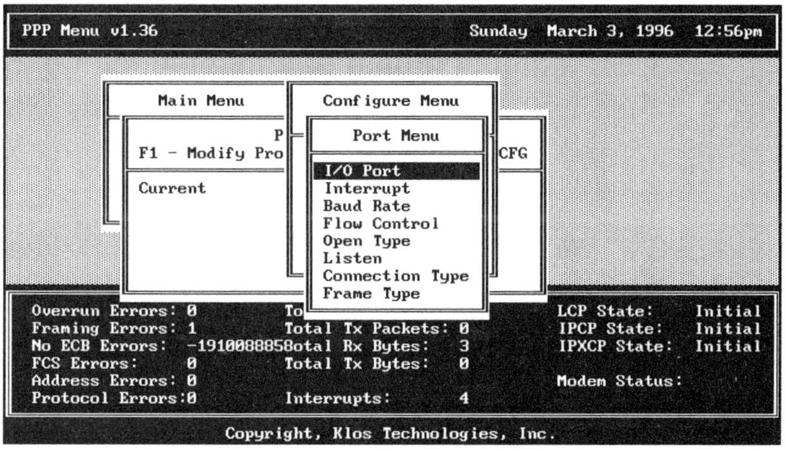

Figure 10.6
The Port Menu.

You can modify the configuration of the following items:

- ✔ **I/O Port.** You can set the port to COM1, COM2, COM3, COM4, or Special. If you choose Special, you are prompted to type the base port address.
- ✔ **Interrupt.** You can set the interrupt to any number between 2 and 15 inclusive.
- ✔ **Baud Rate.** You can set the baud rate to any valid baud rate from 300 to 114,200 inclusive.
- ✔ **Flow Control.** You can choose to use hardware, software, or both for flow control.
- ✔ **Open Type.** You can choose to set the open type to either Active or Passive.
- ✔ **Listen.** You can set the listening status to either Auto-Answer or Don't Answer.
- ✔ **Connection Type.** Opens the Connection Type menu from which you can choose Direct, Modem, Modem - Auto dial, Modem - Demand Dial, or Modem - Terminal (see fig. 10.7).

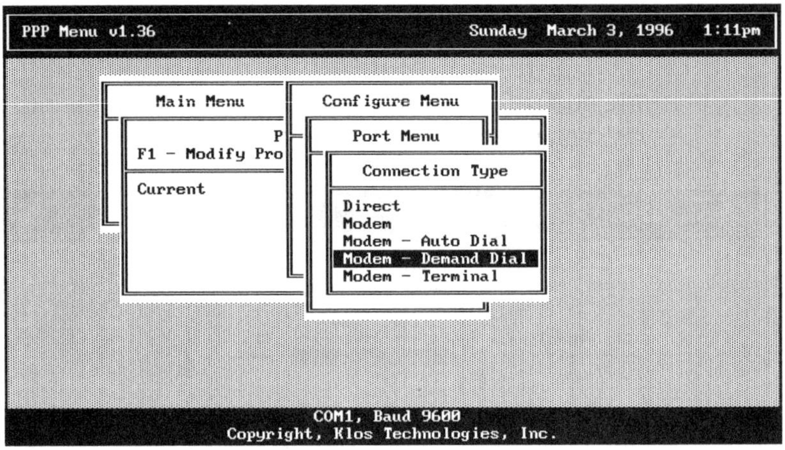

Figure 10.7 The Connection Type menu.

- ✔ **Frame Type.** You can choose the frame type (such as PPP, Ethernet 802.2, Ethernet 802.3, and so on).

✔ **The modem.** Choose Modem from the Configure Menu Current menu to open the Modem Menu (see fig. 10.8). From the Modem Menu, you can set the modem's phone number, name, command strings (see fig. 10.9), and timers and counters (see fig. 10.10).

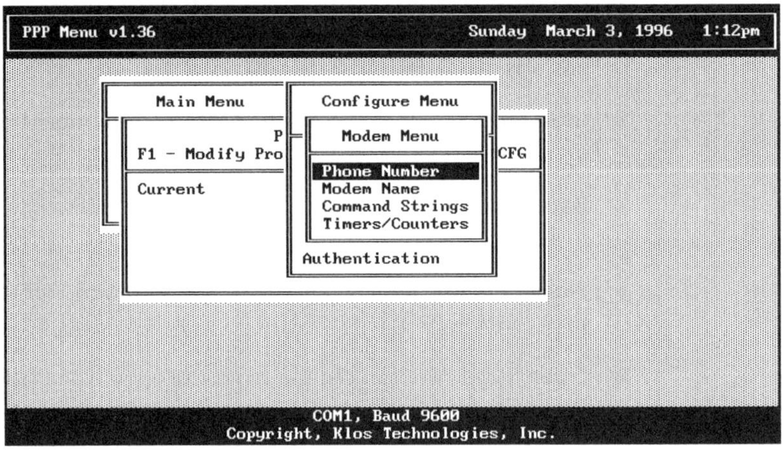

Figure 10.8 The Modem Menu menu.

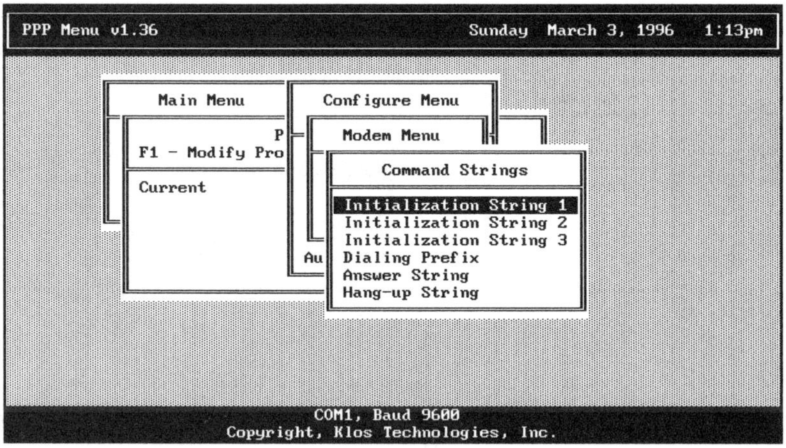

Figure 10.9
The Command Strings menu.

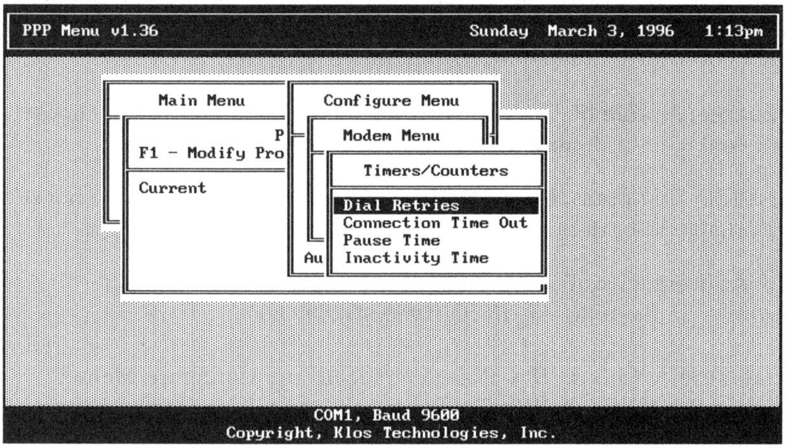

Figure 10.10
The Timers/Counters menu.

- ✔ **Scripting.** Choose Scripting from the Configure Menu Current menu to specify a script.
- ✔ **LCP Parameters.** Choose LCP Parameters from the Configure Menu Current menu to open the LCP Configuration Menu (see fig. 10.11), from which you can choose any of the following options:
  - ✔ Maximum Receive Unit
  - ✔ Async-Control Map
  - ✔ Magic Number
  - ✔ Protocol Compression
  - ✔ Address/Control Compression

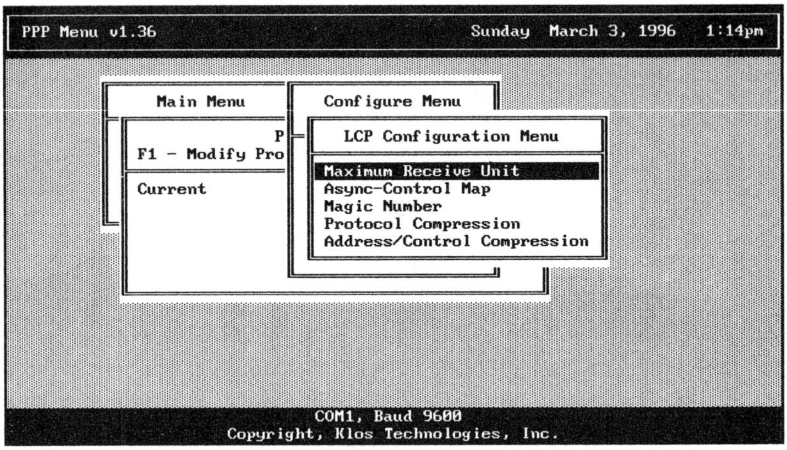

Figure 10.11
The LCP Configuration Menu.

- ✔ **IP Parameters.** Choose IP Parameters from the Configure Menu Current menu to open the IP Configuration Menu. From the IP Configuration Menu, you can choose any of the following options:
  - ✔ **Enable/Disable IP.** Opens another menu from which you can choose to enable IP or disable IP.
  - ✔ **Header Compress.** Opens another menu from which you can choose to enable VJ or disable VJ.
  - ✔ **IP Address.** Provides an area in which you type the 15-character IP address in the following format: 000.000.000.000.
- ✔ **IPX Parameters.** Choose IPX Parameters from the Configure Menu Current menu to open the IPX Configuration Menu, from which you can choose any of the following four options:
  - ✔ **Enable/Disable IPX.** Opens another menu from which you can choose to enable IPX or disable IPX.
  - ✔ **Header Compress.** Opens another menu from which you can choose to enable CIPX or disable CIPX.
  - ✔ **Node Address.** Enables you to set or change the hexadecimal IPX node address, such as 00000000A270.
  - ✔ **Network Number.** Enables you to set or change the hexadecimal network number, such as 00001CD1.

- **Authentication.** Choose Authentication from the Configure Menu Current menu to open the Authentication Menu (see fig. 10.12). From this menu you can choose the type of authentication to use when you load the PPP ODI driver:

  - None
  - Password Authentication Protocol
  - Challenge-Handshake Authentication Protocol
  - Id and Password

  The last option—Id and Password—enables you to set the name of the user and a password for that user. Then, when the user loads the PPP ODI driver, the user is prompted for her password.

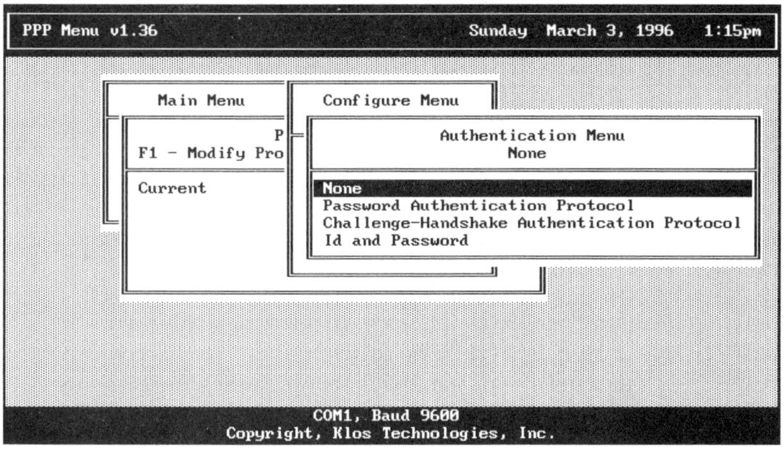

Figure 10.12 The Authentication Menu.

PacketView v1.18/SerialView v1.18 Utilities

PacketView is a network protocol analyzer. You can use PacketView with a variety of standard network adapters. PacketView enables you to capture network packets and decode them.

Like PacketView, *SerialView* also is a protocol analyzer. SerialView, however, is an asynchronous analyzer. It captures its information from PC-to-PC connections made through serial cables connected to the COM ports on various PCs. With SerialView, users can capture and decode asynchronous Point-to-Point (PPP) and Serial Line Internet Protocol (SLIP) traffic.

PacketView v1.18

Because PacketView is a DOS-based utility, you start it by changing to the directory in which PacketView is located, typing **PV** and pressing Enter. When you run PacketView, a screen opens, and after a brief period of time, information about network packets appears, one packet at a time, on the packet screen (see fig. 10.13).

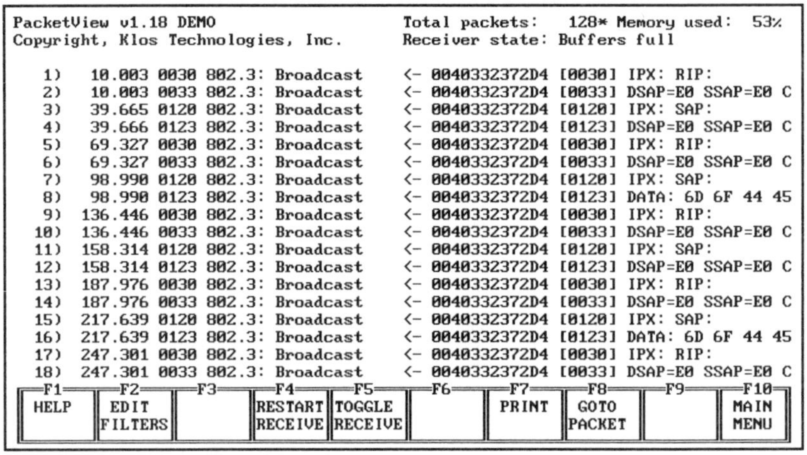

Figure 10.13 The PacketView packet display screen.

Packets are initially displayed one line at a time, in the *Line screen/mode.* A Line screen is displayed when you start PacketView. The Line screen shows limited information about each packet, but shows multiple packets on a single screen.

You can view more detailed information about any particular packet, however, by switching to the Detail screen (see fig. 10.14). To switch to the Detail screen from the Line screen, press Enter. Alternatively, you can toggle between these two screens by pressing D when you are viewing the Line screen, or L when you are viewing the Detail screen.

The Detail screen shows a variety of information not available on the Line screen. Information on the Detail screen includes, but is not limited to, the following:

- ✔ **Frame type**—Such as IEEE 802.3
- ✔ **Destination**—Such as Broadcast
- ✔ **Source**—Such as 0040332372D4
- ✔ **Size**—Such as 0120
- ✔ **Checksum**—Such as FFFF
- ✔ **Hop count**—Such as 0

- ✔ **Protocol—**Such as Service Advertisement Protocol (SAP)
- ✔ **Server—**Such as CP_410

```
PacketView v1.18 DEMO                         Total packets:    22  Memory used:  10%
Copyright, Klos Technologies, Inc.            Receiver state: Enabled

    IEEE 802.3:
        Destination: Broadcast      Size: 0120  Number:       1
        Source:      0040332372D4   Type: 0120  Time:    15.835

    IPX:
    Checksum = FFFF, Packet length = 0120, Hop count = 0
    Protocol type is 0 (Unknown)
    Destination address: 2D699C8D.Broadcast
    Destination socket:  0452 (Service Advertising Protocol)
    Source address:      2D699C8D.0040332372D4
    Source socket:       0452 (Service Advertising Protocol)

    SAP:  Service advertisement
          Type  Network   Node           Socket  Hops  Server
          ----  --------  ------------   ------  ----  ------
          0278  00CAD001  000000000001    4006     1   CADY_LHC
          0047  00CAD001  000000000001    8060     1   PS1
          0107  00CAD001  000000000001    8104     1   CP_410
 F1       F2       F3       F4       F5       F6       F7       F8       F9       F10
 HELP     EDIT              RESTART  TOGGLE            PRINT    GOTO              MAIN
          FILTERS           RECEIVE  RECEIVE                    PACKET            MENU
```

Figure 10.14
The Packet Detail screen.

To see a specific packet's Detail screen, from the Line screen, press F8 (GO TO PACKET). When prompted, provide the packet number. Then press Enter or D to switch to this packet's Detail screen.

In addition to seeing a list of packets (in the Line screen) or details about a particular packet (in the Detail screen), you can press F10 (MAIN MENU) to open PacketView's Main Menu (see fig. 10.15). The Main Menu provides information about current workstations, such as whether or not base memory is available on them, and if so, how much is available. In addition, the Main Menu shows the same information about expanded memory. It also indicates which ODI driver, network board, and media type are being used, among other information.

```
PacketView v1.18 DEMO                         Total packets:    24  Memory used:  10%
Copyright, Klos Technologies, Inc.            Receiver state: Disabled


                                   Main Menu

                       F1  - Help
                       F2  - Load Configuration from Disk
                       F3  - Save Configuration to Disk
                       F4  - Load Packet Buffer from Disk
                       F5  - Save Packet Buffer to Disk
                       F10 - Display Protocol List


                      Serial number: 99999999
                      Registered to: DEMONSTRATION COPY
                                     DISTRIBUTE FREELY


    Available base memory: 51K                Using AE-200JL ODI driver (board 1)
    No expanded memory available              Packet list contains 128 entries
    24 node symbols using 576 bytes           Current media type is Ethernet
    208 host symbols using 4992 bytes
```

Figure 10.15
The PacketView Main Menu.

With the Main Menu open, you can perform different tasks by choosing the function key associated with each task. Because the version of PacketView on the CD is a demo version, however, some of the associated functionality is limited.

The following are the function keys specified on the PacketView Main Menu, and their associated tasks:

- ✔ **F1—Help.** Enables you to view PacketView's online help information.
- ✔ **F2—Load Configuration from Disk.** Enables you to use a predefined configuration file currently stored on disk.
- ✔ **F3—Save Configuration to Disk.** Enables you to save to disk a configuration that you created.
- ✔ **F4—Load Packet Buffer from Disk.** Enables you to choose a predefined packet buffer and load it.
- ✔ **F5—Save Packet Buffer to Disk.** Enables you to save to disk a packet buffer that you created.
- ✔ **F10—Display Protocol List.** Enables you to view a detailed list of protocols and related information which PacketView is able to track and present.

If you choose either F2 or F3 to open (load) or save a configuration file, the `Enter configuration file name:` prompt appears (see fig. 10.16). You can type a configuration file name, or press Enter to choose the default name PV.CFG, and open that file, when the name is displayed. The PV.CFG file, however, is not available with the demo version of PacketView.

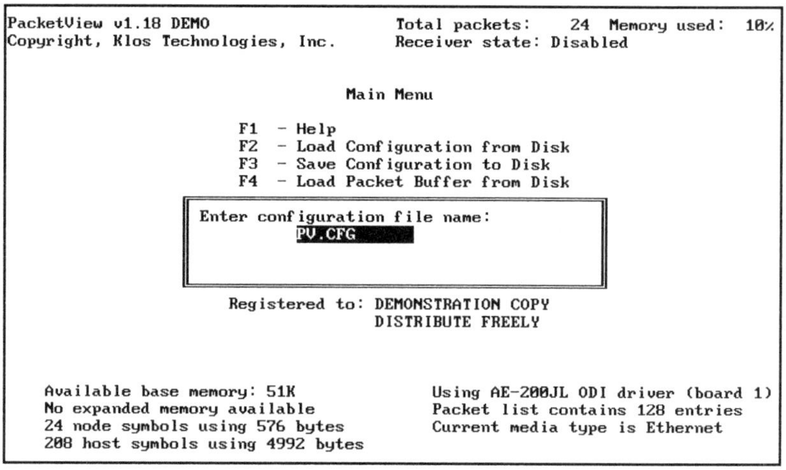

Figure 10.16 Type a configuration file name or press Enter to choose the default.

If you choose F3 to save a configuration, after you enter a configuration file name and press Enter, a confirmation appears. You then are prompted to press Esc to close the `Enter configuration file name:` prompt box (see fig. 10.17).

```
PacketView v1.18 DEMO                        Total packets:    24  Memory used:   10%
Copyright, Klos Technologies, Inc.           Receiver state: Disabled


                                   Main Menu

                        F1  - Help
                        F2  - Load Configuration from Disk
                        F3  - Save Configuration to Disk
                        F4  - Load Packet Buffer from Disk
                  ┌──────────────────────────────────────────┐
                  │ Enter configuration file name:           │
                  │          PV1.CFG                         │
                  │ Configuration saved                      │
                  │ Please press ESC                         │
                  └──────────────────────────────────────────┘
                       Registered to: DEMONSTRATION COPY
                                      DISTRIBUTE FREELY


    Available base memory: 51K               Using AE-200JL ODI driver (board 1)
    No expanded memory available             Packet list contains 128 entries
    24 node symbols using 576 bytes          Current media type is Ethernet
    208 host symbols using 4992 bytes
```

Figure 10.17
You are prompted to press Esc to close the prompt box.

The F4 and F5 keys function similarly to F2 and F3; however, they retrieve or save the contents of the Packet Buffer. The *Packet Buffer* is the area in memory in which the information received by the PacketView utility about each packet is temporarily stored. To store that information to disk, save it using the F4 key. You can then retrieve that information at a later date using the F5 key. The demo version of PacketView, however, does not allow you to save the Packet Buffer to disk.

If you choose F10 to display the protocol list, a multi-page display of the protocols that PacketView can decode is displayed. The information that appears depends on the type of decoder. Figures 10.18 and 10.19 show examples of the first two pages of the protocol list.

```
PacketView v1.18 DEMO                        Total packets:     0  Memory used:    0%
Copyright, Klos Technologies, Inc.           Receiver state: Disabled

   PRIMARY PROTOCOL DECODERS:

   Protocol       Ethertype  802.2  ARCNET  show_line()  show_packet()
   ---------      ---------  -----  ------  -----------  -------------
   ARP              0806               F1    1B10:193C     1B10:000C
   IP               0800       06      F0    1B10:1ACB     1B10:027E
   SNMP             814C                     1D0E:0079     1D0E:0000
   IPX              8137       E0            1F8A:13E8     1F8A:0008
   ARP                                 D5    1B10:1E49     1B10:1F19
   IP                                  D4    1B10:1CB3     1B10:1D83
   AppleTalk        809B                     1AD6:036D     1AD6:000E
   Vines IP                    BC            1E54:116A     1E54:000A
   Vines IP         80C4                     1E54:1126     1E54:0093
   Vines IP         0BAD                     1E54:1126     1E54:0093
   SMB              FF53                     2178:028D     2178:02C6
   NETBIOS          EFFF       F0            2178:0000     2178:0039
   XNS              0600                     20FA:0701     20FA:0000
   IPX                                 FA    1F8A:1617     1F8A:154A
   Vines IP         FF00                     1E54:11E2     1E54:1293

   IP PROTOCOL DECODERS:
  ▼
```

Figure 10.18
The first page of the protocol list display.

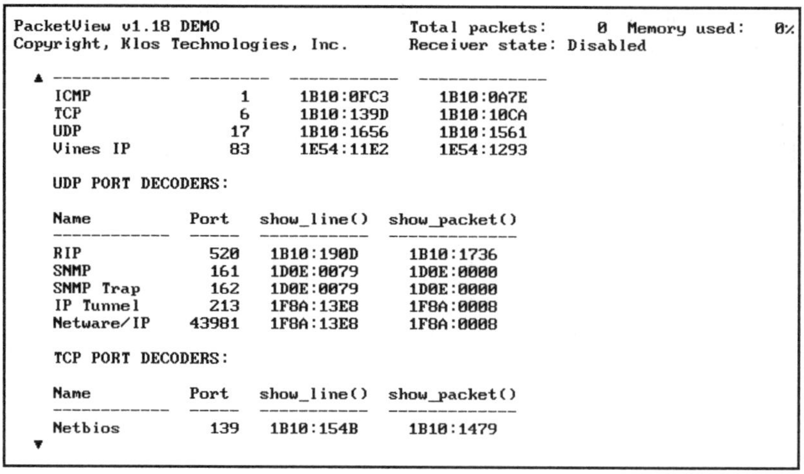

Figure 10.19 The second page of the protocol list display.

The first protocols, displayed in figure 10.18, are the primary protocols such as ARP, IP, SNMP, IPX, AppleTalk, Vines IP, SMB, NETBIOS, XNS, and so on. Figure 10.19 shows the display of IP Protocol Decoders (the heading of which appears in figure 10.18), UDP Port Decoders, and TCP Port Decoders. The show_line() and show_packet() fields display the memory address in the packet buffer of the related information.

You also can create and subsequently choose a filter for limiting the types of packets that are captured and decoded, or displayed by the PacketView utility. To create or use a filter, choose F2 (EDIT FILTERS) while the Line or Detail screen is open to open the Edit Filter Menu (see fig. 10.20).

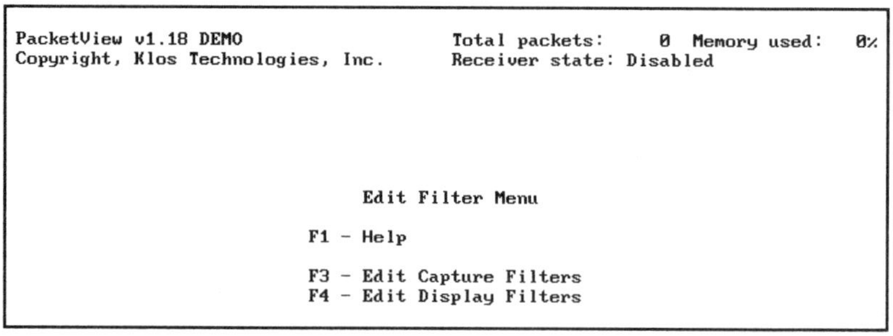

Figure 10.20 The Edit Filter Menu.

From the Edit Filter Menu, you can view online help by pressing F1, edit a Capture filter by pressing F3, or edit a Display filter by pressing F4. If you press F3, the Capture Filters screen shown in figure 10.21 opens.

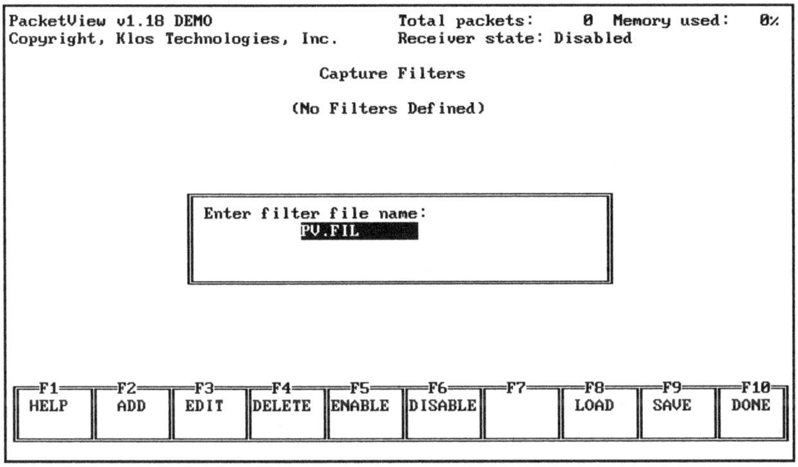

Figure 10.21
The Capture Filters screen.

If you choose F3 or F4 from the Edit Filter Menu, you can then choose another function key to perform the following tasks:

- ✔ **F1—Help.** Choose this key to view online help.
- ✔ **F2—Add.** Choose this key to create a new filter.
- ✔ **F3—Edit.** Choose this key to modify an existing filter.
- ✔ **F4—Delete.** Choose this key to erase an existing filter from disk.
- ✔ **F5—Enable.** Choose this key to activate a specific filter.
- ✔ **F6—Disable.** Choose this key to deactivate a specific filter.
- ✔ **F8—Load.** Choose this key to load a filter.
- ✔ **F9—Save.** Choose this key to save an edited filter.
- ✔ **F10—Done.** Choose this key to finish creating, editing, activating, or deactivating filters and close the filter menu.

If you choose to create a new filter by pressing F2, a screen opens from which you can choose up to five items for filtering (see fig. 10.22). Choose which type to match by pressing the associated function key.

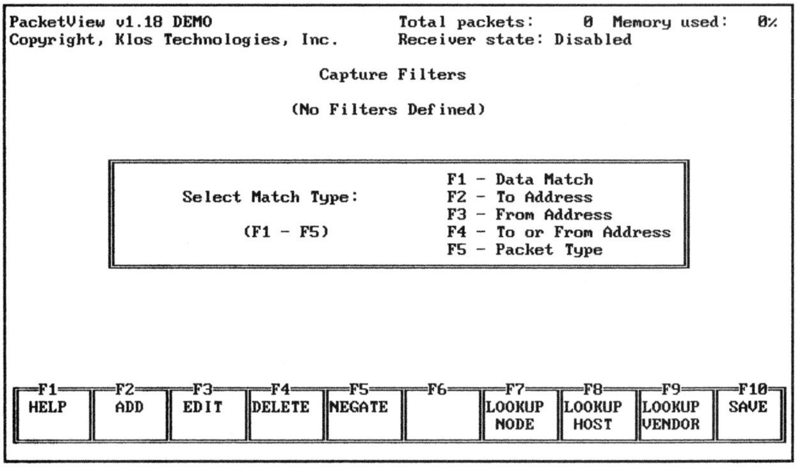

Figure 10.22 The Capture Filters Select Match Type box.

The following are the five Match Type options:

- ✔ Data Match
- ✔ To Address
- ✔ From Address
- ✔ To or From Address
- ✔ Packet Type

The PacketView utility also enables you to temporarily disable or suspend the capture of network packets. To temporarily disable, and then later enable the capture of network packets, press F5. F5 functions as a toggle switch.

With the PacketView utility, you can view a variety of network packet information. In addition, you can store packet information for later review. PacketView provides much versatility of information. It even lets you choose what types of packet information are captured and displayed.

SerialView v1.18

The SerialView utility is almost identical to the PacketView utility. The differences are not noticeable in the user interface (screens presented to you as the user of the utility). Because the utility presents the same information, using the same screens and keys, the information in this chapter about PacketView, except where otherwise noted, also applies to SerialView. For this reason, and because PacketView is more commonly used than SerialView, information about SerialView is not duplicated in this chapter.

Starting the SerialView utility is, however, different from starting the PacketView utility. To start the SerialView utility, use the SV instead of PV command.

CHILAGA
NORVMBEGA
MARATA
CVLIACAN
CALICVAS
CAPASCHI
TERLICHICHIMECHI
HISPANIA NOVA
TOVA
LA FLORIDA
CVBA
HISPANIOLA
MAR DEL SVR, quod
PACIFICVM
CHILI
ICAE SIVE
ORBIS, NO
SCRIPTIO.
Archipelago del C. desseado

11

CHAPTER

MCROHOUS

The MCROHOUS directory on the CD contains several subdirectories. Together these subdirectories contain a version of the Micro House Technical Library and a drive setup utility, both in demonstration mode. Both demonstrations are contained in the DEMOS subdirectory. The files that run them are CDDEMO.EXE and DPDEMO.EXE. This chapter discusses how to run the Micro House Technical Library demonstrations.

Before running the demos, you can copy the software to your local hard disk or to a drive on the network. You also can run it from the CD, although it might run slower than from your hard disk or a network drive.

Note Some of the information in this chapter is adapted from the information provided on the CD by the manufacturer of Micro House Technical Library.

Running the CDDEMO

You must run the CDDEMO file from Windows. To run the CDDEMO file, complete the following steps:

1. Start Windows, then choose **R**un from the **F**ile menu to open the Run dialog box.

2. Type the path to the CDDEMO.EXE file in the Command Line, or use the **B**rowse button to search for the file, then choose OK. A Welcome window opens, providing information about the restrictions related to this demonstration version of the Micro House Technical Library.

3. Choose OK to continue. The Micro House Technical Library main screen opens (see fig. 11.1).

Figure 11.1 The Micro House Technical Library main screen.

4. Choose one of the options provided.

The options from which you can choose on the Micro House Technical Library main screen are as follows:

- ✔ KEYWORD
- ✔ COMPANIES
- ✔ ABOUT
- ✔ EXIT
- ✔ The Four Micro House Technical Library documents:

  The Encyclopedia of Hard Drives

  The Encyclopedia of Main Boards

  The Encyclopedia of Network Cards

  The Encyclopedia of I/O Cards

KEYWORD

Choose KEYWORD to open the Search the Micro House Technical Library dialog box (see fig. 11.2). In this window you can type up to 10 words, separated by spaces. The words you enter are used to search the database of technical information for matches. For example, if you want information about a hard drive, you can search using "hard drive". If you want information about a specific type of hard drive, you can put in more detail, such as the name of the specific hard drive.

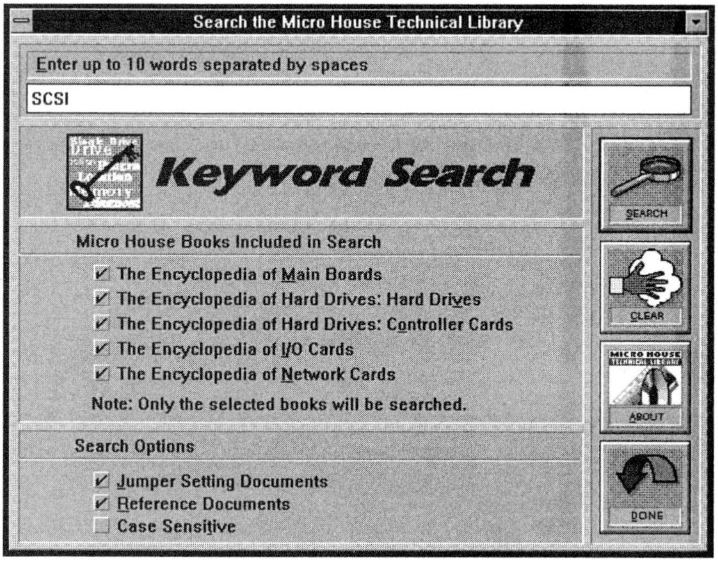

Figure 11.2
The Search the Micro House Technical Library dialog box.

To use the Keyword Search, type the keyword(s), then choose the **S**EARCH button. The Hit List opens, revealing a list of finds (see fig. 11.3). Choose the find you want to read.

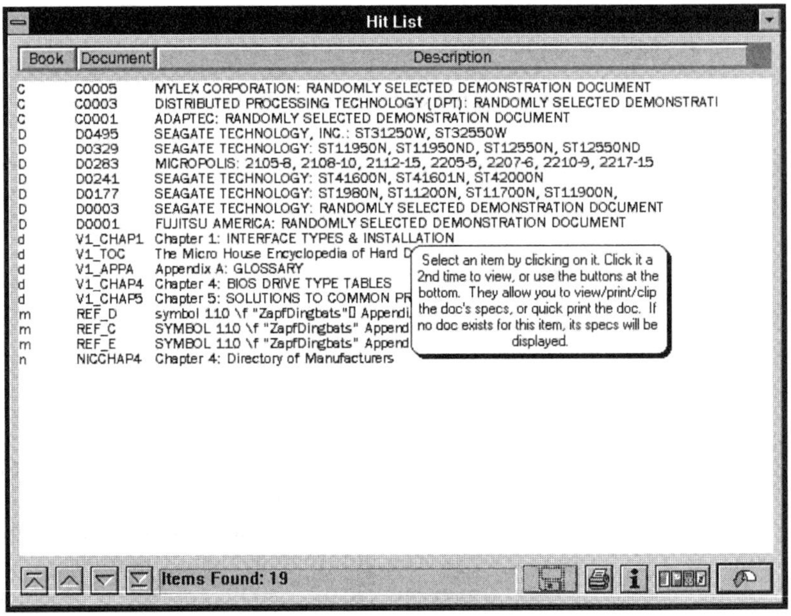

Figure 11.3
The keyword search Hit List.

COMPANIES

Choose **C**OMPANIES to open the Manufacturer Information dialog box. Open the list of companies to choose a company about which you want to see information (see fig. 11.4).

From the Manufacturer Information dialog box, you can print the company information or cut it to the Clipboard so that you can paste it into a document later.

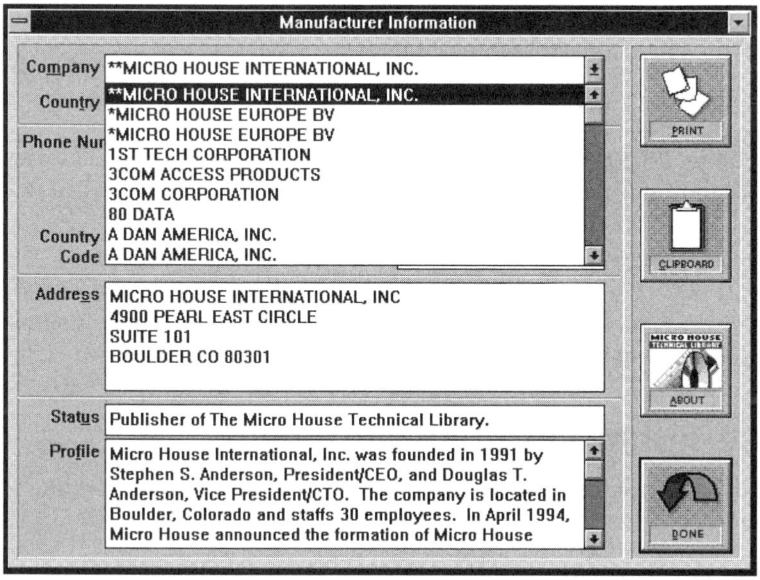

Figure 11.4
The Manufacturer Information dialog box with the Company list open.

ABOUT

Choose ABOUT to open the About the Micro House Technical Library dialog box (see fig. 11.5). Information related to the Micro House Technical Library is presented.

The About the Micro House Technical Library dialog box displays information about the Micro House Technical Library, including the following:

Figure 11.5
The About the Micro House Technical Library dialog box.

- ✔ **CREDITS.** Choose CREDITS to open a list of people who worked on this version of the Micro House Technical Library.
- ✔ **HELP.** Choose HELP to open the online help screen.
- ✔ **DONE.** Choose DONE to close the About the Micro House Technical Library dialog box and return to the main screen.

EXIT

Choose EXIT to close the Micro House Technical Library. Most Micro House Technical Library dialog boxes contain an equivalent Done button.

Micro House Technical Library Documents

You can choose any of the four buttons that represent various Micro House Technical Library documents:

- ✔ The Encyclopedia of Hard Drives
- ✔ The Encyclopedia of Main Boards
- ✔ The Encyclopedia of Network Cards
- ✔ The Encyclopedia of I/O Cards

Choose The Encyclopedia of Hard Drives, for example, to open a dialog box that displays the contents of the encyclopedia (see fig. 11.6).

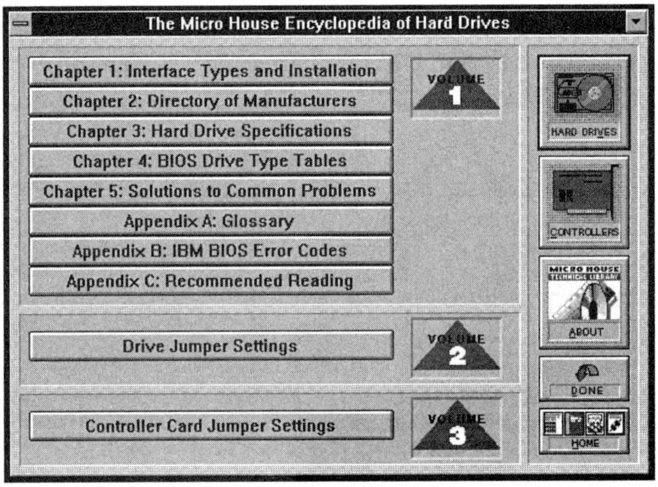

Figure 11.6 The table of contents screen for the Micro House Encyclopedia of Hard Drives.

From this main screen, you can choose a chapter, appendix, and so on, or you can choose one of the buttons (such as HARD DRIVES) to search for specific information.

Running DPDEMO

You can start DPDEMO from Windows, too; however, you should start it from DOS. Before you start DPDEMO, be sure to rename your AUTOEXEC.BAT and CONFIG.SYS files, then reboot your workstation so that no TSRs are loaded. Otherwise, an error message appears.

To start DPDEMO, complete the following steps:

1. Copy the DPDEMO directory from the CD to a directory on your local hard disk, then change your default drive to the DPDEMO directory on the hard disk.

2. Type **DPDEMO** and press Enter. The Micro House Professional Driver Setup utility window opens.

3. Press Enter twice to open the main window, which contains three separate areas (see fig. 11.7): BASIC MODE FUNCTIONS, RESULTS, and BIOS DATA.

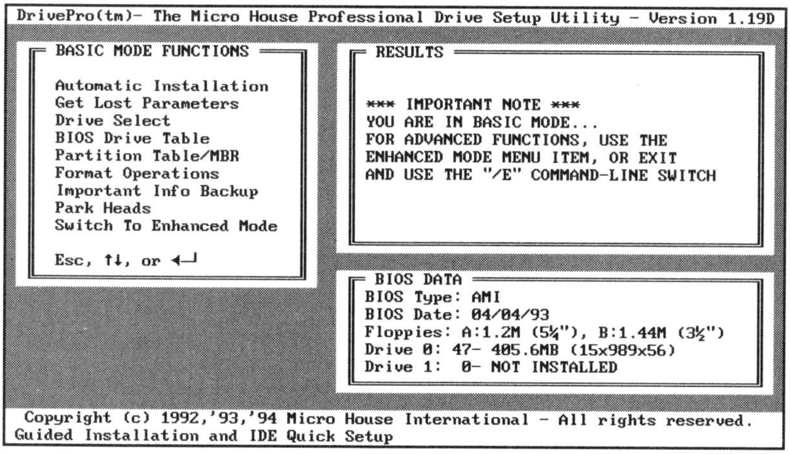

Figure 11.7 The DrivePro Setup Utility main screen.

Note

If the main window does not open, and instead you see an error message indicating that the software cannot find the BIOS table, you have not successfully removed all TSRs. Make certain you modify any files needed to prevent any TSRs from loading, then reboot your PC and start DPDEMO again.

DrivePro Setup

From the Basic Mode Functions menu of the DrivePro Setup Utility main screen, you can choose any of the following options:

- ✔ **Automatic Installation.** Opens a menu called AUTOMATIC INSTALLATION, from which you can choose Guided Installation or IDE Quick Setup (see fig 11.8). Choosing Guided Installation walks you through installing a new hard drive. The IDE Quick Setup option automatically installs an IDE drive.

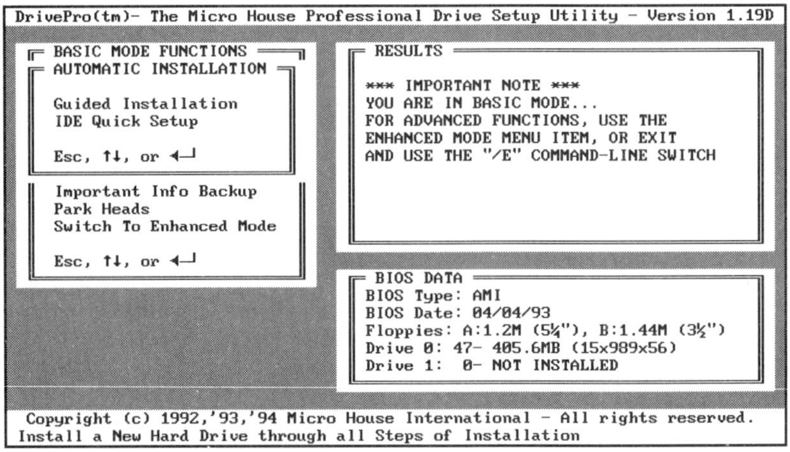

Figure 11.8 The AUTOMATIC INSTALLATION menu.

- ✔ **Get Lost Parameters.** Displays in the RESULTS field the results of a search of the PC's physical drives (see fig. 11.9) and can find system information lost by the system CMOS.

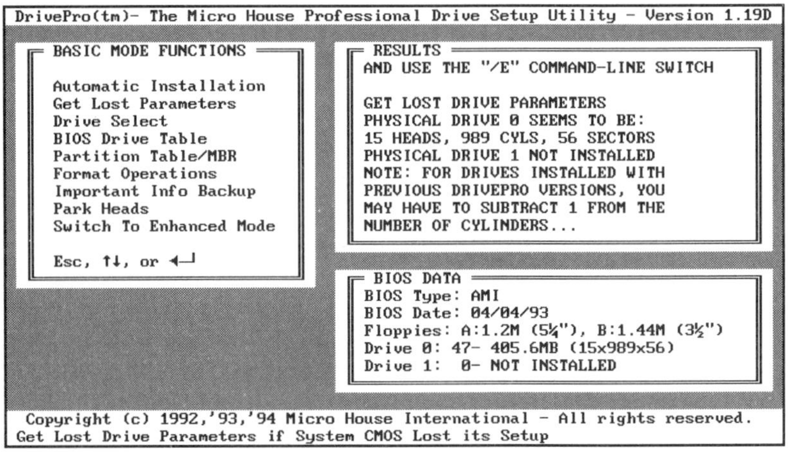

Figure 11.9 RESULTS field contents.

- ✔ **Drive Select.** Opens the DRIVE SELECT menu, from which you can choose a variety of menu options. (See the section "DRIVE SELECT" later in this chapter for more information about the DRIVE SELECT menu.)

- ✔ **BIOS Drive Table.** Provides information about the drive table including drive size, number of heads, number of cylinders, number of sectors, and so on. It also sets the CMOS drive type (see fig. 11.10).

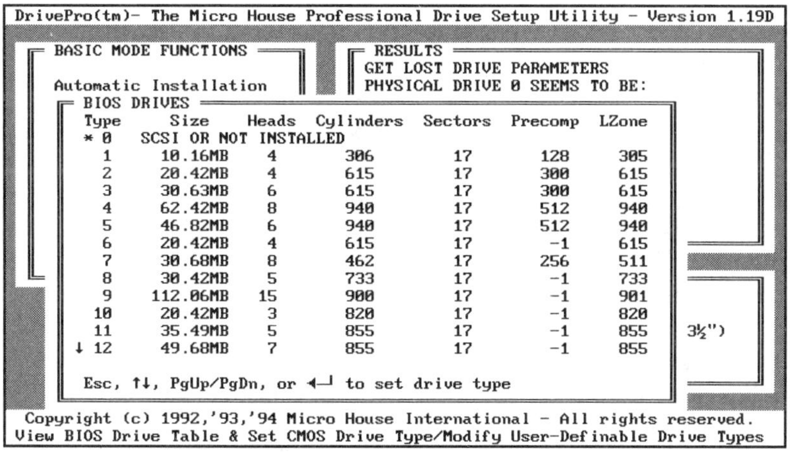

Figure 11.10
BIOS DRIVES window.

- ✔ **Partition Table/MBR.** Opens the SET UP PARTITIONS menu from which you can choose a variety of menu options. (See the section "SET UP PARTITIONS" later in this chapter for more information about the SET UP PARTITIONS menu.)

- ✔ **Format Operations.** Opens a menu from which you can choose to perform a high-level (DOS) format or a low-level format, or relocate a cluster (see fig. 11.11).

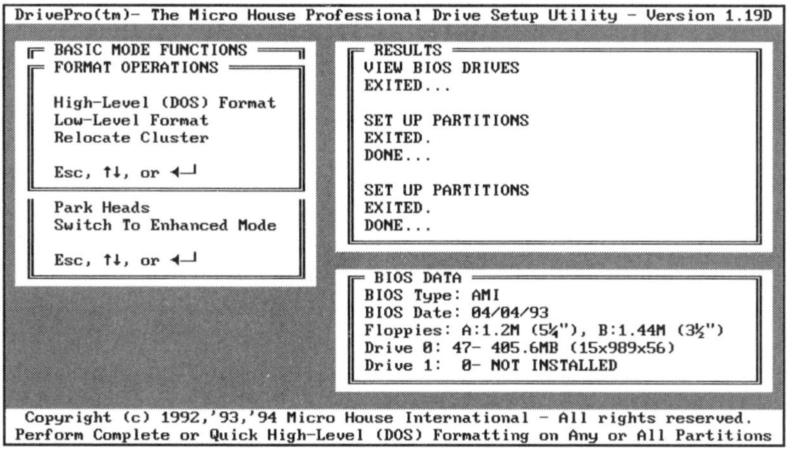

Figure 11.11
The FORMAT OPERATIONS window.

- **Important Info Backup.** Opens a menu from which you can choose to back up important system information to a drive that you specify (see fig. 11.12).

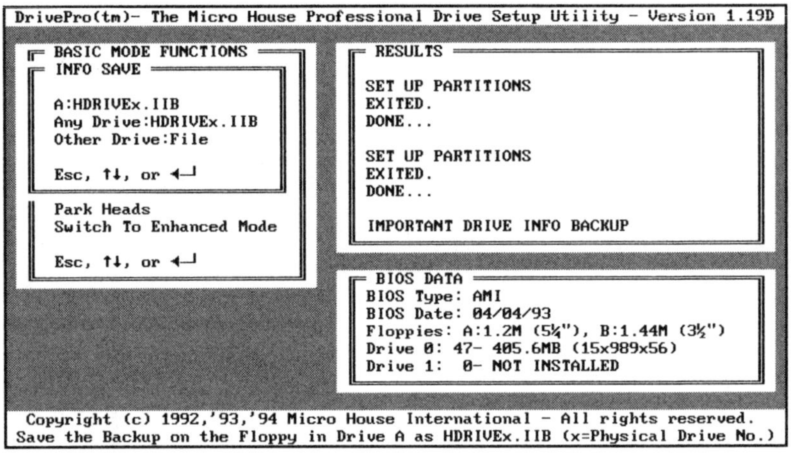

Figure 11.12 The INFO SAVE menu.

- **Park Drive Heads.** Parks the heads and prompts you to turn off the system, but also gives you the option to abort this function (see fig. 11.13).

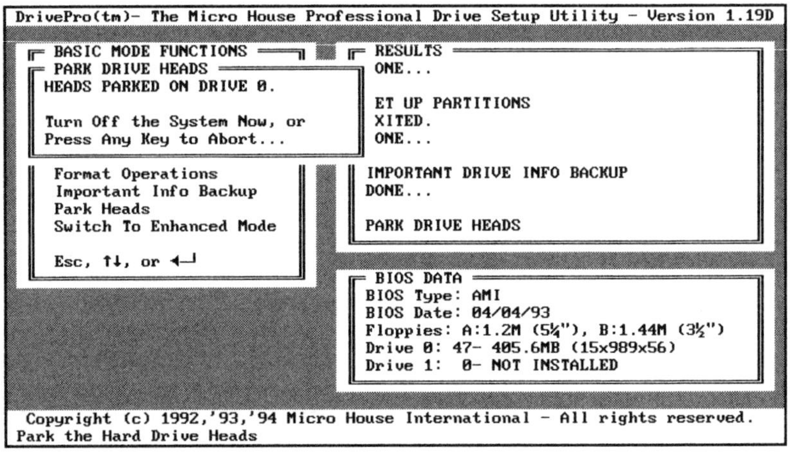

Figure 11.13 The PARK DRIVE HEADS window.

- **Switch To Enhanced Mode.** Opens the Enhanced Mode Functions menu. (See the section "Enhanced Mode Functions" later in this chapter for more information about the ENHANCED MODE FUNCTIONS menu.)

DRIVE SELECT

To view a variety of hard drive options, choose Drive Select from the BASIC MODE FUNCTIONS menu. The DRIVE SELECT menu opens (see fig. 11.14) from which you can choose the following:

- ✔ **Select by Make and Model.** Enables you to view drive specifications by make and model. It also enables you to set the CMOS drive type.
- ✔ **IDE Automatic Selection.** Performs an IDE drive inquiry, shows drive specifications, and sets the CMOS drive type.
- ✔ **ESDI Automatic Selection.** Performs an ESDI drive/device inquiry, shows drive/device specifications, and sets the CMOS drive type.
- ✔ **SCSI Automatic Selection.** Performs a SCSI drive/device inquiry, shows drive/device specifications, and sets the CMOS drive type.
- ✔ **Install Custom Drive Type.** Enables you to create a DrivePro user-definable drive type, even if BIOS does not have one.
- ✔ **Reinitialize Drive/DOS.** Reinitializes the drive parameters and reboots DOS for full access to the drive.

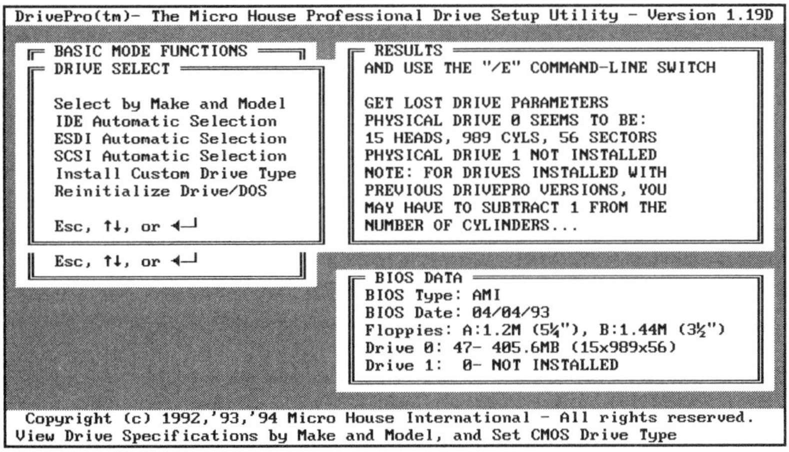

Figure 11.14 The DRIVE SELECT menu.

SET UP PARTITIONS

To view a list of partitioning options, choose Partition Table/MBR (Master Boot Record) from the BASIC MODE FUNCTIONS menu. The SET UP PARTITIONS menu opens (see fig. 11.15), from which you can choose the following options:

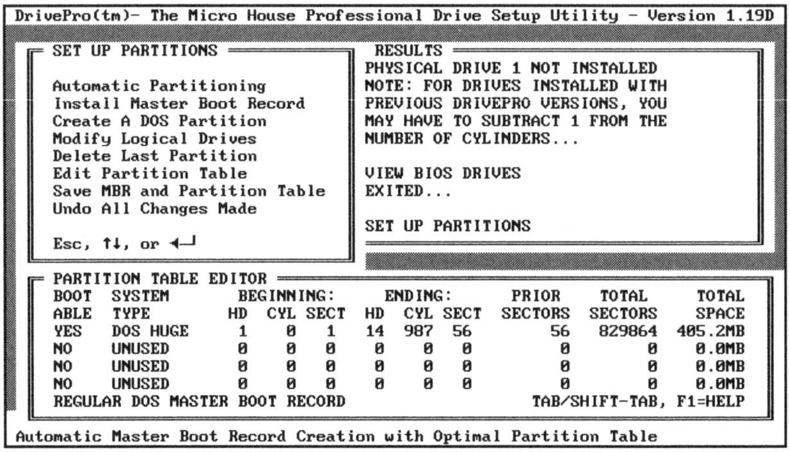

Figure 11.15
The SET UP PARTITIONS menu.

- ✔ **Automatic Partitioning.** Automatically creates the Master Boot Record with the optimal partition table.
- ✔ **Install Master Boot Record.** Creates a new Master Boot Record and enables you to wipe the partition table clean.
- ✔ **Create A DOS Partition.** Creates a DOS Huge (BigDOS), regular (<=32MB), or extended partition.
- ✔ **Modify Logical Drives.** Enables you to edit the logical drive setup in the DOS extended partition.
- ✔ **Delete Last Partition.** Wipes clear the last partition entry, also eliminating all data on the partition.
- ✔ **Edit Partition Table.** Enables you to edit the partition table to set up special partitions or change the active partition.
- ✔ **Save MBR and Partition Table.** Saves changes to the drive.
- ✔ **Undo All Changes Made.** Resets changes to original settings.

ENHANCED MODE FUNCTIONS

The ENHANCED MODE FUNCTIONS menu contains several of the options in the BASIC MODE FUNCTIONS menu (see fig. 11.16). Options in the ENHANCED MODE FUNCTIONS menu that you do not find in the BASIC MODE FUNCTIONS menu nor any of its submenus are as follows:

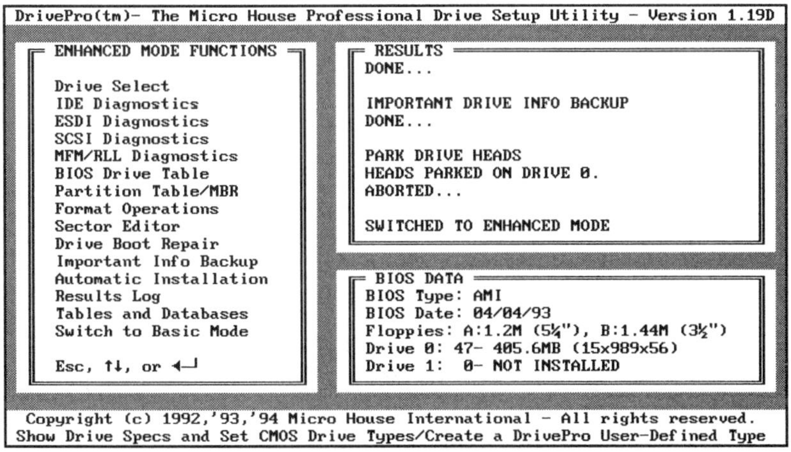

Figure 11.16
The ENHANCED MODE FUNCTIONS dialog box.

- ✔ **IDE Diagnostics.** Runs a diagnostic utility on the disk drive to determine information such as the average seek time, the drive's interleave, and throughput.
- ✔ **ESDI Diagnostics.** Runs a diagnostic utility on the disk drive to determine information such as the average seek time, the drive's interleave, and throughput.
- ✔ **SCSI Diagnostics.** Runs a diagnostic utility on the disk drive to determine information such as the average seek time, the drive's interleave, and throughput.
- ✔ **MFM/RLL Diagnostics.** Runs a diagnostic utility to determine information such as the average seek time, interleave, and throughput.
- ✔ **Results Log.** Enables you to save, read, print, or clear the results log.
- ✔ **Tables and Databases.** Enables you to view controller specifications, manufacturer address/phone/FAX information, system data, and program configuration.
- ✔ **Switch to Basic Mode.** Enables you to switch to basic mode from enhanced mode.

After you finish using this demo, press Esc until you see the prompt `Do you want to save the results log?`. Type **Y** to save the results log, or accept the default of **N** to not save the log.

CHILAGA
NORVMBEGA
MARATA
CVLIACAN
CAPASCHI
TERLICHICHI
HISPANIA NOVA
LA FLORIDA
CVBA
MAR DEL SVR, quod
PACIFICVM
CHARCAS
CHILE
PATAGONES
CAE SIVE
ORBIS, NO
SCRIPTIO.
Archipelago del C.
delleado

12

CHAPTER

NOVELL

The NOVELL directory on the CD contains a copy of the July 1995 issue of *Novell Application Notes.* This issue is used on the CD with Novell, Inc.'s permission.

Table 12.1 in this chapter contains a list of the back issues of *Novell Application Notes.* This list of back issues is also included on the CD. A single article from the July 1995 issue is provided in this chapter to demonstrate the type of informative articles you can find in each issue of *Novell Application Notes.* You can, however, read all articles from the July 1995 issue from the CD. In addition, the CD contains an order form you can use to order *Novell Application Notes.*

To access the information on the CD, first create a directory in which you have the rights required to create new files. Then extract the information.

Extracting the July 1995 Issue of *Novell Application Notes*

To read the entire July 1995 issue, you must extract the required files by completing the following steps:

1. Create a directory into which you can extract the files.
2. Change your default drive to point to that directory.
3. From the DOS prompt, type **W0795A** and press Enter.

   The W0975A.EXE file is a self-extracting file that will place all articles from the July 1995 issue of *Novell Application Notes* into the specified directory.

You now can use WordPerfect 6.1 to read the files. You also can convert the files from WordPerfect to another word processing software, if the software has the capability to do so.

Note

The UnixWare article in this chapter, "Installing and Configuring UnixWare 2.0," which begins immediately after following this note, is adapted from the CD. In some instances, minor changes were made to accommodate format differences between the CD and the book. This article was written by two members of the UNIX Systems Group: **Kurt Spiegel**, Technical Marketing Support Specialist, and **Lester Temple,** Senior Software Engineer. It is reproduced here with only slight editorial and formatting modifications.

Installing and Configuring UnixWare 2.0

UnixWare 2.0 installation has been re-engineered to give you a simpler, faster installation process. In fact, Novell is aware of a claim that you can install the base system on a Pentium machine in about 18 minutes. We're not suggesting that you should expect this result yourself; we're just pointing out that the process is probably not as difficult as you might assume. As you read this AppNote, notice how many times the word "automatic" appears.

First, we'll look at installation features new to UnixWare 2.0. Next, we'll take a look at hardware requirements. Then we'll go step-by-step through the installation process. After that, we'll tell you where to obtain further help if you need it.

This AppNote is designed as a supplement to the UnixWare installation guide. The most important step in ensuring a successful installation is also the most neglected: read the manual. Your installation manual provides detailed information on installation procedures. This documentation is quite good, so don't set it aside and ignore it. The Release Notes are also required reading. They contain last-minute documentation changes, discuss software notes, and specify how to get UnixWare support.

This AppNote assumes you have a working familiarity with UnixWare, but have never installed it. You need not have a background in NetWare to perform this installation.

New Installation Features

In terms of installation, several changes in the 2.0 version make installation easier.

The installation process has a new user interface (it isn't a GUI, but it is better).

- ✔ You need only one boot diskette rather than three.
- ✔ User interaction takes place up front. Since all questions are provided at the beginning, no intervention is required during file installation.
- ✔ The installation process is faster, via CD-ROM, tape, or the network. (If you plan to do a network installation, be sure you have an install server, properly configured, on your network.)
- ✔ Hardware support is improved.
- ✔ You can perform a network installation via TCP/IP as well as IPX/SPX.
- ✔ The autoconfiguration feature simplifies setting up your system.
- ✔ The Device Configuration Utility (DCU) simplifies some tedious installation tasks.

Autoconfiguration

UnixWare's new autoconfiguration utility works for EISA, MCA, and PCI controllers. (ISA cards are limited in that they carry no information on board.)

This new utility provides several advantages:

- ✔ Automatic detection of boards and their configuration parameters
- ✔ Dynamic assignment of drivers to new boards
- ✔ New administrative tools to change configuration
- ✔ Dynamic configuration of drivers during their initialization
- ✔ Installation using multiple SCSI boards
- ✔ No user prompting required in most cases
- ✔ New Device Configuration Utility (DCU)
- ✔ Platform hardware configuration setup assumed
- ✔ Minimizes hardware knowledge required of user
- ✔ Simplifies hardware configuration and system installation

How Autoconfiguration Fits into System Installation

Here is the process that autoconfiguration performs:

- ✔ Boots the installation diskette
- ✔ Installs host bus adapter (HBA) diskettes (as needed)
- ✔ Optionally runs DCU interactively
- ✔ Loads HBA drivers
- ✔ Specifies network card (if card is readable, reconfigures it)

The Device Configuration Utility (DCU)

Like the new autoconfiguration, the new DCU is important enough to UnixWare 2.0 installation to discuss separately. The DCU is an interactive administrative tool that's called during network installation. The DCU provides several useful functions:

- ✔ Provides an interface during installation
- ✔ Runs from /etc/inittab to assign drivers to new boards
- ✔ Lets you select and deselect software drivers during installation
- ✔ Lets you modify your hardware configuration information

- ✔ Lets you enable or disable hardware instances
- ✔ Lets you perform hardware parameter conflict checking
- ✔ Is called by pkgadd post-install scripts to update configuration files

The DCU rarely asks you to alter values. If fact, we advise that under normal conditions, you make no changes. If you enter incorrect values, your installation may fail, or the system may be unable to recognize your devices. You may even disable your devices by using incorrect values. On the other hand, if a device halts your installation process, rather than physically removing the board you can use the DCU to "logically" remove the device, allowing installation to proceed.

Hardware Requirements

The minimum hardware requirements specify what you need for successful installation and execution of UnixWare (see fig. 12.1). These minimum requirements may be inadequate under certain conditions. Keep your specific needs in mind when you make decisions about minimum hardware configurations.

Application Server	Intel 386 25MHz processor 16MB of RAM 160 MB available disk space
Personal Edition	Intel 386 25MHz processor 12MB of RAM 140 MB available disk space

Figure 12.1
Minimum hardware requirements for a successful UnixWare 2.0 installation.

Adequate RAM and Disk Space

Minimum disk requirements refer to the space required to successfully install the operating system; this minimum space requirement doesn't include adequate space for file storage. If you plan to use an application server as a file server, you'll have to make a judgment call to gauge the actual space requirements. You might base the disk requirements on past configurations, or discuss your needs with software vendors.

Basing a multiuser system on a minimum CPU configuration such as a 386/25 will lead to poor performance. A Personal Edition supporting one user, running a non-graphic application or serving as a NetWare client, might work satisfactorily with such a CPU, but a more realistic system sports a minimum 486/33 or Pentium CPU.

Available RAM is critical to performance. More RAM allows for less swapping and provides better support for users and for development efforts. Swapping occurs when RAM becomes full. The system uses swap space to transfer portions of RAM to disk, so reducing the swapping that occurs leaves the system free to concentrate on user production instead of on system overhead.

The Installation Process

You will need to know ahead of time your system IP values, DNS, and network frame type. You'll have to enter these values when you reach the network adapter configuration stage of the installation.

Let's look at the installation process for UnixWare 2.0. Figure 12.2 shows you an installation roadmap to help you find your way through the procedure.

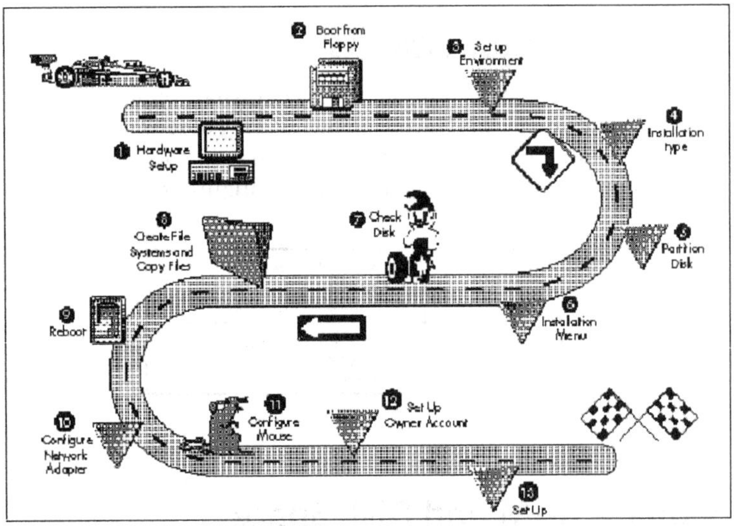

Figure 12.2
An installation roadmap for UnixWare 2.0.

As you can see from figure 12.2, installing and configuring UnixWare 2.0 involves a series of procedures you can logically follow from one step to the next. UnixWare 2.0 lets you gather the information you need at the proper time. You shouldn't have to abort an installation in the middle to go find information you didn't know you would need.

Let's look briefly at each of the steps identified in figure 12.2. Some of them are so basic they require little discussion.

Performing the Hardware Setup

Complete the following steps to set up your hardware before you install UnixWare 2.0.

1. Before beginning the actual installation of UnixWare 2.0, be sure that all your network devices are properly attached and powered up.
2. Configure all devices, making certain that no hardware conflicts exist to create problems during installation.
3. If your system is EISA, PCI, or MCA, make certain the device configuration utilities are accurate.
4. If appropriate, register any ISA boards so you can take advantage of UnixWare's autoconfiguration abilities.

Booting from Floppy Diskette

Complete the following steps to boot from diskette.

1. Power off the system.
2. Place the UnixWare Install diskette into the appropriate drive and turn the power on. This process installs the minikernel and begins the installation process.

Setting Up the Environment

Complete the following steps to set up your environment.

1. To set up the environment, you must configure and designate the keyboard type.
2. You also have the option to load host bus adapter (HBA) drivers. If your system has a SCSI adapter, you must load the HBA diskette when prompted. If you're unsure of the configuration, load the HBA diskette anyway; the installation process automatically loads and configures the drivers.

Note A new feature of UnixWare 2.0 is that the device drivers are dynamically bound to the hardware configuration. This means that you no longer must set the hardware at specific values during installation.

3. At this point, the installation process gives you the option to invoke the DCU. This interactive administrative tool facilitates the installation process. You can choose to invoke the utility or to proceed.
4. The installation process automatically loads and checks the hardware drivers.

Choosing the Installation Type

You've completed the necessary access to the installation diskette. You can now choose to do a local installation, with a CD-ROM or QIC tape device, or to do a network installation over either TCP/IP or SPX. Only installed devices will appear as choices; for example, if there is no QIC tape drive, such a device won't appear as an installation choice.

To install UnixWare 2.0 over a network connection, an install server must be enabled somewhere on the network. If you need to set up an install server, you can use the icon located on the UnixWare Application Server in the Administration Tools window. Online help is available, but the utility is reasonably straightforward.

If your network supports both protocols, choose the TCP/IP option. If the install server has been properly configured with the network host names, IP addresses, and IP router information, all networking values will be supplied automatically to the local installation. This information further simplifies the installation process.

Partitioning the Disk

To place an operating system on the hard drive, you must allocate the appropriate system partition and size. The installation process lets you choose to use the entire hard disk as the active UNIX partition, or to select a custom disk configuration. The custom option gives you an FDISK utility you can use to view and change the partitions on the hard drive.

Remember to reserve enough disk space for the operating system as well as for user and application space.

Using the Installation Menu

The installation menu gives you a final opportunity to make final changes to the system before any modifications are written to the hard drive. The choices on the menu are Package Selection, Disk Configuration, Disk Operations, and Return to Previous Menu.

1. The Package Selection option lets you customize the UnixWare operating system. Packages are software modules that add functionality to the OS. (Appendix D of the Installation Handbook discusses these packages in detail.)

Note

The installation process can recognize package dependencies. In other words, if you select a package that depends on a package you haven't yet selected, the system makes you either select the independent package or deselect the dependent package. The installation process also informs you if the number of packages you've selected exceeds the disk space available. You must then deselect some packages.

2. The Disk Configuration submenu gives you three options. The Disk Partitions option is actually the FDISK utility. The File Systems option lets you customize file system types and file system sizes. If you have more than one hard drive, it lets you place the file systems on selected disks.

Note The default file system for the root and user file systems is vxfs, a journaling file system that provides system fault tolerance and the recommended file system type. However, if you need backward compatibility with a legacy file system, the s5 and ufs file systems are available to you.

3. The Disk Operations option lets you disable the scanning of the hard drive.

4. The Return to Previous Menu option needs no explanation.

At this point in the installation process, all options and parameters are complete. Once you select the Accept All Settings and Install Now option on this menu, the system begins the unassisted operating system installation.

Checking the Disk

Next, this automatic utility simply shows you a bar graph indicating what percentage of the task has been completed. It requires no user intervention. The capacity of the hard drive determines how long this process takes.

We recommend that you do not disable this step. It maps the bad blocks on the hard drive so the OS won't use them. A complete check of a 511 MB SCSI disk drive, for example, takes five minutes.

Creating File Systems and Copying Files

This automatic process also requires no user intervention. Once the bad blocks are mapped, the system begins to create file systems and to copy files. How long this process takes is determined by the speed of the I/O subsystem and the number of packages you selected. Copying the default packages on a 486/50, for example, takes about half an hour.

Rebooting the System

When all files have been copied to the hard drive, the system automatically reboots. When it comes back up, the kernel rebuilds. Installation continues.

Configuring the Network Adapter

Complete the following steps to configure your network adapter.

1. Choose the "NICs" package. You'll see the Network Interface Card Selection screen. This screen lists all network adapters supported on UnixWare 2.0.

2. Choose the appropriate adapter and quantity. UnixWare's installation process then loads the drivers.

3. If the adapter is EISA, PCI, or MCA, UnixWare's installation process automatically configures it. If you have an ISA adapter, you'll be prompted for configuration values.

4. At this point, you can enter system IP values, DNS, and network frame type. If there is a bootup server in the network, you can prompt it at this point for the appropriate values. Press F8 for the reboot server, and it will let you enter these values.

Configuring the Mouse

The mouse selection screen gives you an interactive setup utility, complete with test. UnixWare supports bus, serial, and PS/2 mice.

Setting Up the System Owner

UnixWare installation lets your system define two users: the system owner and the root user. When you set up the system, you become the system owner. You choose your user ID, user name, user number, and password.

Setting Up the Root Account

The root account is the most powerful user on the system. The installation process automatically sets up this account. Only the password is then required in order to use it.

Ensuring Hardware Compatibility

Since UnixWare has many dependencies on the hardware, it's imperative that you use compatible hardware. This requirement represents a paradigm shift from operating systems such as DOS and NetWare, where hardware support is taken for granted.

To ensure compatible hardware, you can pursue several avenues. For example, Novell has instituted the "YES, It Runs with UnixWare" branding program to assure compatibility with the UnixWare operating system. Look for the certification "branded" on the product.

To distribute Novell product certification information, Novell Labs offers a FaxBack system. Novell's FaxBack is online 24 hours a day, seven days a week. You can reach it in the U.S. at (800) 414-LABS or at (801) 429-2776. By calling the FaxBack and obtaining the Master Index catalog, you can quickly obtain specific information on UnixWare and NetWare when you call back and request a specific document number.

Conclusion

With UnixWare 2.0, installation is easier and faster than ever. Thanks to several new utilities, much of the installation process has been automated. Make sure your hardware is compatible, use the installation manual, and make the choices you need to make before you start. Your UnixWare installation will be smooth and problem-free.

Reviewing the List of *Novell Application Notes* Back Issues

Table 12.1 contains a list of back issues of *Novell Application Notes.* Reprints of these issues, along with the list, are available from Novell Research Publications.

For information on how to order these publications, refer to the Novell Research Order Form on the CD.

Prices for reprints are $15 per copy in the United States (U.S.) and $20 per copy in all other locations. Price includes shipping and handling. To obtain an updated list of publications, call the Novell Research Order Desk at (800) 377-4136. Outside the U.S. and Canada, call (303) 297-2725.

Each of the back issues listed in table 12.1 includes an issue date, a part number to use for ordering, and associated titles.

Table 12.1
Back Issues of Novell Application Notes

Date	Part Number	Titles
Jul 95	164-000047-007	Installing and Configuring UnixWare 2.0
		Understanding the NetWare UNIX Client (NUC) NLM 2.0
		Configuring Asynchronous Connections with the NetWare MultiProtocol Router 3.0 Software

continues

Table 12.1, Continued
Back Issues of Novell Application Notes

Date	Part Number	Titles
Jun 95	164-000047-006	Centralized Multiserver Backup over 100VG-AnyLAN Networks
		Using Novell's NetWare User Tools (NWUSER.EXE) for MS Windows Clients
		Anatomy of a Voice Processing NLM
		ABEND Recovery Techniques for NetWare 3 and 4
May 95	164-000047-005	The Benefits of Using Intelligent LAN Adapters in NetWare Servers
		Using the NTSWD Utility to Diagnose MS Windows Workstation Problems
		Upgrading to NetWare 4.1 Across a LAN/WAN Using RCONSOLE
		Using NDS User Object Properties in NetWare 4.1 Login Scripts
Apr 95	164-000047-004	Integrating the NetWare DOS Requester (VLMs) with Windows for Workgroups
		Importing User Information into NetWare Directory Services Using UIMPORT
		Unified Messaging: Paving the Road to Pervasive Computing
		Using NetWare/IP Over Satellite Networks
		Understanding NetWare HostPrint 1.1*x*
		The NetWare 4 Memory Architecture/ Understanding Memory Fragmentation in NetWare Servers
		Using MONITOR to Track NetWare 4 Memory Allocation

Date	Part Number	Titles
Mar 95	164-000047-003	Using the DSMERGE Utility in NetWare 4.1
		Support Issues for the NetWare DOS Requester (VLM) 1.2
		Black Screen of Death Explained
		NetWare Workstation Security Architecture
		What's New in UnixWare 2
		NetWare for SAA 2.0: An Overview of Novell's Next Generation SNA Connectivity Product
		Tuning Cache with the NetWare 4 LRU Sitting Time Statistic
Feb 95	164-000047-002	Inside Novell's High Capacity Storage System (HCSS)
		Resolving Critical Server Issues
		Computer Telephone Integration: Call Control vs. Voice Processing
		Wide Area Networking with Frame Relay and NetWare MultiProtocol Router
Jan 95	164-000047-001	What's New in NetWare 4.1
		NetWare 4.1 CIT Interoperability Testing Overview
		NetWare 4.1 Interoperability Test Configurations and Troubleshooting
		Planning an NDS Tree
		Understanding and Using NDS Objects
Dec 94	164-000036-012	NetWare IPX Routing Enhancements
		Customizing Your NetWare Link Services Protocol Routing Configuration

continues

Table 12.1, Continued
Back Issues of Novell Application Notes

Date	Part Number	Titles
		Managing Basic MHS
		Printing to Network Printers in Windows 3.1
		Configuring UnixWare's Point-to-Point Protocol (PPP)
Nov 94	164-000036-011	Characteristics of TCP/IP, IPX/SPX, and NCP Protocols Over VSAT
		NetWare Management System (NMS) Components and Functionality
		Upgrading to NetWare 4.01: A Case Study of Canadian Tire Corporation, Ltd.
Oct 94	164-000036-010	Migrating from NetWare Name Services to NetWare Directory Services
		Understanding the Role of Identification and Authentication in NetWare 4
		Managing and Using FirstMail
		Configuring NetWare Connect with TCP/IP Remote Clients
		Installing and Configuring UnixWare 1.1
Sep 94	164-000036-009	Using Novell's CDROM.NLM to Run CD-ROM Drives as NetWare Volumes
		What's New in NetWare 4.02
		Effectively Managing RIP and SAP Traffic with Filtering
		UnixWare 1.1 as a NetWare Client
		Troubleshooting Printing in a NetWare for Macintosh Environment

Date	Part Number	Titles
		Novell Research Publications
Aug 94	164-000036-008	An Introduction to Novell's Open Security Architecture
		Using DOS Batch Files with NetWare 4 to Ease the Transition from NetWare 3
		Installing Basic MHS and FirstMail
		TUXEDO System Release 4.2.2: The Path to Reliable Client/Server Computing
		Unattended OS/2 CID Installation Using NetWare Navigator
Jul 94	164-000036-007	Configuring NetWare 4 for the Mobile User
		Key Issues Surrounding Enterprise E-Mail
		Testing Performance of NetWare SNA Remote Host Connectivity Products
		Customizing Autodiscovery Using NMS
		Records Management: Document Storage and Retrieval Challenges in an Enterprise Network
		Application of Networked Multimedia in Business and Education
Jun 94	164-000036-006	NET.CFG Parameters for the NetWare DOS Requester 1.1
		Using Network-Direct Print Devices in NetWare 4
		Compression and Suballocation in NetWare 4
		Managing the Branch Office: Part 2

continues

Table 12.1, Continued
Back Issues of Novell Application Notes

Date	Part Number	Titles
		Implementing NetWare MultiProtocol Router Products in an IBM Source-Route Bridged Environment
May 94	164-000036-005	The Functions and Operations of the NetWare DOS Requester v1.1
		Managing the Branch Office: Part 1
		Performance Tuning NetWare Connect 1.0
		Optimizing NetWare Wide Area Networks
		NetWare Link Services Protocol: Link-State Routing in a NetWare Environment
Apr 94	164-000036-004	SPECIAL EDITION: Building and Auditing a Trusted Network Environment with NetWare 4
Mar 94	164-000036-003	An Introduction to AppWare and Visual AppBuilder
		Management Procedures for Directory Services in NetWare 4.01
		Optimizing NetWare as a Database Platform
		Providing DOS and MS Windows User Access to UNIX/NFS Files
		Ghardenstone: A Novell Methodology for Network Performance Evaluation
		A Review of Bridging and Routing Techniques
Feb 94	164-000036-002	Implementing Naming Standards for NetWare Directory Services
		Implementing and Configuring Novell/AT&T Telephony Services

Date	Part Number	Titles
		NetWare Distributed Management Services: An Integrated Approach for Managing Network Computing Environments
		Certification Programs for Networking Professionals
Jan 94	164-000036-001	Novell's Corporate-Wide Upgrade to NetWare 4
		Upgrading to NetWare 4: The Chase Manhattan Bank's CC and FMI Groups
		Time in the NetWare Environment
		Computer-Telephone Integration with Novell's Telephony Services
		An Overview of Multimedia Technologies
Dec 93	164-000032-012	Installing NetWare 3.12 from CD-ROM
		Wide Area Networking with VSAT: A Customer Installation
		Workstation Memory Management: Using QEMM386, 386 To The Max, and MS-DOS 6
		IBM AS/400 Connectivity Using NetWare for SAA 1.3 in an Ethernet Environment
Nov 93	164-000032-011	Time Synchronization in NetWare 4.*x*
		Designing NetWare 4.*x* Security
		Packet Burst Update: BNETX vs. VLM Implementations
		Multi-Segment LAN Imaging: Departmental Configuration Guidelines
Oct 93	164-000032-010	NetWare 4.*x* Performance Tuning and Optimization: Part 3

continues

Table 12.1, Continued
Back Issues of Novell Application Notes

Date	Part Number	Titles
		What's New in NetWare 4.01
		NetWare 3.12 Enhancements
		Using NetWare HostPrint for AS/400 Host Printing
		Managing Memory in a DOS Workstation: Using Novell DOS 7
Sep 93	164-000032-009	Optimizing Printing with NetWare 4.*x* and 3.1*x*
		Understanding and Using NDS Alias Objects
		NetWare Migration Utilities Part 2: The Across-the-Wire Migration Utility
		An Introduction to Network Workflow
		Migrating Ethernet Frame Types from 802.3 Raw to IEEE 802.2
		Multilingual PC Setup with DR DOS
Aug 93	164-000032-008	NetWare for Macintosh 3.*xx* Printing: A Configuration Tutorial
		Exploring Hard Disk Compression
		NACS 3.0 and NetWare Access Server 1.3 Integration
Jul 93	164-000032-007	Using NETADMIN to Create and Administer NDS Objects
		A Test Workload Analysis of LANQuest Lab's Application Benchmark (LAB) Test Suite
		Multi-Segment LAN Imaging Implementations: Four-Segment Ethernet
		A NetWare Interface for Visual Basic

Date	Part Number	Titles
		Understanding Relational Theory
Jun 93	164-000032-006	NetWare 4.0 Performance Tuning and Optimization: Part 2
		NetWare 4.0 Bindery Emulation: An Overview
		Bindery Emulation and NetWare for Macintosh
		NetWare Migration Utilities Part 1: The In-Place Upgrade NLM
		Administering DOS Paradox 4.0 and Paradox for Windows 1.0 on NetWare
		Virtual Server Technology and DataClub File Sharing
May 93	164-000032-005	NetWare 4.0 Performance Tuning and Optimization: Part 1
		Tips and Techniques for Troubleshooting Drive Deactivation in NetWare 3.1*x*
		Imaging Test Results: Retrieval Rates on Single- and Multiple-Segment LANs
		An Introduction to Videomedia and NetWare
Apr 93	164-000032-004	Overview of NetWare 4.0 New Features
		An Introduction to NetWare Directory Services
		Planning a NetWare 4.0 Directory Tree
		Understanding NetWare Directory Services Rights
		Planning for NetWare 4.0 Installation, Server Migration, and Coexistence
		Using the DOS Requester with NetWare 4.0

continues

Table 12.1, Continued
Back Issues of Novell Application Notes

Date	Part Number	Titles
		Migrating to NetWare 4.0: An Example
Mar 93	164-000032-003	An Introduction to Developing Cross-Platform Client/Server GUI Applications
		Installing and Configuring NetWare TCP/IP on a NetWare 3.11 Server
		NetView LAN Management: RUNCMDs Made Easy
		NetWare and Windows for Workgroups 3.1 Interoperability
		Using Production Workload Characteristics to Validate Performance Evaluation Studies
Feb 93	164-000032-002	Mapping Between UNIX Permissions and NetWare Rights in NetWare NFS
		ODINSUP Interoperability Configurations for DOS Workstations
		Imaging Configuration Performance Test Results
Jan 93	164-000032-001	The State of the Infrastructure for Distributed Computing
		IBM AS/400 Connectivity Using NetWare for SAA v1.3
		Imaging Configurations and Process Testing
Dec 92	164-000031-012	NetWare NFS Bidirectional Printing: A Configuration Tutorial
		Upgrading and Configuring NetWare File Servers with Origen v2.0
		NetWare SNA Links v1.0 Rules of Thumb
		NCP Packet Signature Performance Considerations

Date	Part Number	Titles
Nov 92	164-000031-011	NetWare and LAN Server Client Interoperability via ODINSUP: Part 2
		Organizing Users and Applications with Saber Menu System for DOS
		Communication Basics and Open Data-Link Technology
		Corporate Downsizing: A Case Study of PIEFCU (Pacific IBM Employees Federal Credit Union)
Oct 92	164-000031-010	NetWare v3.*x* Mirroring and Duplexing Tips and Tricks
		Managing Memory in a DOS Workstation: Part 2
		The Past, Present, and Future Bottlenecks of Imaging
		Interfacing Visual Basic for Windows and NetWare
Sep 92	164-000031-009	NetWare and LAN Server Client Interoperability via ODINSUP: Part 1
		Using NetWare SQL to Access Relational Information from Btrieve Data
Aug 92	164-000031-008	Managing Memory in a DOS Workstation: Part 1
		Securing DOS and Windows Workstations with PCGuard
		Accessing Novell Information on the Internet
Jul 92	164-000031-007	Managing SAP Information with the NetWare Service Advertising Filter (SAFILTER) v1.00
		Increasing NetWare Throughput with Large Internet Packet Exchange (LIPX.NLM)

continues

Table 12.1, Continued
Back Issues of Novell Application Notes

Date	Part Number	Titles
		The Hardware of Imaging Technology
		Administering WordPerfect v5.1 on NetWare
		NetWare Asynchronous Communications Services v3.0 Rules of Thumb
Jun 92	164-000031-006	NetWare v3.11 Server Tuning and Optimization
		Dealing with LAN Printing Problem Areas
		Administering Quattro Pro 4.0 on NetWare
		Directory Entry Tables and NetWare for Macintosh
May 92	164-000031-005	Understanding and Troubleshooting Novell's Print Services
		Issues and Implications for LAN-Based Imaging Systems
		NetWare for SAA v1.2 Rules of Thumb
		Identifying Test Workloads in LAN Performance Evaluation Studies
Apr 92	164-000031-004	Running VREPAIR on a NetWare v3.11 Server
		Embedded SQL: How to use NetWare SQL Statements in Your C Code
		AppleTalk Protocol Routing and NetWare
Mar 92	164-000031-003	Detecting Viruses in the NetWare Environment
		LookUp: Implementing a Multiplatform, Multiprotocol Application
		Integrating CAD/CAM and Database Technology

Date	Part Number	Titles
		An Introduction to Novell's Burst Mode Protocol
		STAT.NLM: A Tool for Measuring NetWare v3.11 Server Resource Utilization
Feb 92	164-000031-002	How Referential Integrity Works With Novell's Database Products
		Automating Office Procedures with MHS
		A Comparison of NetWare for UNIX v3.11 With Native NetWare v3.11
		Applying Process Architectures to LANs: Single Segment LAN, Part 1
Jan 92	164-000031-001	A Workstation Inventory Program for NetWare
		Browsing the NetWare Bindery with the BSEARCH Utility
		An Introduction to SQL
Dec 91	164-000030-012	Using NetWare Accounting to Track User Logins
		NetWare v3.*x* System Messages: File System, Part 1
		LAN Application Architectures: Exploring the Distributed Processing Environment
Nov 91	164-000030-011	Logging In to IBM LAN Server and NetWare from a DOS Workstation
		A Comparison of Mainframe and LAN Database Process Architectures
		Printing with NetWare for Macintosh
Oct 91	164-000030-010	Installing and Configuring Novell's Token-Ring Source Routing Drivers

continues

Table 12.1, Continued
Back Issues of Novell Application Notes

Date	Part Number	Titles
		Database Installation and Maintenance: Installing Advanced Revelation on a NetWare LAN
		Getting Started in NLM Development
		Revision History of the NetWare DOS Shell and Windows Device Driver Set
Sep 91	164-000030-009	NetWare v2.*x* Server Memory and File Service Processes (v2.2 Update)
		Using the Asynchronous Event Scheduler in an NLM
		How NetWare Loadable Modules Operate in the NetWare Environment
		Developing Parameters for Extended Print Service Management
Aug 91	164-000030-008	Source Routing and the Spanning-Tree Protocol
		Detecting the Presence of IPX, the NetWare Shell, and NetBIOS from a DOS Application
		Using Personal MHS on Your Laptop
		Using the NetWare 3.*x* Internal Debugger
		The Data and the Base: A Discussion of Database File Structures and Networking Problems
Jul 91	164-000030-007	NetWare v3.*x* Operating System Statistics Exposed!
		Extended Print Services: Obtaining Information for Queue Management
		Workload Characterization of NetWare Clients and Servers Using a Protocol Analyzer

Date	Part Number	Titles
Jun 91	164-000030-006	Measuring Performance in the Extended Print Service Environment
		Analyzing LAN/WAN Internets: Testing IPX Routes Using Novell's LANalyzer 3.0
		Backing Up Macintosh Files on a NetWare Server
		SPX Design Enhancements to the NetWare Requester for OS/2 (v1.3)
May 91	164-000030-005	Understanding Token-Ring Source Routing
		Case Study: Implementing CIM with NetWare at Compaq Corporation
		An Introduction to Workload Characterization
		Code and Concept: How to Allocate IPX Resources and How to Listen for IPX Packets Using CLIB
Apr 91	164-000030-004	NetWare Print Service Performance
Mar 91	164-000030-003	Resolving Performance Problems on a NetWare Network
		Code and Concept: How to Gracefully Load and Unload a Multi-Threaded NLM
		Code and Concept: Creating and Controlling a Thread That Polls a Queue or Some Other Entity
Feb 91	164-000030-002	The NetWare DOS Client Environment
		Running SQL Server in the NetWare Environment
Jan 91	164-000003-001	NetWare and Microsoft Windows Integration
		OVERVIEW: LANalyzer Applications for NetWare File Server Access Characterization

continues

Table 12.1, Continued
Back Issues of Novell Application Notes

Date	Part Number	Titles
		FILEVIEW: LANalyzer Applications for NetWare File Service Diagnostics
Dec 90	164-000016-001	Calculating NetWare Routing Table Sizes
		NODEVIEW: LANalyzer Filters for IPX Protocol Diagnostics
		SERVERVU: LANalyzer Filters for Service Advertising Protocol (SAP) Diagnostics
Nov 90	164-000015-001	Understanding VTAM Traces
Oct 90	164-000014-001	3287 Host Printer Emulations
		NetWare 386 System Messages: Bindery, Packet Services, and Queue Management Services
Sep 90	164-000013-001	TRACK [ON/OFF] Console Command, Syntax and Applications
		NetWare 386 Speed Rating
		NetWare Communications Processes
Aug 90	164-000012-001	MAC Layer Bridging Techniques
		A Comparison of NetWare IPX, SPX, and NetBIOS
Jul 90	164-000011-001	NetWare 386 System Messages: Disk, Memory, and Accounting
		An Overview of Virus Prevention Strategies in a NetWare Environment
Jun 90	119-000010-001	286-Based NetWare v2.1x File Service Processes: The Final Word
		Novell NetWare and AT&T Integration
		NetWare Internal and External Bridge Performance Benchmarking

Date	Part Number	Titles
Aug 94	164-000036-014	Enhancing the DOS Desktop Environment with Novell DOS 7
Aug 93	164-000032-013	Implementing Fault Tolerance with NetWare SFT III
Dec 92	164-000031-016	NetWare Application Notes for Macintosh
Jul 92	164-000031-014	Integrating NetWare and Windows 3.1
Feb 92	164-000031-013	Inside NetWare for UNIX v3.11
Nov 91	164-000030-015	NetWare Security: Configuring and Auditing a Trusted Environment
Jan 90	479-000063-001	Network Backup

To read descriptions and page counts of some of the back issues of *Novell Application Notes* listed in table 12.1, open the file on the CD.

CHILAGA
NORVMBEGA
TEAC.
MARATA.
CVLIACAN.
CALICVAS.
CAPASCHI
HISPANIA NOVA
TOVA
LA FLORIDA
MAR DEL SVR, quod
PACIFICVM
CHILE
PARANA
Archipelago del C. deseado
CAE SIVE
ORBIS, NO
SCRIPTIO.

13

CHAPTER

NTWRKINS

The NTWRKINS directory on the CD contains demonstration versions of various applications that you can run, subdivided into the following four subdirectories:

- ANAPROBE
- FARPRINT
- NIPRINT
- OBSERVER

The applications that these directories contain are designed to run on the Windows 95 interface, but you can still run them on Windows if you don't have Windows 95. If you do have Windows 95, refer to the Readme file for information about installing the demo software. This chapter explains the installation process for Windows v3.*x*.

Note Some information in this chapter is adapted from the help and text files included on the CD, with only minor editing and format changes applied.

The software in the NTWRKINS directory on the CD is manufactured by Network Instruments, LLC. For more information on this demo software, you can reach the manufacturer at the following numbers and e-mail address:

(800) 526-7919 (US Toll free)
(612) 932-9899 Voice
(612) 932-9545 FAX

(612) 932-9590 BBS
support@netinst.com

Installing Software from the Subdirectories under the NTWRKINS Directory

Only three of the directories contain INSTALL.EXE programs. You can use MS Windows to install the software in those three directories. To install the software, follow these steps:

1. Start MS Windows.
2. Choose File from the menu bar.
3. Choose Run from the File menu.
4. Choose the Browse button.
5. Scan through the directory structure on your CD drive to find the NTWRKINS directory, then choose the subdirectory whose files you want to install.
6. Choose the INSTALL.EXE file.
7. Choose OK.
8. Choose OK again, and then follow the screen prompts.

When you choose the INSTALL.EXE file to install the Analyst/Probe software, for example, the first screen informs you that this is a demonstration version of the software, not a shareware or freeware product. You then follow its prompt, and that of the subsequent screen. The prompt on this first screen is the Continue button.

Choosing the Continue button then opens another screen. If you are installing the Analyst/Probe software, the next screen prompts you to choose to install either the Analyst or the Probe software (see fig. 13.1). You must choose an option from this screen, then choose Continue again to move to the next step of the installation.

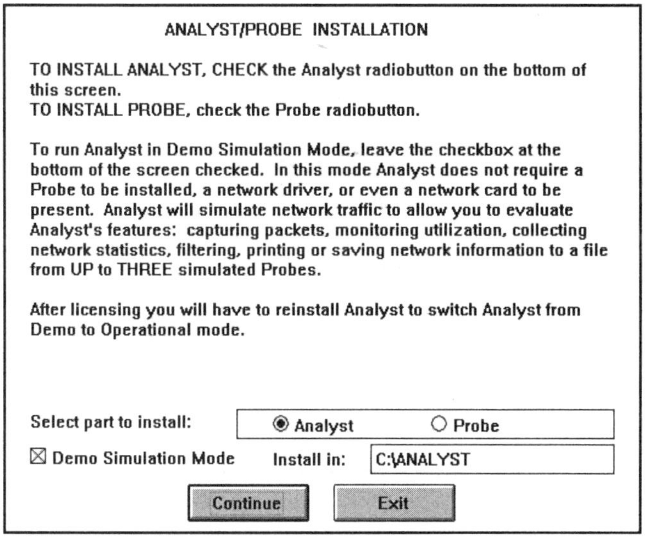

Figure 13.1
The ANALYST/PROBE INSTALLATION screen prompts you to choose to install either Analyst or Probe.

After you choose an option to install, the installation program copies the files to the specific directory. It then creates a Windows program group, and creates icons in that group.

Installing the other software products that have INSTALL.EXE files in a subdirectory in the NTWRKINS directory on the CD follows much the same steps. The screens might differ, but if you follow the prompts and respond as requested, the installations should all go rather smoothly.

Understanding the Demo Software

You already know that the NTWRKINS directory has four subdirectories, each containing demo software. Each software performs its own related tasks. This section briefly describes the respective software products to help you understand what they are and how to use them. To truly understand this software, however, you must work with it. This chapter gives you enough information to help you get started.

The ANAPROBE subdirectory contains Analyst and Probe software. To run the Analyst software, choose the Analyst icon from the Analyst program group. Running Analyst requires a copy of WINSOCK.DLL (not provided with the software) in your Windows directory.

Other programs you can run are contained in the different subdirectories under the NTWRKINS directory on the CD. You can run the Discover software, for example, by choosing the Window **R**un option under the **F**ile menu. When you run the Discover software, a screen opens that resembles the screen shown in figure 13.2. You should be aware, however, that the amount of time you can run these demos might be extremely limited (sometimes measurable in just minutes). So be prepared to explore the software rather quickly.

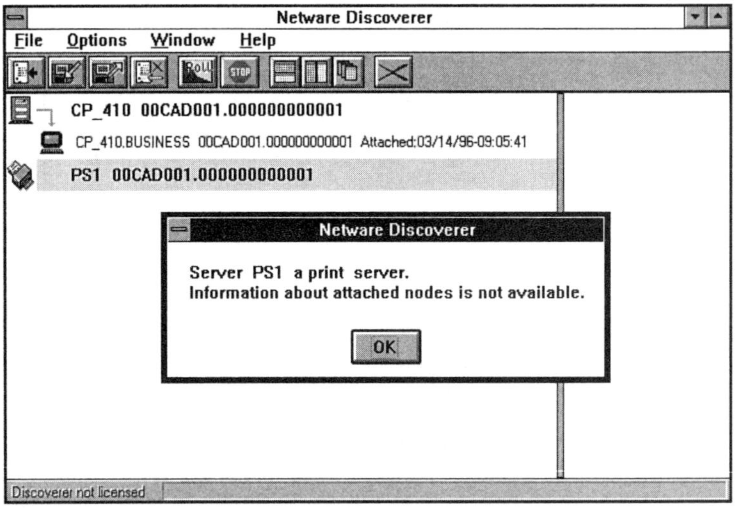

Figure 13.2
The Discover software demo screen.

Another utility you can run is the Observer utility. It captures packets from the network and displays information about them in a graphic format.

The Observer utility also provides a menu bar from which you can choose options for performing such tasks as saving the information to a file, copying it to the Clipboard, and creating or editing filters.

As with most software programs, the best way to become familiar with them is to try them.

CHILAGA
NORVMBEGA
FRANCIA
MOCOSA
AVACAL
APALCHEN
CALICVAS
CAPASCHI
TERLICHICHI MECHI
TEAC
MARATA
CVLIACAN
ASTATLAN
HISPANIA NOVA
TOVA
LA FLORIDA
CVBA
HISPANIOLA
Suali mons
MAR DEL SVR, quod
Circulus Æquinoctialis
240
250
260
270
280
290
PACIFICVM
CHARCAS
PARANA
CHILI
PATAGONES, vel REGIO GIGANTVM
FRETVM MAGELLANICVM
Archipelago del C. deileado
CAE SIVE
ORBIS, NO
SCRIPTIO.

14

CHAPTER

OFFSITE

The OFFSITE directory on the CD contains software called the *WorkStation Clone* (WSClone). WSClone is a management tool that you can use to clone a network workstation. You use it to organize files on a PC and network. WSClone enables you to create a model (clone) of a workstation's configuration, from which you can make a disk to use to identically configure other workstations.

Note Some of the information in this chapter is taken from the information provided by the manufacturer on the CD.

The installation disk you create will contain the files you need for attaching and logging in to the network, creating target directories, and copying the files you need to their appropriate locations. This chapter explains how to install the WSClone software on a workstation and how to configure it for a specific workstation.

The online help provided with the WSClone software provides more information about WSClone. You can access help after you install the WSClone software from the CD and choose the WorkStation Clone icon from the WorkStation Clone group.

This version of the software is a 30-day trial version. To use it beyond 30 days you must contact the manufacturer at the following address:

PsL
P.O. Box 35705
Houston, TX 77235
(800) 242-4775

You can find additional information about registering this software and technical support for this product in its respective online help.

Installing the WorkStation Clone Software

Before you install the software that the OFFSITE directory contains, copy the files to a local hard disk or a network directory so that you can install the software from a drive other than the CD drive. You need to use a different drive because the software of many of the programs on the CD has been compressed into either an executable decompression program or a PKWARE ZIP file. You need to make sure that the software has room to expand and explode the files.

To install the software, complete the following steps:

1. Start Windows, then choose **R**un from the **F**ile menu to open the Run dialog box. Type the path to the SETUP.EXE file, or use the **B**rowse button to search for the file, then choose OK.

2. In the WorkStation Clone Setup dialog box (see fig. 14.1), provide the path to SETUP.EXE and other related files, then choose **C**ontinue.

3. When prompted to provide a directory into which to place the software, choose the default of C:\WSCLONE or provide a different path and directory. Then choose **C**ontinue.

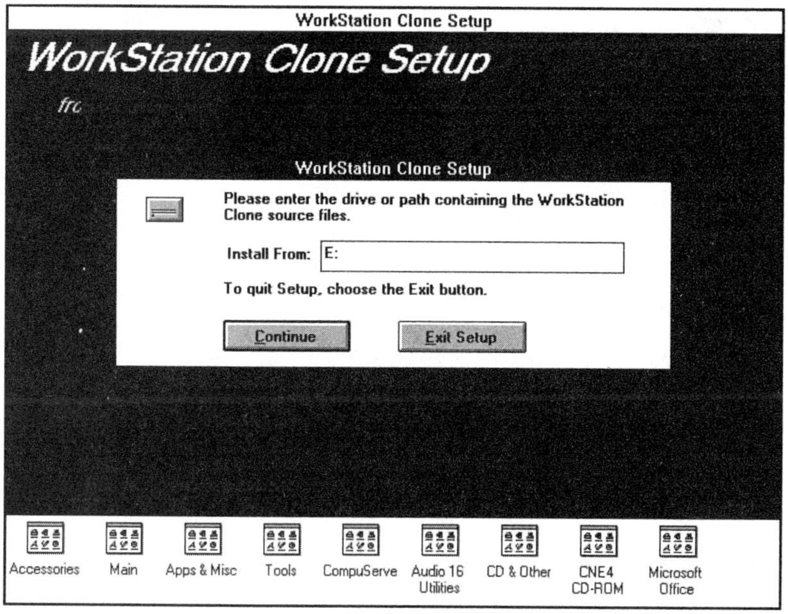

Figure 14.1
The WorkStation Clone Setup dialog box.

4. After you install the files and set up the WorkStation Clone group, a screen appears telling you the installation is complete. Choose OK.

Configuring the WorkStation Clone Software

To run the WorkStation Clone software and configure it for a workstation, choose the WorkStation Clone icon from the WorkStation Clone group. Because this is a 30-day trial version, a message informs you that you are running an unregistered copy of the software, and that you are granted a 30-day license to use and explore the software. If after 30 days you want to continue to use the software, you must register it with the manufacturer. To close this message screen, choose OK. The WorkStation Clone [UNREGISTERED] window then opens.

Complete the following steps to configure a workstation:

1. Choose Configure from the Setup menu to open the Configuration dialog box (see fig. 14.2).

2. Choose the Network Attachment Files radio button (activated by default the first time this window opens).

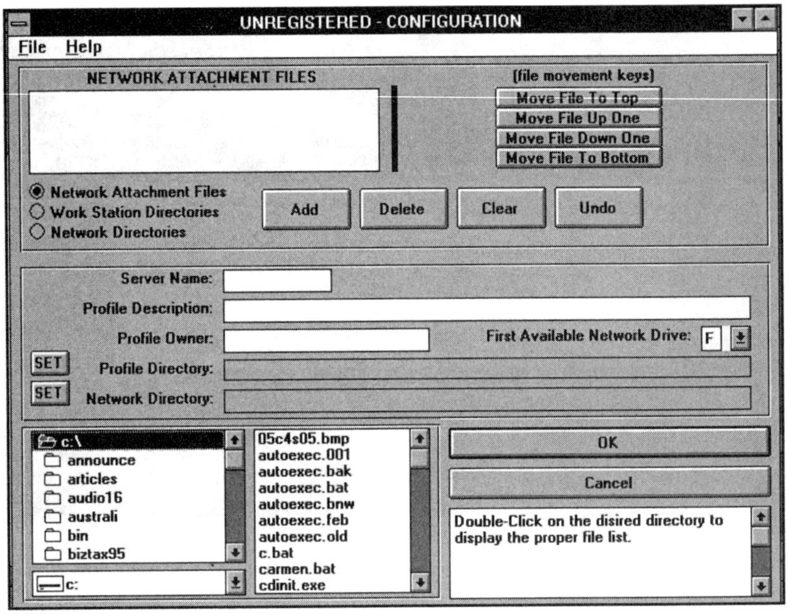

Figure 14.2 The Configuration dialog box.

3. Scroll through the directory structure (at the lower left corner of the screen) until you find the location of the client connection files, then select them. Select the workstation connection files from the list of files to the right of the directory structure scroll box.

   Select the files one at a time, pressing the Add button after each one. The files then appear in the Network Attachment Files list. (For a NetWare DOS or Windows client, the files are LSL.COM, a LAN driver such as NE2000.COM, IPXODI.COM, and VLM.EXE. Choose them in the order listed.)

Note If the workstation is a NetWare DOS or Windows client and the default directory was used when the client software was installed, that directory is C:\NWCLIENT.)

4. Choose Work Station Directories.

5. Choose first the Source then the Target Directories.

   To choose these directories, select a directory from the list displayed in the box at the bottom left of the dialog box. Then choose Add. Do this for both directories.

6. Choose Network Directories, then specify which directories to place in the user's home network directory.

7. In the Server Name field, type the name of the file server from which to copy the information. The copied information is used to create the AUTOEXEC.BAT file on the installation disk.

8. In the Profile Description field, enter a brief description that describes the profile's information or the type of configuration stored in this profile.

9. In the Profile Owner field, enter the name of the person responsible for maintaining the profile. This name can be any assigned user, including the LAN administrator.

10. In the First Available Network Drive field, specify the drive letter you want to represent the first available network drive. Usually, you would set this drive to G.

    If you select F to be the first available network drive, for example, the CONFIG.SYS file would read `LASTDRIVE=E`.

11. In the Profile Directory field, enter a value to use to search for the CONFIG.PRF or AUTOEXEC.PRF files. If either one or both of these files are found, they are used on the installation disk instead of creating new files. (These files are used only for networks other than NetWare.)

12. Choose OK after you finish if you want to accept all changes. If you do not want to accept the changes you made, choose Cancel rather than OK.

After you create a configuration, you can create installation disks that enable you to *install* (copy the same configuration to) multiple workstations using that same configuration.

Creating Installation Disks

To create installation disks, complete the following steps:

1. Choose Install Disks from the menu to open the Installation dialog box (see fig. 14.3).

2. Change the drive letter to the drive that contains the disk that you intend to become the installation disk. If you prefer, you can use a network drive as the installation disk.

3. Choose OK to create the installation disks and copy the required files to the disks. If you do not provide all the necessary information before you start creating the disks, you are prompted for the missing information, as shown in figure 14.4.

After you finish creating the installation disks, the clone program closes. You now can use the installation disks you created to configure other workstations.

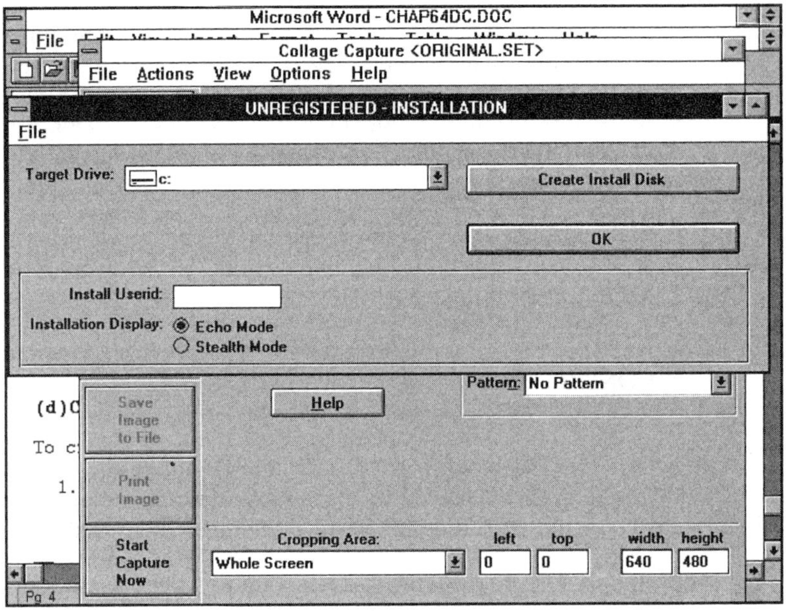

Figure 14.3 The Installation dialog box.

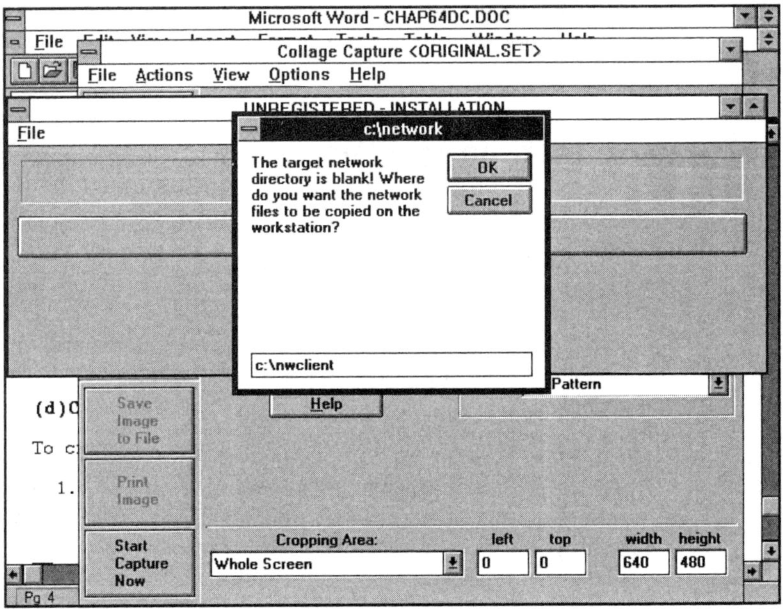

Figure 14.4 If you do not provide all the necessary information before you start creating the disks, you are prompted for the missing information.

CHILAGA
FRANCIA
NORVMBEGA
MOCOSA
AVACAL
APALCHEN
TEAC
MARATA
CALICVAS
CVLIACAN
CAPASCHI
TAGIL
LA FLORIDA
TERLICHICHI MECHI
HISPANIA NOVA
TOVA
TOPIRA
MEXICO
MECHVACAN
CVBA
HISPANIOLA
IVCATAN
MAR DEL SVR, quod
Circulus Æquinoctialis
240
250
260
270
280
290
PACIFICVM
Caribana
Paguana
CHARCAS
PARANA
CHILE
PATAGONES
REGNVM GIGANTVM
Archipelago del C. desseado
CAE SIVE
ORBIS NO
SCRIPTIO

15

CHAPTER

ONDEMAND

The ONDEMAND directory on the CD contains files for WinINSTALL, a software distribution program. You can use the software for a free 15-day trial period from the time you install it. After 15 days, you are expected to register and pay for the software to continue to use it.

WinINSTALL is available from ONDEMAND Software, Inc. You can phone or FAX them for more information at the following numbers:

(800) 368-5207
(941) 261-6678
(941) 261-6549 FAX

You also can register the software when prompted with the registration option during the installation process.

Note Although the author prepared much of this chapter and all of the figures, some information is adapted from the information provided by the manufacturer on the CD.

This chapter explains how to install and use the WinINSTALL software distribution software.

Running WinINSTALL

To install WinINSTALL, you must run the setup for the WinINSTALL utility. Before installing WinINSTALL, copy all files from the following directory on the CD, into a single directory on your hard drive:

Ondemand\Wininstl\Disk1

Alternatively, you can create diskettes from the separate directories. The install will not run from CD.

To run setup, complete the following steps:

1. Start Windows, then choose **R**un from the **F**ile menu to open the Run dialog box. Type the path to the SETUP.EXE file, or use the **B**rowse button to search for the file, then choose OK.

2. When the `Would you like SETUP to install sample WinINSTall.DAT files?` prompt appears, choose **Y**es.

3. Choose **C**ontinue to accept the default path and directory, or specify an alternative directory in which to install the files by typing the path and directory name and then choose **C**ontinue.

4. The files are installed to the specified directory, and you are given the option to register the software now, or to continue without registering (see fig. 15.1). Because the software is designed to let you try it before registering it, go ahead and choose **C**ontinue for now.

5. The balance of the remaining files are installed and prepared (see fig. 15.2), then the program group and related icons are created (see fig. 15.3). When the installation screen reappears, choose OK to exit the install program.

Before the install program closes, you are given the option to read the related WRI file. If you do not read it immediately, you can read it later simply by choosing the WinINSTALL Readme File icon from the WinINSTALL 5.0 program group.

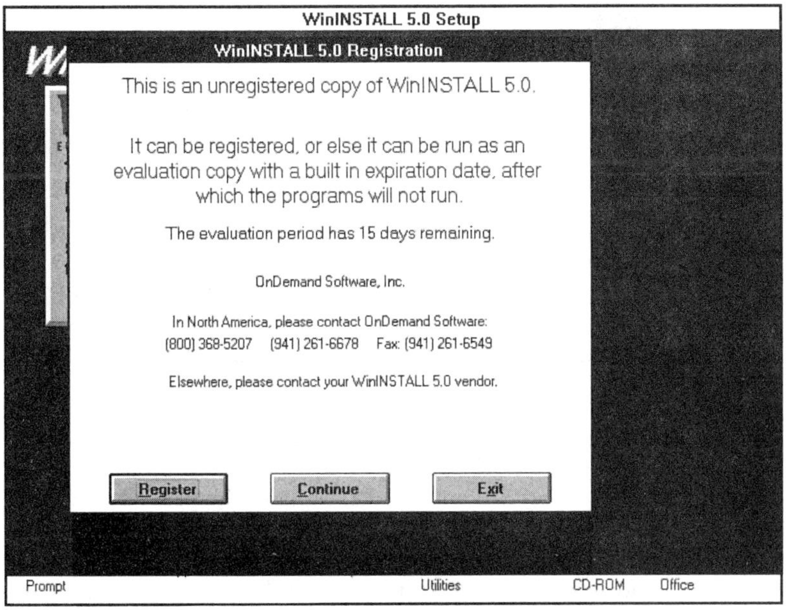

Figure 15.1
The WinINSTALL 5.0 Registration prompt.

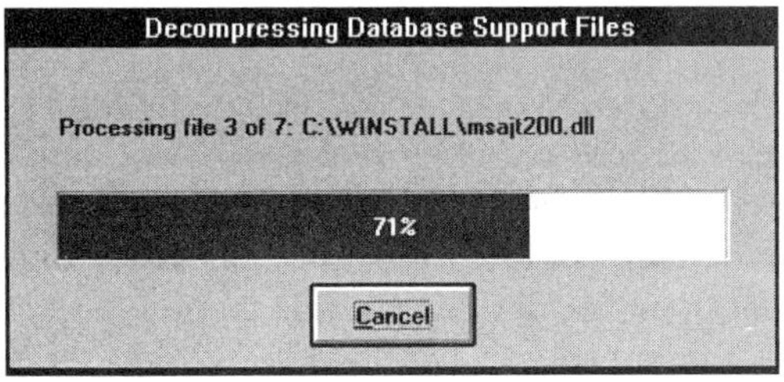

Figure 15.2
The screen showing the installation of related files.

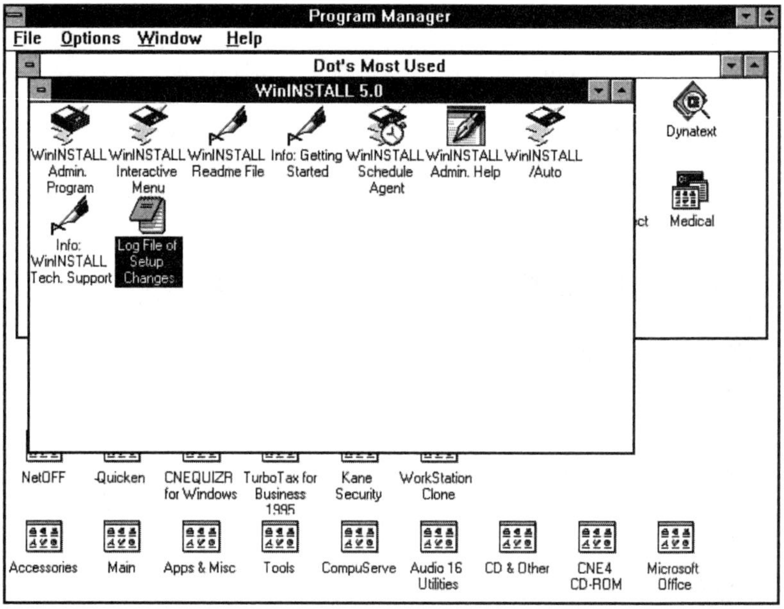

Figure 15.3 The WinINSTAll 5.0 program group window.

Getting Started with WinINSTALL

The GETSTART.WRI file included with WinINSTALL explains the procedure for starting WinINSTALL. You can read the GETSTART.WRI file by choosing the Info: Getting Started icon from the WinINSTALL 5.0 program group. To read the file online (from the screen), however, you must switch back and forth between the file and the process you are trying to complete. To enable you to access the information more easily, this chapter includes an abbreviated version of GETSTART.WRI.

Note NetWare users, note that one of the provided WinINSTALL.DAT files looks for the files NWCALLS.DLL, NWLOCALE.DLL, and NWNET.DLL in the directory in which WinINSTALL resides on the server. Copy these files to that directory before running WinINSTALL, and make sure they are not older than the files listed in this chapter in the section "Required Components."

The steps in this section are in outline form. They are explained in detail in the ensuing sections. Complete the following steps to start WinINSTALL:

1. Set up a workstation on which WinINSTALL will run as "Administrator."

2. Determine the method of software distribution (delivery).

3. Enable the USER's DELIVERY METHOD(S).

4. Implement your delivery choice(s), installing the WinINSTALL User Node, using WinINSTALL.

These steps are briefly explained in the following sections.

Setting Up a Workstation as the Administrator

After the initial installation, WinINSTALL has enough functionality to perform the necessary DAT file editing and initial node installations of the product. First, however, you must set yourself as the Administrator. You work from the WinINSTALL Interactive Menu dialog box, which contains the following eight options:

- ✔ 1 - WinINSTALL Administrator Node Installation
- ✔ 2 - Administrator MAPI compliant E-Mail Initialization
- ✔ 3 - Administrator VIM compliant E-Mail Initialization
- ✔ 4 - WinINSTALL Automatic
- ✔ 5 - WinINSTALL E-Mail
- ✔ 6 - WinINSTALL Interactive User Menu
- ✔ 7 - WinINSTALL Scheduler
- ✔ 8 - Required Files for ALL NOVELL Admin/Users

From the WinINSTALL 5.0 program group, complete the following steps:

1. Double-click on the WinINSTALL Interactive Menu icon to open the WinINSTALL Interactive Menu dialog box (see fig. 15.4).

2. From the Available Applications window choose 1 - WinINSTALL Administrator Node Installation.

3. If you are not sure about your type of e-mail system, you can skip this step for now. If you do not already see a SEND button on the WinINSTALL main menu and you have a MAPI- or VIM-compliant e-mail system and want to enable the e-mail integration function of WinINSTALL, hold the Ctrl key and click on option 2 - Administrator MAPI Compliant E-Mail Initialization or option 3 - Administrator VIM Compliant E-Mail Initialization.

4. If you are on a Novell LAN, highlight option 8 - Required Files for ALL NOVELL Admin/Users by holding the Ctrl key and clicking on it.

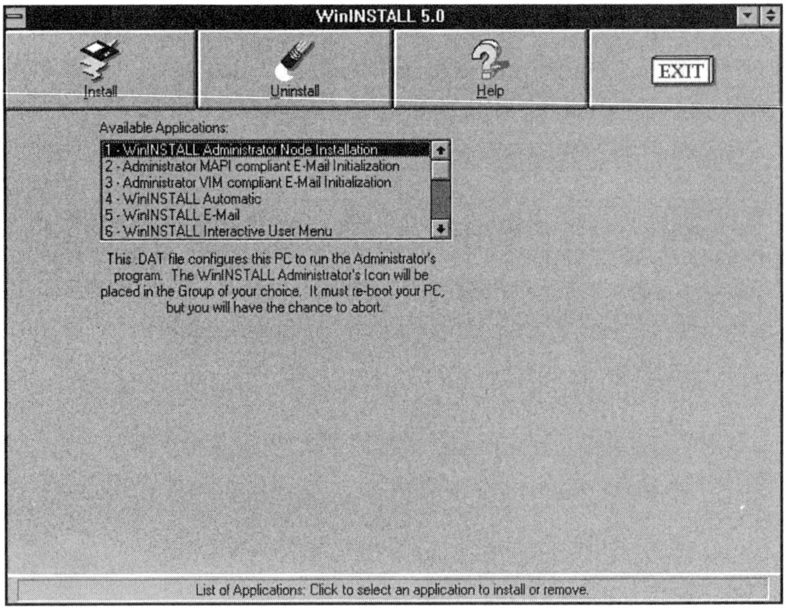

Figure 15.4 The WinINSTALL interactive menu dialog box.

Note If you do use a Novell LAN, the three files mentioned previously—NWCALLS.DLL, NWLOCALE.DLL, and NWNET.DLL—must already be copied to the WinINSTALL directory before this step will work.

5. Click on Install to perform the highlighted installations.

WinINSTALL performs the necessary steps to make this workstation ready for the WinINSTALL Administrator to use. After it finishes, reboot the workstation so the changes can take effect.

Determining the Method of Software Distribution

As the WinINSTALL Administrator, you need to determine which of the methods WinINSTALL offers you want to use to distribute (deliver) applications to your users. Choose from the following Windows-based distribution methods:

- ✔ **Automatic.** Occurs at Windows startup with no user intervention. To set up WinINSTALL so that distribution is automatically carried out at Windows startup, specify the WinINSTALL Automatic Installer (WINSTALA.EXE), either on the WIN.INI `Run=` line or in the startup group. Because the `Run=` line does not support command-line parameters, to specify command-line parameters for WINSTALA.EXE, you must run WINSTALA.EXE from the startup group and specify the parameters on the command line in the icon properties box.

A WinINSTALL DAT file automatically performs the following required changes to the WIN.INI file, via the WinINSTALL menu:

[WINDOWS]

RUN=*path*\AUTONAI.EXE

- ✔ **E-Mail.** Applications are sent as icons with attachments to designated users. WinINSTALL also offers the capability to send a special form of a DAT file (an NAI—Network Automatic Installation—file) as an attachment to an e-mail message. Properly configured, the Automatic Installer (WINSTALA.EXE) is launched by a user by double-clicking (or shift-double-clicking, depending on how your e-mail application launches an application) on the attachment icon, upon which it immediately installs the application. This method of distribution works with many Windows-based e-mail packages.

  The following changes to the WIN.INI file are accomplished automatically with WinINSTALL:

  [Extensions]

  NAI=*path*\WINSTALA.EXE ^.NAI

  [Mail]

  MAPI=1

  SMI=1

  RUN=*path*\ONDSCHED.EXE

  Substitute *path* with the full DOS path to the WINSTALA.EXE or ONDSCHED.EXE program.

- ✔ **Active or Menu Driven.** Enables users to choose from a controlled list.
- ✔ **Scheduled.** Applications are delivered at a pre-determined time.
- ✔ **Remote.** Applications are installed without being connected to a server.

Enabling the User's Delivery Method(s)

WinINSTALL comes with several *DAT* files (WinINSTALL **DAT**A files) that enable you to custom configure your users delivery method(s). You create your users delivery method by modifying one or more of the DAT files (items 4 through 8) in the Administrator's list of Available Applications in the WinINSTALL main menu.

Warning Novell users must run item 8 on all node installations.

To enable users to receive installation of one or more of the available delivery methods you must modify the associated WinINSTALL DAT file to remove the installation restriction that prevents the DAT file(s) from running or being available to users. To accomplish that task, complete the following steps:

1. Start the WinINSTALL Administrator.
2. Choose one of the items on the menu (see fig. 15.5).

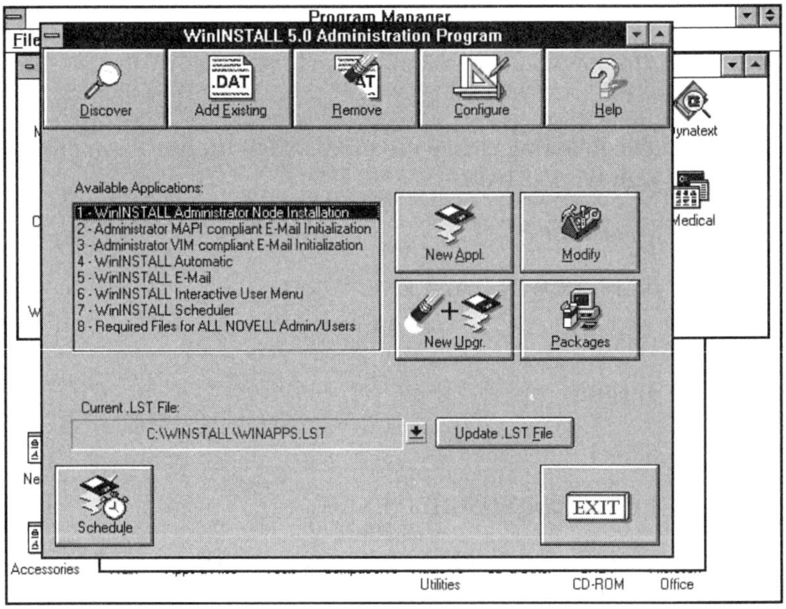

Figure 15.5
The WinINSTALL Administration Program dialog box.

3. Choose **Modify** to open the Modify Existing Application dialog box.
4. Choose Pre\Post Options.
5. Choose the Software Prerequisites tab.
6. Choose Desktop to remove the **X**.
7. Choose OK to save the modifications and exit the Pre\Post Options screen.
8. Choose OK to save the modifications and exit the Modify Existing Application dialog box.

9. Choose OK to exit the Modify Application Completed screen, and return to the WinINSTALL 5.0 Administration Program dialog box.
10. Choose Update .LST File to save any modifications to the LST file.
11. Choose OK to acknowledge the `.LST File Update Complete` message.

You can now go on to implementation.

Implementation Methods

With most networks, you can call a BAT file from the login script. This capability enables you to start Windows along with WinINSTALL, and have WinINSTALL immediately perform its user node installation.

The following is an example of a WINAUTO5.BAT file that can be called during the login process:

```
@ECHO OFF
IF EXIST C:\WINDOWS\SYSTEM\ONDNET.DLL GOTO THEEND
IF EXIST C:\WINDOWS\NWCALLS.DLL REN C:\WINDOWS\NWCALLS.DLL
C:\WINDOWS\*.OND
IF EXIST C:\WINDOWS\NWLOCALE.DLL REN C:\WINDOWS\NWLOCALE.DLL
C:\WINDOWS\*.OND
IF EXIST C:\WINDOWS\NWNET.DLL REN C:\WINDOWS\NWNET.DLL C:\WINDOWS\*.OND
rem THE LINE BELOW PERFORMS THE SAME AS THE 3 ABOVE, ONLY MUCH FASTER
rem FOR %%A IN (NWCALLS NWLOCALE NWNET) DO IF EXIST C:\WINDOWS\%%A.DLL
rem REN C:\WINDOWS\%%A.DLL C:\WINDOWS\%%A.OND
:\WINSTALL\WINSTALA.EXE
:THEEND
```

If you are using a batch file similar to the one in the example, be sure to change the paths where needed to reflect the actual paths that contain the files on your workstation or network.

Note Explanations of the commands used in this example are included in the write file that opens when you choose the INFO: Getting Started icon from the program group.

After Windows is started, you can still perform updates to files. The standard method of distributing the WinINSTALL client components is to place a call to a batch file in the user/system login script. The specified batch file contains a call to start Windows and execute WINSTALA.EXE, executing a DAT file that configures the client to receive WinINSTALL-generated application packages. These login scripts generally are executed prior to Windows startup, so this is perfectly legal. Several networks, however, either allow or require login scripts to be executed after Windows startup. Therefore, an error message is generated: `You are already running Microsoft Windows.`

To solve this problem, modify the user/system login batch file to include steps that temporarily replace the STARTUP.GRP file on the client workstation with one that contains only one icon (a call to WINSTALA.EXE). The DAT file specified on this command line will install the client components the next time the user starts Windows.

The following is a sample login batch file:

```
REM Step 1
REM  Check if WinINSTALL has already been installed, if so, check to see
REM  if the STARTUP.GRP needs to be restored.
if exist c:\windows\winstall.don goto CHECK_STARTUP
REM Step 2
REM  Backup and then Replace users STARTUP.GRP with a new one that
REM  will automatically evoke "f:\winstall\WINSTALA.EXE".
if exist c:\windows\startup.grp copy c:\windows\startup.grp
➥c:\windows\startup.bak
copy f:\winstall\startup.grp c:\windows
echo WinINSTALL successfully installed... >> c:\windows\winstall.don
goto EXIT
REM Step 3
REM  Restore STARTUP.GRP to its original state, if WinINSTALL has been run.
REM
:CHECK_STARTUP
if not exist c:\windows\system\nai.dll goto EXIT
copy c:\windows\startup.bak c:\windows\startup.grp
:EXIT
```

The following is an example command line for the related icon in temporary STARTUP.GRP:

> *path*\WINSTALA.EXE

You now are ready to use the DISCOVER feature of WinINSTALL to help create DAT or NAI files to distribute applications to your network users. Before using the DISCOVER feature, however, there are several caveats of which you should be aware. To read about these caveats, open the Info: Getting Started icon from the program group window, then scroll to section V, "CAVEATS."

DISCOVER

DISCOVER is a utility within WinINSTALL that compares the state of your Windows configuration before and after an application is installed, then builds a DAT file that enables you to perform the same procedure quickly, automatically, and effortlessly on users workstations.

To run DISCOVER the first time, complete the following steps from the WinINSTALL 5.0 program group:

1. Double-click on the WinINSTALL Admin. Program icon to open the WinINSTALL 5.0 Administration Program dialog box.
2. Choose Discover.
3. In the WinINSTALL List Name box, type a meaningful description of the application you are about to install or of the changes you are about to make.
4. Press Tab.
5. In the DAT File Name box, type **myfirst** (without regard to case). Do not type .DAT after myfirst.
6. Choose Before to initiate a Before snapshot.
7. If you did not exclude any files/directories, choose OK.
8. Choose OK from the Before Snapshot completed screen.
9. Choose Cancel from the Run Application Setup Program dialog box.
10. Choose Exit Discover.
11. Choose EXIT. You are now completely out of WinINSTALL.
12. Install something or copy icons or files and make some harmless INI file changes to see the results of your changes now that you have run DISCOVER and exited WinINSTALL.
13. From the WinINSTALL 5.0 program group, choose the WinINSTALL Admin. Program icon to open the WinINSTALL 5.0 Administration Program dialog box.
14. Choose Discover.
15. Choose After to perform an After snapshot.
16. Choose Yes.

17. If the after snapshot found any new files, choose NO.
18. If you installed an application you want to keep select Create New Directory Structure.
19. If you selected Create New Directory Structure pick a location for the new directory structure to be placed.
20. Choose OK.
21. Choose My First Discover.
22. Choose Modify.

You can now explore. The blue labels indicate WinINSTALL found a change. Be sure to check it for possible anomalies caused by the creation of BAK files or applications running in the background. You can customize this DAT file or deliver it to users as-is. Please refer to the manual for more details.

Now that you have seen WinINSTALL at work, you can undo your work by completing the following steps:

1. From the WinINSTALL 5.0 program group, double-click on the WinINSTALL Menu icon.
2. Scroll down until you see My First Discover and select it.
3. Choose UnInstall.

Your machine's environment is now back to its original state.

ICAE SIVE
ORBIS, NO
SCRIPTIO.
MAR DEL SVR, quod
PACIFICVM
Circulus Æquinoctialis
HISPANIA NOVA
MARATA
CVLIACAN
ASTATLAN
CHILAGA
NORVMBEGA
MOCOSA
CALICVAS
CAPASCHI
TERLICHICHIMECHI
LA FLORIDA
CVBA
HISPANIOLA
CHARCAS
CHILI
PATAGONES, vel REGIO GIGANTVM
FRETVM MAGALLANICVM
Archipelago del C. delleado

16

CHAPTER

ONTECH

The ONTECH directory on the CD contains software called SofTrack, manufactured by ON Technology. *SofTrack* enables you to meter software usage on your network, helping you keep track of the software on your network so you can ensure you are staying within the license agreement for each software package used on your network.

Note

Much of the information in this chapter is taken from the help and text files included on the CD which were provided by ON Technology. Minor editing and format changes have been made to keep this chapter consistent with the other chapters in this book, and to enable you to read and follow the text more easily. The author also has provided the figures and some of the text in this chapter.

If you have questions or problems that are not explained in the online help system, contact ON Technology for support. Record as many details of your problem as possible.

You can reach ON Technology through any of the following means:

- ✔ Phone/Fax: Call SofTrack product support at (617) 374-1400. The FAX number is (919) 319-7091. Hours are 9:00 a.m. to 5:30 p.m., EST.
- ✔ CompuServe: At any CompuServe prompt, type **GO ONTECHNOLOGY** to reach the ON Technology forum.
- ✔ MHS: Send your inquiries to `SUPPORT @ ON`. The Host number at ON Technology is (617) 374-1425. Modem speeds up to 14,400 kbps are supported.
- ✔ Internet: Send messages to `support@on.com`.

Although distributed by ON Technology, SofTrack is copyrighted by Integrity Software, Inc.

You can use SofTrack on NetWare 3 *and* NetWare 4 file servers.

Installing SofTrack

Before installation, log in to your NetWare 3.*x* server as Supervisor or equivalent. Log in to your NetWare 4.*x* server as Admin or equivalent (with full rights to modify the Root).

Some files are compressed on disk to enable the product to fit. The Windows Installer decompresses these files automatically. The installation process is discussed in the next section of this chapter.

Automated Installation

To automatically install the SofTrack software from CD, complete the following steps:

1. Load Windows and choose **F**ile, **R**un to run the INSTALL.EXE program in the ONTECH\SOFTRACK directory of the CD from the Windows Program Manager.

Figure 16.1
The SofTrack Welcome screen.

2. Wait while the program initializes, then choose **C**ontinue when prompted (see fig. 16.1).

3. When prompted, select the file server in which you want to install SofTrack, then choose **C**ontinue.

4. When prompted (see fig. 16.2), specify the network directory in which you want to install SofTrack's administration files, then choose **C**ontinue.

5. When the screen indicating where to install the SofTrack NLM and administrative files opens, answer **Y**es to indicate these are the correct locations for the files to be installed.

6. After the files are decompressed and copied, the related program group and icons are created. Choose the Exit icon to exit the installation program.

Figure 16.2 The screen in which you specify the network directory to which to install the SofTrack administration files.

Now you are prompted to set up SofTrack. Figure 16.3 shows the SofTrack opening window.

Figure 16.3 SofTrack's main window.

Manual Installation

For instructions on how to manually install SofTrack, refer to the README.TXT file on the CD.

Setting Up SofTrack

Before you set up any specifications for SofTrack, you must load the related NLM on the file server. To load the NLM, type **LOAD SOFTRACK** at the console prompt, and press Enter. SofTrack notifies you when the load is successful with the `SOFTRACK successfully completed initializations` message.

In addition, from Windows Program Manager, use the **R**un option in the **F**ile menu to run the STTECH.BAT program. Run it from the directory in which you installed SofTrack, not from the CD. Running STTECH.BAT automatically records workstation and system configuration information.

From the SofTrack menu, you can set up SofTrack parameters and use SofTrack's other features. The following section discusses using SofTrack.

Using SofTrack

To start the SofTrack utility, choose the SofTrack icon from the related program group window, or use it when it opens automatically after you exit the installation utility.

The SofTrack main window provides the following four menu options:

- ✔ Administration
- ✔ Licenses
- ✔ Reports
- ✔ Server

The following sections serve as discussions for each of these options in turn.

Administration

To set up various parameters for SofTrack, open the Administration menu (see fig. 16.4), then choose the appropriate menu option and provide the necessary information.

Figure 16.4
The Administration menu.

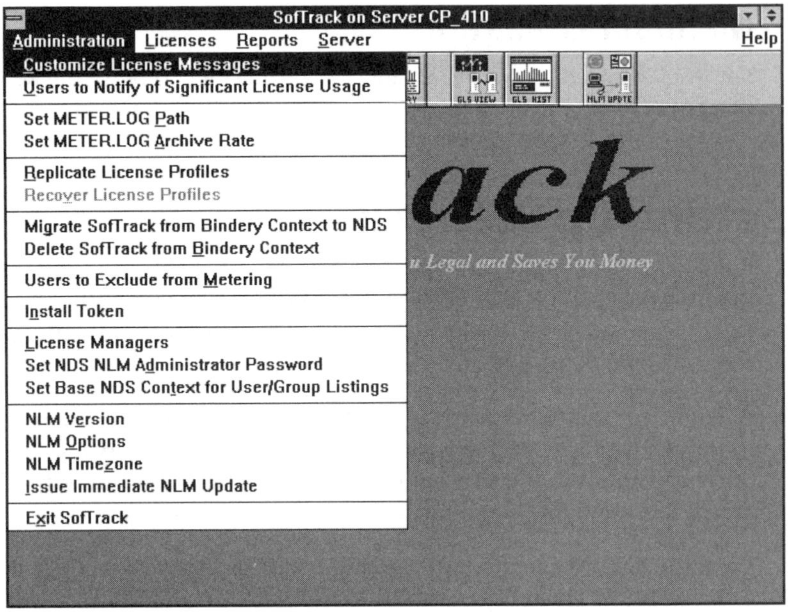

You can choose from a wide variety of options in the Administration menu. Which option you choose depends on what you want to accomplish. Choosing a specific option opens related windows. SofTrack prompts you for information as necessary. You also can access the online help information for additional assistance when working with any of the options.

To track license usage, one of the options you want to choose from the Administration menu is Set METER.LOG **P**ath, to open the Set METER.LOG Path dialog box (see fig. 16.5).

From this window, choose a volume from the **V**olumes area. Then walk through the directory structure in the **D**irectories area and choose the directory in which you want the meter log file to be stored. The final path then appears in the **P**ath for METER.LOG field at the top of the dialog box.

The best way to learn about the options in the Administration menu is to open the menu, choose one, and work with it. You can use online help for additional information about any item in the Administration menu.

Licenses

Choosing the **L**icenses menu opens the License Registry window, from which you can add, delete, edit, rename, and copy license information for different software packages. To add a license, choose the **A**dd button to open the Add New License dialog box (see fig. 16.6).

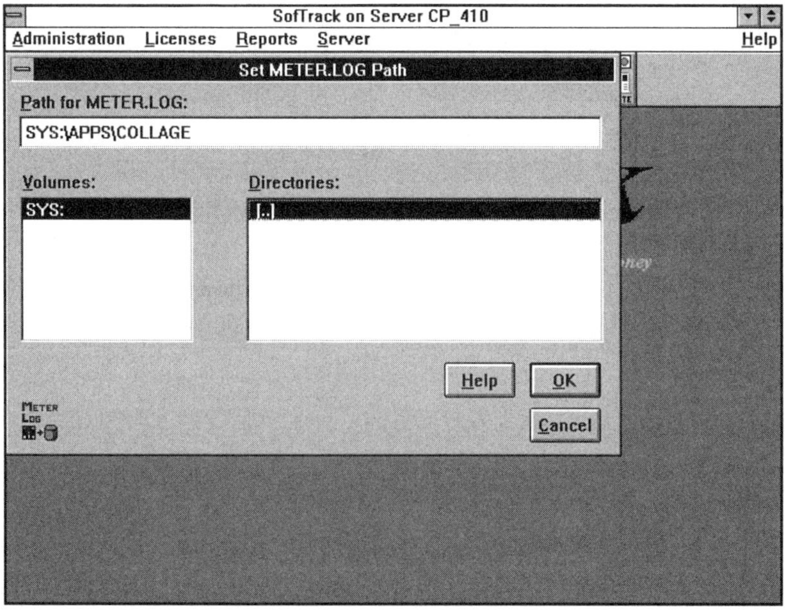

Figure 16.5
The Set METER.LOG Path dialog box.

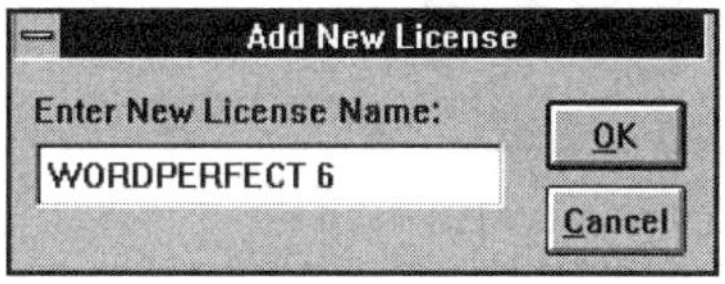

Figure 16.6
The Add New License dialog box.

After you provide a license name and choose OK, the License Profile dialog box for the new license you are adding opens (see fig. 16.7).

From the License Profile dialog box, you can provide various types of information, such as notes in the Application Note 1 or Application Note 2 fields.

If you are not sure what information to add to the fields in the License Profile dialog box, choose Help. To find help for the License Profile dialog box, scroll through the table of contents until you find the License Profile Options section (see fig. 16.8).

To see specific information about a particular field in the License Profile dialog box, double-click on the corresponding title. To see specific information about what information to add to one of the Application Note fields, for example, choose Application Note 1 & 2 from the table of contents, which opens the screen shown in figure 16.9.

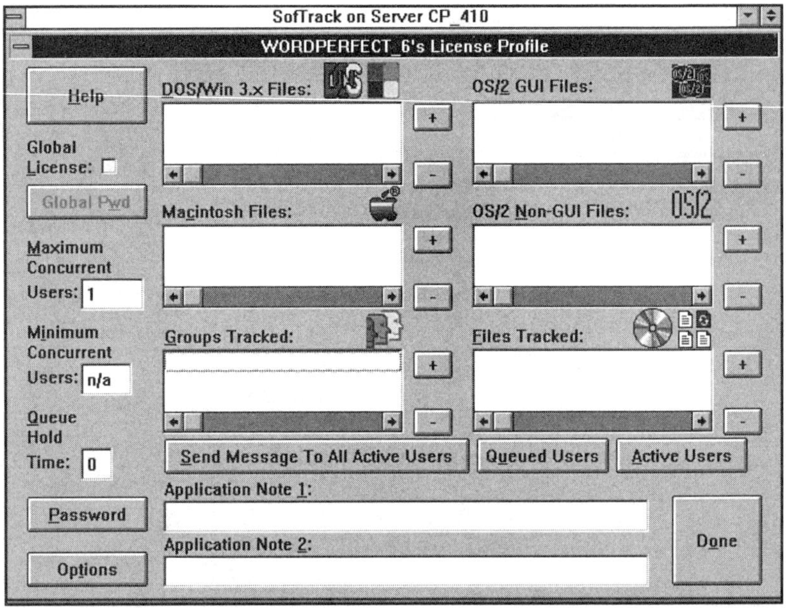

Figure 16.7 The WordPerfect 6 License Profile dialog box.

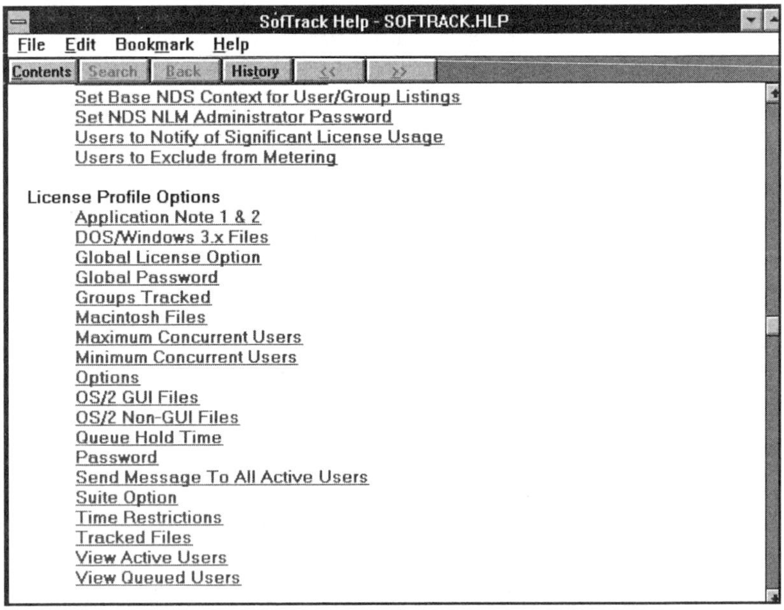

Figure 16.8 The SofTrack Help table of contents showing the License Profile Options section.

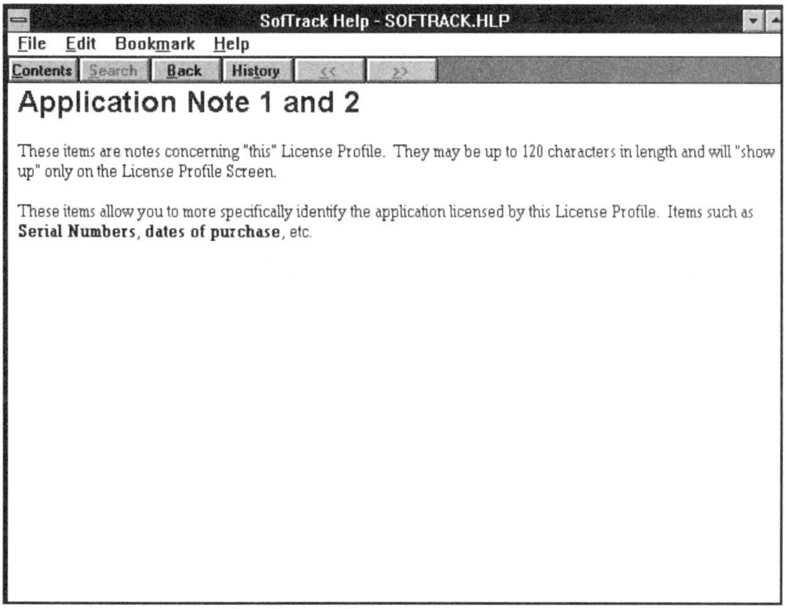

Figure 16.9
The SofTrack help screen for the Application Note 1 and Application Note 2 fields.

After you enter profile information, choose D<u>o</u>ne, which returns you to the Select License Profile window. This time, the License Registry list shows the title of the license information you just added (see fig. 16.10).

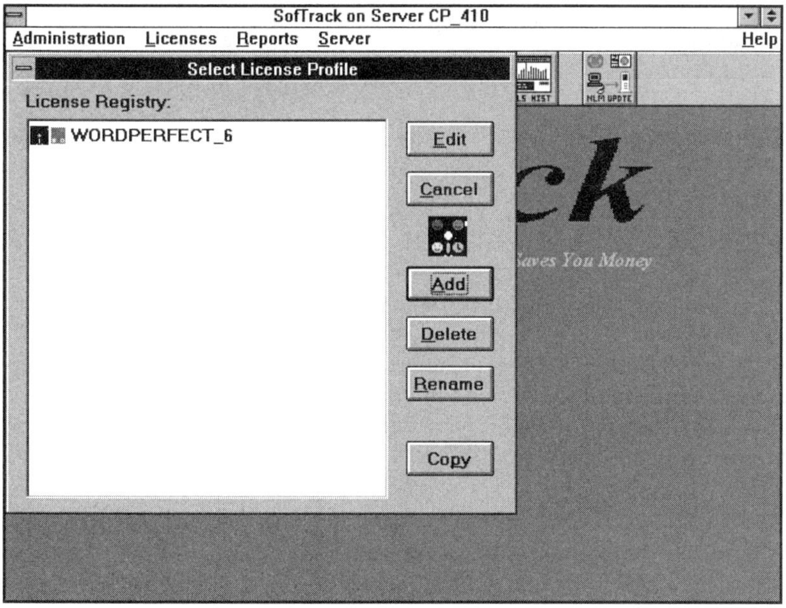

Figure 16.10
The Select License Profile window with the WORDPERFECT_6 license registry added.

Reports

Choosing the **R**eports menu option drops down the Reports menu (see fig. 16.11), from which you can choose to view the current METER.LOG file. You also can print various reports, including a usage report and license profiles report. The Report menu also enables you to recall report definitions, graph a history of a license, view summaries, and view online global licenses.

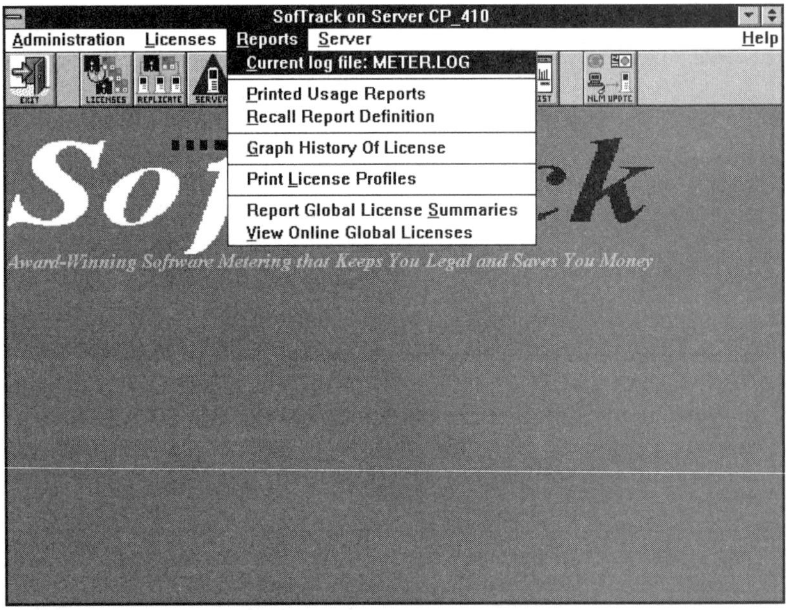

Figure 16.11 The Reports menu.

As with the Administration menu, the best way to learn more about these options is to choose one and work with it.

Server

Choosing the **S**erver menu option opens the Change Current Server dialog box (see fig. 16.12), from which you can view the names of the servers to which you currently are connected (note the Connected Servers area). You also can connect to other servers by selecting the name of the server from the Resources list, then clicking on the **L**ogin button and filling in the Login **N**ame and **P**assword fields. To log out of a server from this screen, select the server, then click on the Logou**t** button.

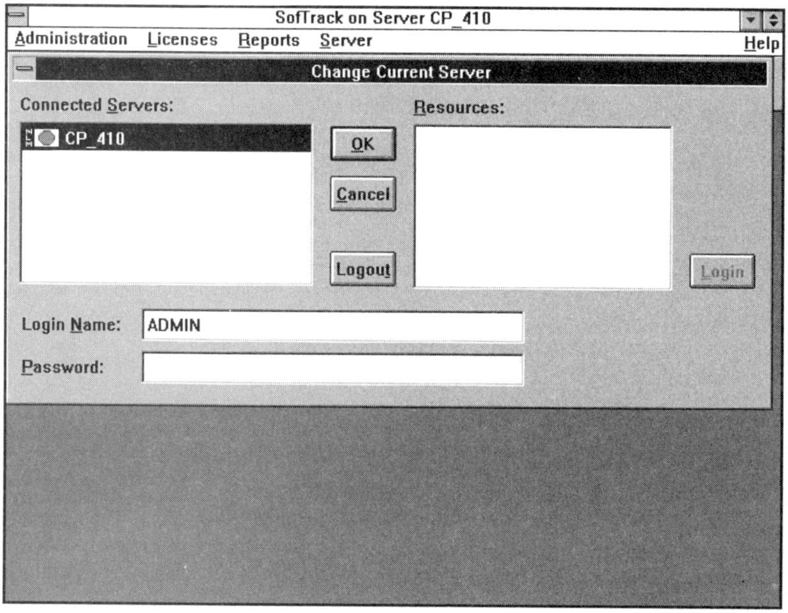

Figure 16.12
The Change Current Server dialog box.

To exit the SofTrack utility, choose E**x**it SofTrack from the **A**dministration menu.

CHILAGA
FRANCIA
NORVMBEGA
TEAC
MARATA
CVLYACAN
TERLICHICHI MECHI
HISPANIA NOVA
CALICVAS
CAPASCHI
AVACAL
LA FLORIDA
CVBA
MAR DEL SVR, quod
CHILE
PATAGONES
REGIO GIGANTVM
CAE SIVE
ORBIS, NO
SCRIPTIO.
Archipelago del C. desseado

17

CHAPTER

SECRDESN

The SECRDESN directory on the CD contains software called QView Pro by Secure Design. *QView Pro* is designed to control Novell print queues, enabling you to delete, view, and move between queues. You also can use QView Pro to monitor queues to locate duplicate or oversize print jobs.

The SDLPD subdirectory also contains print server software. To use this software, any workstation that accesses the network must be running the NetWare DOS Requester (VLM files) as workstations running the NetX file will not be able to access this software.

> **Note** Much of the information in this chapter is taken from the help and text files included on the CD as provided by Secure Design. Some minor editing and format changes have been made to keep this chapter consistent with the other chapters in this book, and to enable you to read and follow the text more easily. The author also provided the figures and some of the text in this chapter.

You can reach Secure Design at the following address, phone numbers, and e-mail addresses:

Secure Design
P.O. Box 475
Corvallis, OR 97339
USA

Phone: (541) 752-5988
FAX/BBS: (541) 752-5990

Internet: Support@sdesign.com
MCI Mail: sdesign@mcimail.com
WWW: http://www.peak.org/~sdesign

Installing the Secure Design Software

This QView Pro software is an evaluation copy and may be used for 60 days from the time of installation. To install the software, change to the directory that contains the QVINS.EXE file (*CD_drive*:\SECRDESN\QviewPro), then type **QVINS** and press Enter. The Introductory screen opens. Press Esc to continue the installation as follows:

1. When prompted, choose the file server onto which you want to install the software (see fig. 17.1).

2. When prompted for a serial number, do not enter one because this copy is an evaluation copy. Instead, choose Ok.

3. From the main menu that opens, choose Install Queue to open the Select a Print Queue menu. Select a print queue to install from the Select a Print Queue list (see fig. 17.2).

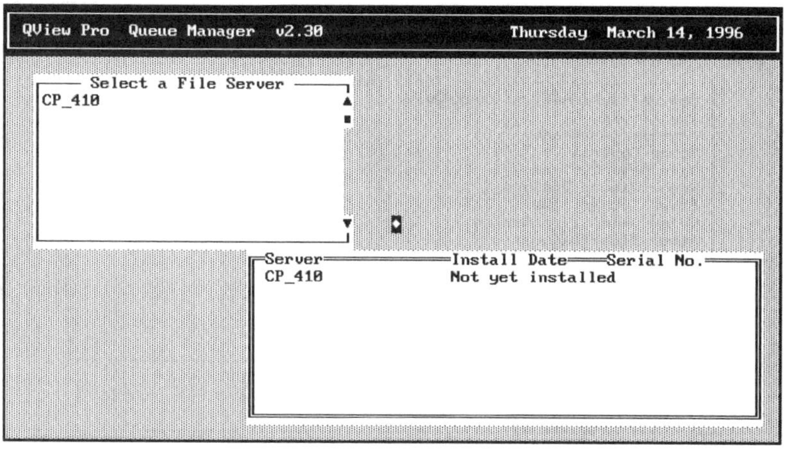

Figure 17.1
The area from which to select a file server onto which to install the software.

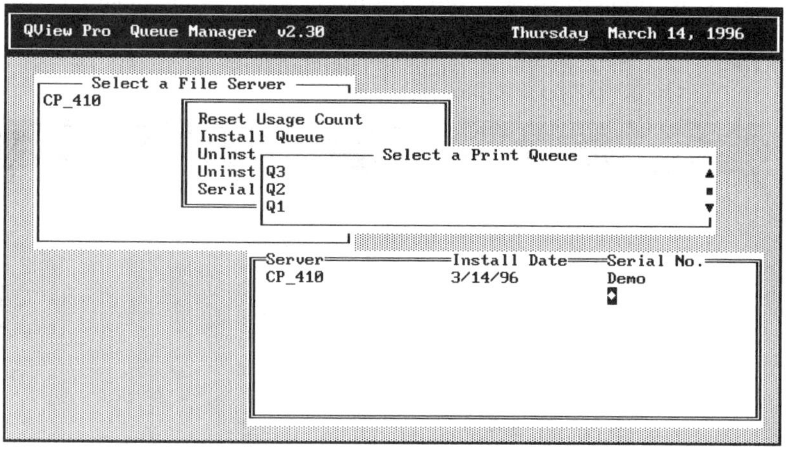

Figure 17.2
The Select a Print Queue menu.

4. You then can reset the usage count for duplicates deleted and jobs removed by choosing Reset Usage Count from the main menu, then choosing OK.

Running QView Pro

To use QView Pro, start it by typing **QVIEW** and pressing Enter. When prompted, provide a name. The QView screen opens. From this screen press F1 for a list of topics on which you can receive help information (see fig. 17.3)

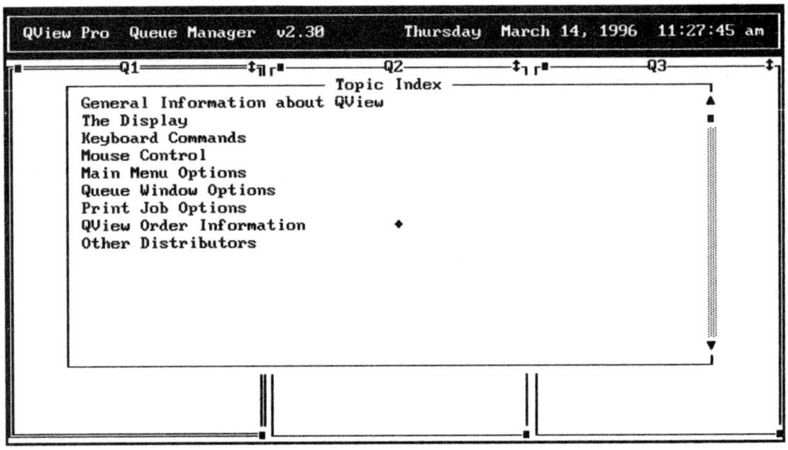

Figure 17.3 The Help Topic Index.

Most of QView Pro's functionality comes from the options in the utility's main menu (see fig. 17.4). To open this menu, either click the mouse pointer on the top of the screen or press Esc.

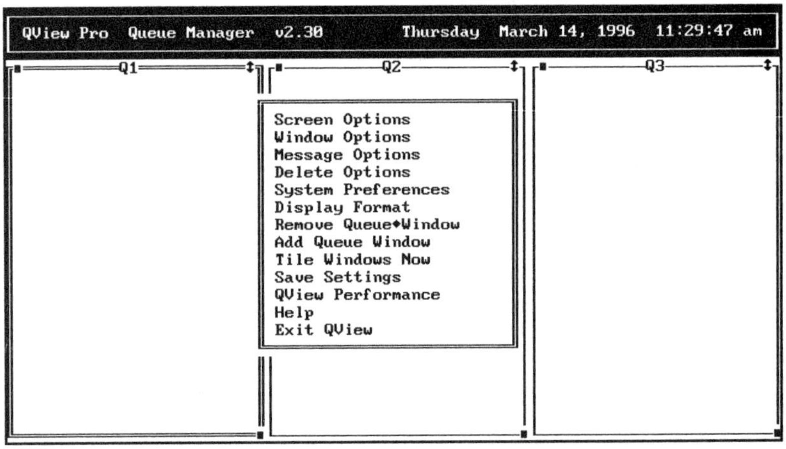

Figure 17.4 QView Pro's main menu.

The following sections explain the QView Pro main menu and its subsequent options and fields. The information in these sections also has been provided by the manufacturer in the QV_HELP.TXT file. It has been reproduced with minor editing and formatting changes to enable you to read and follow it more easily.

Screen Options

Screen options are Animation Speed, 43/50 Line Mode, Screen Saver, Screen Message, Auto Tile Windows, and Show I/O Status Character (see fig. 17.5).

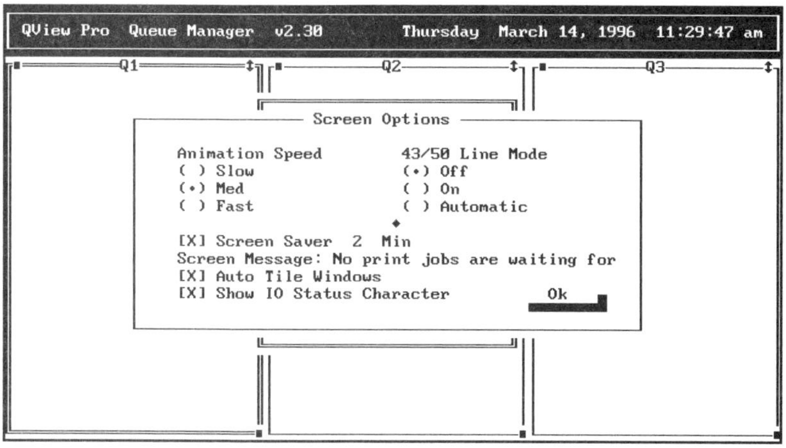

Figure 17.5
The Screen Options dialog box.

The following list describes the options in the Screen Options dialog box:

- ✔ **Automation Speed.** Sets the speed at which screen characters are animated.
- ✔ **43/50 Line Mode.** Enables you to set the line mode to on, off, or automatic.
- ✔ **Screen Saver.** Opens a screen saver after two minutes when jobs exist in the queues.
- ✔ **Screen Message.** Displays a message when the screen saver is activated.
- ✔ **Auto Tile Windows.** Automatically re-tiles windows when new windows are displayed.
- ✔ **Show IO Status Character.** Blinks a status character in the upper left corner of the screen. The following characters are used to display status:

>	Scanning print queues
û	Checking for overage print jobs
#	Checking for files in the service directory
+	Calculating print job CRC

Window Options

The Window Options dialog box includes Data Query Speed, Show Windows From, Close Off Line Windows, Re-Open Active Windows, Queue Status Change Alarm, and Auto Hold Jobs During Edit. (see fig. 17.6).

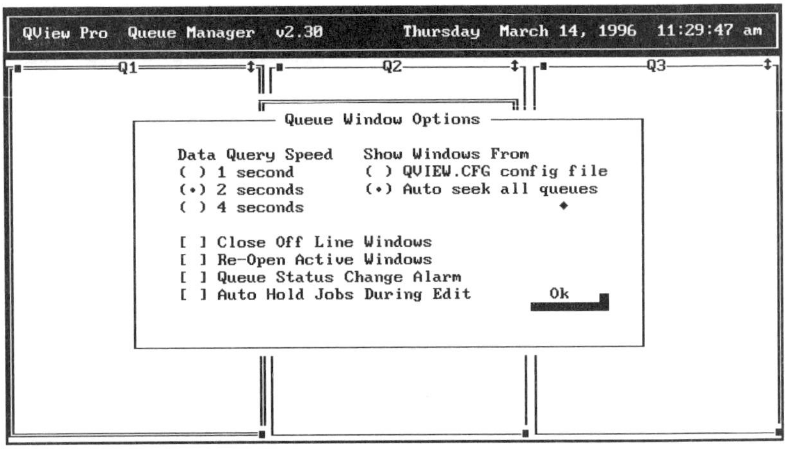

Figure 17.6
The Queue Window Options dialog box.

The following list describes the options in the Queue Window Options dialog box:

- ✔ **Data Query Speed.** Controls how often QView queries the print queues. A fast query speed enhances QView's accuracy but taxes the server's resources.
- ✔ **Show Windows From.** Enables you to select the method that QView uses to display queue windows on startup. If QView is to read from the config file, the window settings and placement are preserved. If QView is to auto seek all queues, the queues use the default queue settings and the windows are tiled.
- ✔ **Close Off Line Windows.** When a queue window's status is offline, QView closes the window. Windows that are closed cannot perform automatic functions.
- ✔ **Re-Open Active Windows.** Monitors windows that were closed because they were off line. If the queue status changes such that the windows are not off line, the windows are re-opened. This option must be on at the time the windows are closed.
- ✔ **Queue Status Change Alarm.** Causes QView to make a chirping sound when a window changes status.
- ✔ **Auto Hold Jobs During Edit.** Used with the edit or view commands in the Job Options Dialog to hold the print job. This feature enables QView to automatically set a hold on a job while you edit or view it.

Message Options

QView can make use of Novell's broadcast message functions to keep users informed about their print jobs (see fig. 17.7).

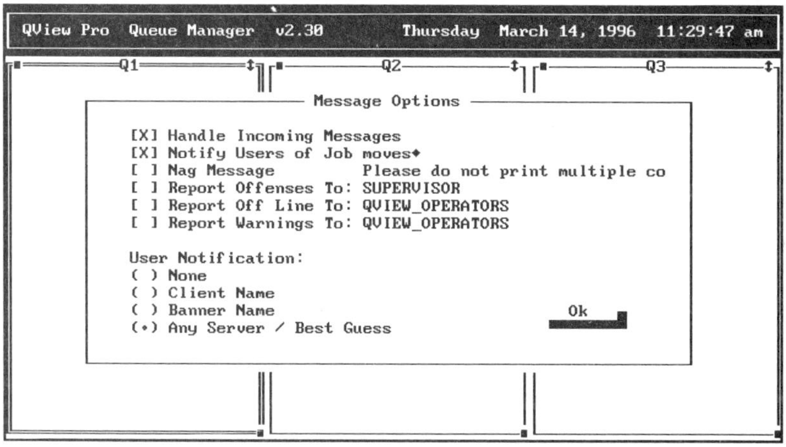

Figure 17.7
The Message Options dialog box.

The following list describes the options in the Message Options dialog box:

- ✔ **Handle Incoming Messages.** Enables QView to display broadcast messages instead of the standard "PRESS CTRL - ENTER" message that is usually displayed.
- ✔ **Notify Users of Job moves.** Enables QView to send a broadcast message when a print job is successfully moved from one queue to another.
- ✔ **Nag Message.** When a duplicate job is found, this option enables QView to notify the user twice that a duplicate job has been found. User Notification also must be on. Check the option on the left, and change the message on the right.
- ✔ **Report Offenses To.** Enables QView to send a message stating print job offenses (such as duplicates) to the user or group specified in the field to the right of the option.
- ✔ **Report Off Line To.** Enables QView to send a message when a print queue's status changes to offline to the user or group specified in the field to the right of the option.
- ✔ **Report Warnings To.** Enables QView to send a message when a print queue's status changes to "warning" to the user or group specified in the field to the right of the option.
- ✔ **User Notification.** Enables you to select the method by which the print job owner is notified when the print job is complete.

Delete Options

You can configure QView to delete duplicate print jobs. The Delete Options dialog box enables you to configure the handling of duplicate print jobs.

The following list describes the options in the Delete Options dialog box:

- ✔ **Duplicate Job Criteria.** The information provided for indicating what constitutes a duplicate job are used to specify how QView finds a duplicate print job. All the criteria of the checked options must be met before a print job has duplicate status.

- ✔ **Check Between Queues.** Checks for duplicates between queues. If this option is off, the duplicates must be located in the same print queue.

- ✔ **Use CRC check.** Calculates a CRC for each print job. This method is optimal for determining whether a job is a duplicate. Print jobs of the same size (such as Print Screens and MacPaint bitmaps) are deleted when this option is off. Using this option, however, slows down QView considerably. With this option on, QView might pause for up to 20 seconds when it is working on a print job larger than 2,000 KB.

- ✔ **File Size match.** Specifies a range of file sizes to match. If set to 0%, the two print jobs must be exactly the same size.

- ✔ **Job History.** QView stores in memory who printed which job for a specific amount of time after a job arrives in the print queue. This option specifies for how much time QView stores this information.

- ✔ **Manual Delete.** Enables you to turn off the `are you sure` message displayed when a print job is deleted. (No message appears if the print job is deleted automatically.)

System Preferences

QView enables you to edit the data associated with a print job. The System Preferences dialog box (see fig. 17.8) enables you to specify which text editor to use while editing a print job. The default editor is EDIT.COM, which comes as part of DOS 5. If you are using DOS 3.3, you must change the editor program.

When the editor is loaded, QView removes most of itself from memory to allow the editor space to work. QView can swap itself to EMS, XMS, or disk depending on which type of memory is available and the options specified in the System Preferences dialog box.

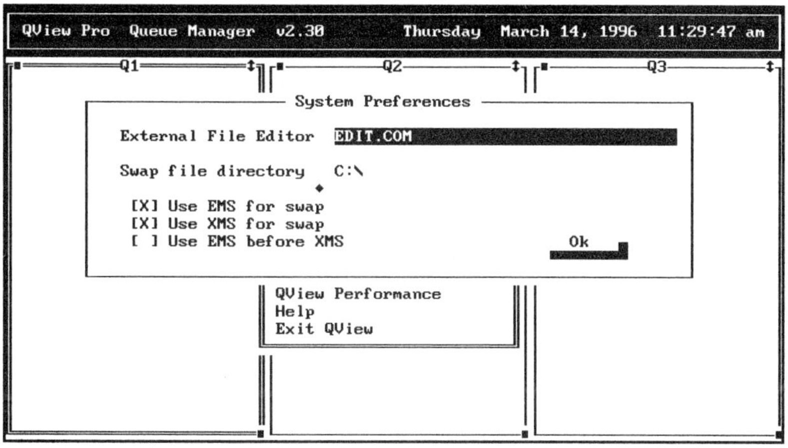

Figure 17.8
The System Preferences dialog box.

Display Format

QView can display several different fields in each window. You can use the Display Options dialog box to specify a variety of information related to how information is displayed (see fig. 17.9). In the width field, for example, you can specify how many characters wide a column should be.

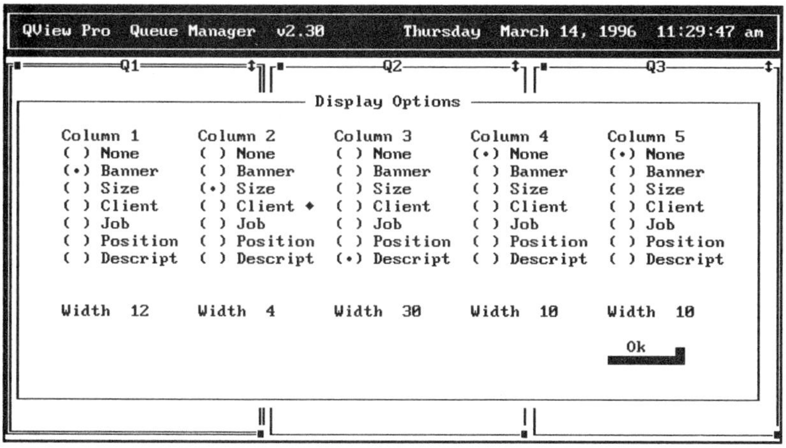

Figure 17.9
The Display Options dialog box.

Saving Settings

QView can save and restore any configuration. Select Save Settings from the main menu to save the current configuration. The default file name is QVIEW.CFG, but you can use any file name.

When QView starts, it searches automatically for a configuration file—either the default configuration file QVIEW.CFG, or a configuration file that you specify at the command line. If you provide the full path and file name to a configuration file, that configuration is used. When loading QView, you may specify the configuration file from the command prompt as shown in the following example:

qview c:\stuff\othrview.cfg

If you do not specify a configuration file at the command line, QView checks the current directory and the search path for the file QVIEW.CFG. If QView finds QVIEW.CFG, QView uses QVIEW.CFG to load the configuration preferences specified in QVIEW.CFG.

QView Performance

You can view QView's performance by choosing the QView Performance option from the main menu. The QView performance information screen shown in figure 17.10 opens.

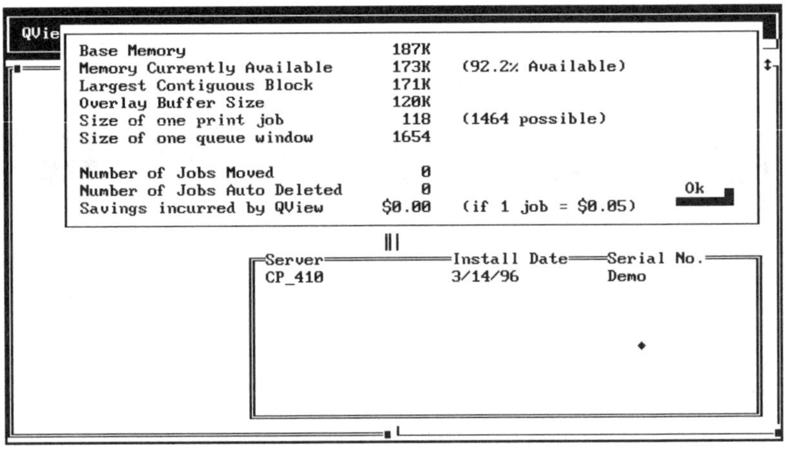

Figure 17.10 The QView performance information screen.

Installing and Using the Print Server

The SDLPD subdirectory of SECRDESN on the CD contains print server software (SDLPCON.NLM). The version on the CD is a restricted version in that it expires after a limited amount of time.

To use this print server software, copy the related files to the file server, then type **LOAD SDLPCON** at the file server console and press Enter. The Options menu shown in figure 17.11 opens. From the Options menu choose Install, and follow the prompts to install the print server.

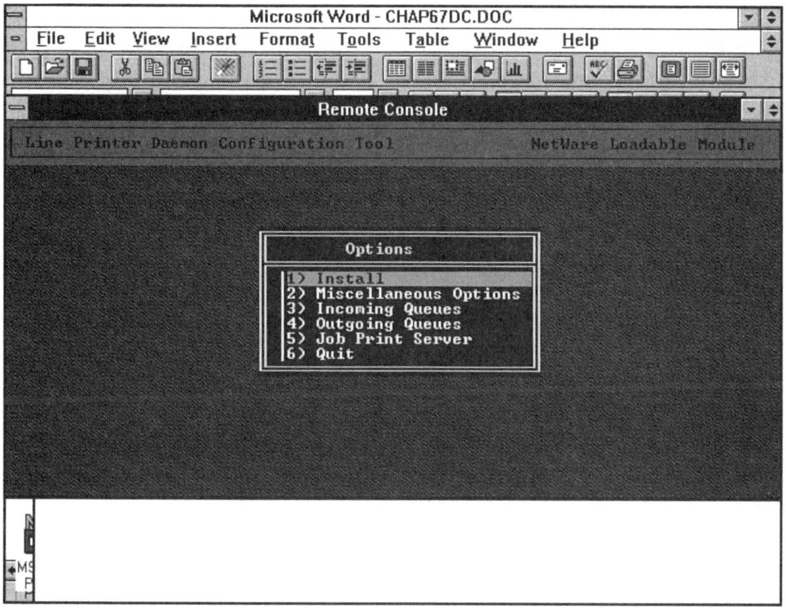

Figure 17.11 The Options menu.

From the Options menu, you can choose to look at incoming and outgoing print queues, print job information, and other miscellaneous information. To view miscellaneous information, choose Miscellaneous Options to open the Miscellaneous Options menu (see fig. 17.12).

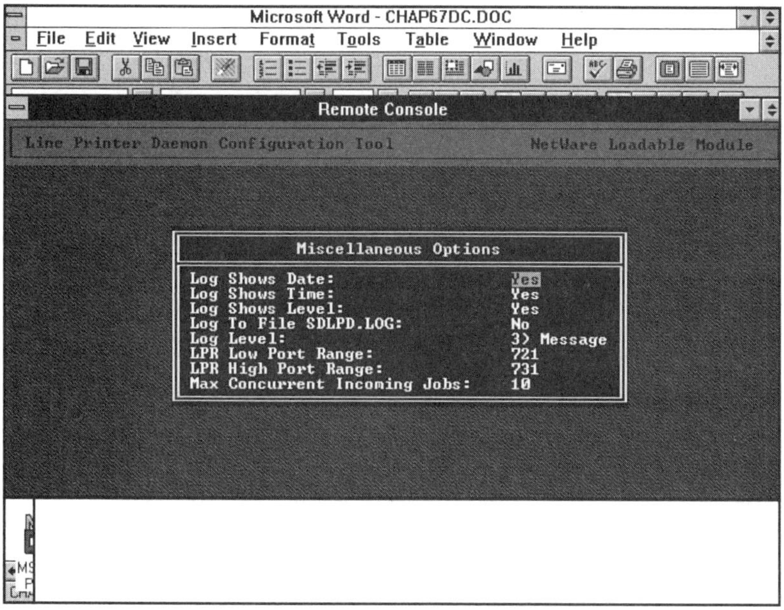

Figure 17.12 The Miscellaneous Options dialog box.

This print server software is very similar to many other print server software products including Novell's; therefore, you should be able to work your way through it easily to obtain an understanding of how it works.

CHILAGA
FRANCIA
NORVMBEGA
MARATA
CVLIACAN
CALICVAS
CAPASCHI
HISPANIA NOVA
TOVA
CVBA
MAR DEL
SVR, quod
Circulus Equinoctialis
CHILI
ICAE SIVE
ORBIS, NO
ESCRIPTIO.
Archipelago del C.

18

CHAPTER

TAC_SYS

The TAC_SYS directory on the CD contains demonstration software for a product called SCSI Shuttle. *SCSI Shuttle* enables you to use up to two CD-ROM drives on your NetWare file server. If you enter an *activation code* (a code the product's manufacturer provides only if you register this product) when prompted during installation, however, you will be unable to run SCSI Shuttle.

SCSI Shuttle was developed by TAC Systems. For more information about SCSI Shuttle or to register or purchase the SCSI Shuttle software, call TAC Systems at (205) 721-1976, or e-mail TAC at sales@tacsys.com.

Note Some of the information contained in this chapter is taken from the online documentation provided with the SCSI Shuttle software on the CD. Minor editing and format changes have been made to enable you to read the information more easily, as well as to make the text fit the format of this chapter. The figures in this chapter are screen shots of the software prepared by the author.

The TAC Systems SCSI Shuttle for NetWare is a NetWare Loadable Module (NLM) that allows access to ISO-9660, ISO-9660 with Apple Extensions, High Sierra, or HFS (Macintosh) CD-ROM drives across a Novell NetWare network. This access is provided through NetWare's standard file system architecture, which enables all the CD-ROM disks to be mounted as a single NetWare volume or as individual volumes. These volumes then can be accessed by any workstation on the network through NetWare's standard mapping commands.

Generally, system administrators place CD-ROM drives on a network to allow any interested user access to the data. If restricted access is necessary, however, the software allows the assignment of group access rights to each CD-ROM drive.

The SCSI Shuttle for NetWare is comprised of the following modules, the last three of which are optional:

- ✔ **TACSYS.DSK.** TACSYS.DSK is the main driver for the SCSI Shuttle system. It is required for the operation of the remaining modules in this list.
- ✔ **TACCDR.DSK.** TACCDR.DSK is the main driver for the CD-ROM drives, giving NetWare the capability to identify and mount CD-ROM disks.
- ✔ **TACCFG.NLM.** TACCFG.NLM is used to configure CD-ROM disks for use on the network as well as display information to the network administrator on the status of each CD-ROM drive.
- ✔ **TACOPT.DSK.** TACOPT.DSK is the driver for the Hitachi 2GB Optical drive.
- ✔ **TACAUTO.NLM.** TACAUTO.NLM is used to automatically configure CD-ROM disks. You can use TACAUTO.NLM to update a set of disks on a regular basis.
- ✔ **TACSTAT.NLM.** TACSTAT.NLM is used for usage statistics and license metering.

The following sections in this chapter discuss the SCSI Shuttle software and how to install and use it.

Installing SCSI Shuttle

The SCSI Shuttle software is installed on your NetWare file server into the SYS:SYSTEM directory. Because this is a demonstration version of the software that you might want to remove later, consider backing up your SYSTEM directory before installing SCSI Shuttle. You can remove SCSI Shuttle later simply by restoring the backup.

To install SCSI Shuttle, complete the following steps:

1. Open a DOS screen in Windows, or close Windows and run the software from the DOS prompt.

2. Change your default directory to the drive letter that represents the CD-ROM drive, making certain the default directory includes the TAC_SYS\SCSIDEMO directory.

3. Type **INSTALL** and press Enter.

4. When the initial screen opens, read it and choose OK to continue (see fig. 18.1).

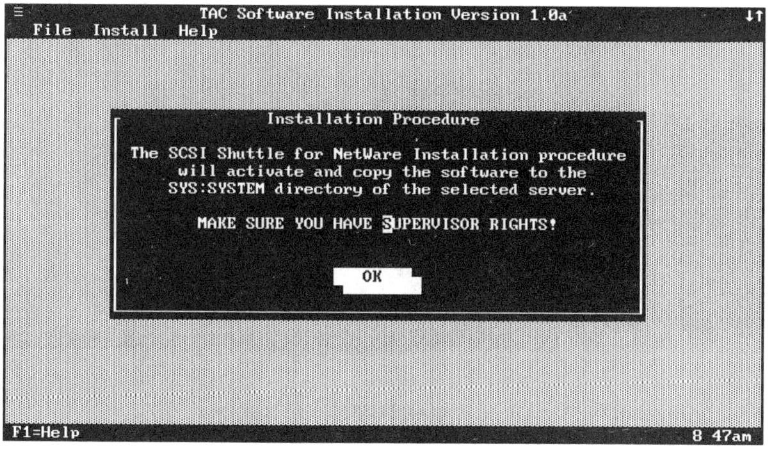

Figure 18.1
The Installation Procedure screen.

5. When the SCSI Shuttle Base Modules dialog box opens, choose the file server into which to install the SCSI Shuttle software demo, then choose OK (see fig. 18.2).

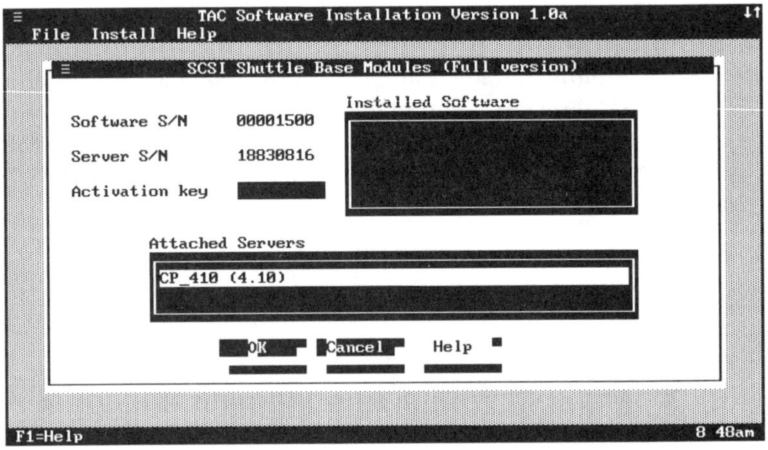

Figure 18.2
The SCSI Shuttle Base Modules dialog box.

6. When the Verifying Options dialog box opens, choose Install (see fig. 18.3).

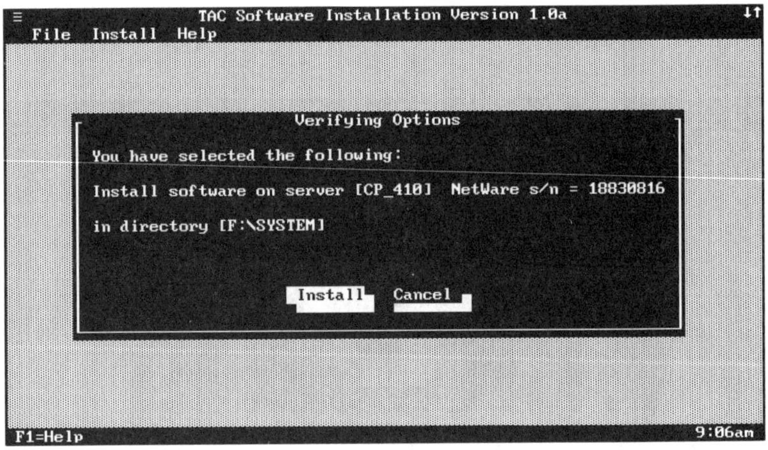

Figure 18.3
The Verifying Options dialog box.

7. When the Installation is Complete dialog box opens, choose OK.

Loading the SCSI Shuttle Demonstration Software

After you install the SCSI Shuttle demonstration software, you can run the software on the file server. First, however, you must complete the following steps:

1. Ensure that the following NetWare support modules are available in the SYS:SYSTEM subdirectory for NetWare 3.11 and 3.12:

AFTER311.NLM v4.10a

A3112.NLM v4.10a

CLIB.NLM v3.12h

NWSNUT.NLM v4.10g

STREAMS.NLM v3.12

For NetWare 4.*x*, no additional modules are needed.

2. Switch to the file server console to complete the remaining steps.

To run the SCSI Shuttle demonstration software, complete the following steps:

1. Ensure that any necessary SCSI adapter drivers are loaded. Examples of such drivers are AHA1540.DSK, AIC7770.DSK, and BT31X.DSK.

2. Ensure that the module ASPITRAN.DSK or BTASPI.DSK, or an equivalent ASPI manager, is loaded. You can verify that the module is loaded by entering the NetWare console command modules.

3. Type the command **LOAD TACCFG** to autoload any necessary modules. Next, complete the following tasks:

   a. Highlight Manage Volumes and press Enter. A list of converted CD-ROMs appears. If none have been converted, an empty box appears.

   b. Press Ins to open a list of CD-ROM drives attached to the server.

   c. Highlight the desired drive or drives and press Enter.

   d. A window opens with the Volume ID and other data. If the you want to edit the Volume ID, you may do so at this time.

   e. Press Esc and answer YES to begin configuring the CD-ROM for use.

   f. The program asks if you want to mount the CD-ROM at this time. Answer YES.

   Repeat steps 3a through 3f for each CD-ROM disk installed in the system.

4. When all the CD-ROMs are configured, switch to the console screen, type **MOUNT ALL**, and press Enter to mount all configured CD volumes.

When all the CD-ROM volumes are mounted, users can begin mapping their local workstation drive letters to these volumes.

After the software is initially installed, place the LOAD TACCFG and MOUNT ALL commands in the AUTOEXEC.NCF file. Adding these commands ensures the

TACCFG NLM is loaded each time the server is brought up, and that all volumes are mounted.

You can configure the CD-ROM drive when the required NLMs are loaded.

Configuring the CD-ROM Drive

Configuration for all the CD-ROM drives and CD-ROM is performed through the TACCFG.NLM module. This module configures each CD-ROM and displays the status of each CD-ROM drive.

Each CD-ROM disk to be accessed through the server must be configured using TACCFG.NLM prior to being mounted by NetWare. You need to configure the CD-ROM disk only once. You cannot configure the same disk more than once: each disk must be unique within that server. When configured, the CD-ROM can be mounted, dismounted, or moved to another CD-ROM drive on the same file server without being reconfigured.

To configure the CD-ROM, complete the following steps:

1. At the file server console screen prompt, type **LOAD TACCFG**, then press Enter.

   After the software is initially installed, you might want to place the preceding load statement in the AUTOEXEC.NCF file.

   When the NLM is loaded, a standard NetWare user interface screen containing an Available Options menu opens. The following menu options are available from the Available Options menu:

   - ✔ **Auto-Configure Titles.** Auto-Configure Titles is an optional module not shipped with SCSI Shuttle. It is used to set up SET NAMES that enable an automatic re-conversion of all the CD-ROMs in the set when they are replaced. For use with subscription CD-ROMs.

   - ✔ **Display Status.** Opens the Display Status window, which lists each CD-ROM unit managed and its status. The Display Status window is used for information purposes and mounting and dismounting of the CD-ROMs only. Press Esc to return to the TACCFG Available Options menu. The TACCFG now has the capability to mount and dismount the CD-ROM for any of the drives listed in the Display Status window.

   - ✔ **Manage Volumes.** The Manage Volumes option enables you to configure new CD-ROM disks (titles) and deletes old volumes. When selected from the Options menu, a list of currently configured CD-ROM titles appears. The appearance of volume names in this list does not imply that any or all of them are mounted, only that these volumes have been configured. If no names appear, no volumes have been configured.

- ✔ **Statistics.** Statistics is an optional module that allows for user access statistics and CD-ROM license metering.

2. To select an option, use the arrow keys to highlight the desired entry, and press Enter.

   In addition to the options on the Available Options menu, which have just been listed and described, TACCFG also responds to the normal Alt+Esc and Shift+Esc NetWare key sequences. For more information on these key sequences, refer to your NetWare documentation.

   When you choose the Display Status option, the following information about each CD-ROM drive appears:

   - ✔ **DEVICE NAME.** The actual device name as returned by the CD-ROM drive to the driver.

   - ✔ **HOST ADAPTER.** Identifies the host adapter to which the CD-ROM drive is attached. Normally the assignment of host adapter numbers is governed by the sequence in which the host adapter drivers are loaded in the STARTUP.NCF (or AUTOEXEC.NCF) file, and are not related to slot numbers (for EISA servers) or port addresses (ISA servers).

Note

All host adapter numbering begins with number zero (0) for the first adapter, as in the following sample STARTUP.NCF file:

```
LOAD AHA1740 slot=1 (HA #0)
LOAD AHA1740 slot=5 (HA #1)
LOAD AHA1740 slot=3 (HA #2)
LOAD AIC7770 slot=7 (HA #3 and #4)
```

This example assumes the adapter in slot 7 is an AHA-274xAT (twin) adapter.

- ✔ **SCSI ID.** The SCSI ID assigned to the drive either by jumpers or DIP switches on the drive itself. Normally SCSI IDs of only 0 to 6 are assigned. The SCSI ID of 7 usually is reserved for the host adapter.

- ✔ **MOUNTED=['Y' or 'N'].** If a configured CD-ROM disk is mounted and accessible as a NetWare volume, "Y" is displayed, otherwise "N" is displayed.

- **VOL:[volume_name].** If a configured CD-ROM disk is installed in the unit, its volume label appears as the volume name. Otherwise, a <<NO MEDIA>> message appears in place of the volume name. To display a prompt to either mount or dismount a volume, go to DISPLAY STATUS, select a CD-ROM volume, then press Enter. If the volume is not mounted, the mount box is displayed. If the volume already is mounted, the dismount box is displayed. If you select a drive that shows <<NO MEDIA>> (no volume has been converted for the CD-ROM in the drive), pressing Enter will do nothing.

When you choose the volume option, you can add (configure) CD-ROMs as volumes. To add a volume, follow the instructions and information provided in the following paragraphs.

To mount a CD-ROM disk as a volume, it must first be configured using the ADD option. To configure a CD-ROM disk, complete the following steps:

1. Press Ins while the Volumes Configured window is in view to open another window similar to the Display Status window. This window contains a list of all known CD-ROM drives.

2. Press Enter if you want to convert the CD-ROMs one at a time. Or, use the arrow keys to highlight and the F5 key to mark or unmark one or more of the drives, then press Enter to convert multiple CD-ROMs. If you choose to mark the CD-ROM drives, you are asked if you want to process the CD-ROMs as individual volumes or as one large NetWare volume. Choose either Individual Volumes or One Large NetWare Volume.

   - **Individual Volumes.** The CD-ROMs will appear as standard volumes. Workstations will map one drive letter per CD-ROM.

   - **One Large NetWare Volume.** The CD-ROMs will be seen as one large volume. Workstations will map one drive letter per multiple CD-ROM Volume. A few minor restrictions apply to this new method of accessing CD-ROM titles. These restrictions do not apply, however, if you use the software in the traditional single volume per CD manner.

3. After all the CD-ROMs have been converted with TACCFG, the CD disks must remain in the same drive. Because a large volume spans several disks, the SCSI unit numbers are locked in.

Note

Only standard ISO9660 or High Sierra formats are supported.

A large volume must consist of CD-ROMs of the same format. In other words, if seven CD-ROMs are being mounted as one volume, all seven discs must be either ISO9660 or HighSierra. The formats cannot be mixed.

Individual CD-ROM volumes and multiple CD-ROM volumes can exist on the same server.

Warning A large volume must consist of discs of the same format. The CD-ROMs must remain in the same drive in which they are converted.

4. A small window appears with the volume name, owner name, group name, set name, and name spaces in an edit box. If necessary, edit these items as explained in the following list:

   ✔ **Volume Name.** The volume label as it appears on the CD-ROM disk itself. The default label might be sufficient. If not, you can edit this field.

   The volume label is the volume name that NetWare recognizes for all subsequent mount/dismount commands. Be aware that the volume label you choose cannot be blank nor be the same as any other volume label that might be mounted later (such as magneto optical cartridges or other hard drives).

   ✔ **Owner Name.** The default owner name is Supervisor. This option is rarely (if ever) used. Like group name, however, this field can be edited. Again, the user name placed here must be established already within NetWare.

   ✔ **Group Name.** The default group name is Everyone, which allows all network users access to the volume. If the volume requires security, however, you can choose another group name. Any group name must have been previously defined.

Note The Everyone group name is not automatically created when you install NetWare 4.*x*. Normally, you should create this group from the file server; however, it can be created anywhere within NDS.

   ✔ **Set Name.** Enables the grouping of CD-ROM volumes into sets. This feature is valid only if you plan to use the auto-configuration module, which automatically re-converts the CD-ROM volumes in the set when they are replaced. Typically, this is a useful tool for those who have subscription services that replace the CD-ROMs on a weekly or monthly basis.

   ✔ **Name Spaces.** Enables support of either plain ISO-9660 or ISO-9660 with Apple Extensions CD-ROMs in name spaces other than DOS. Currently, only the Mac name space is supported; however, future versions will support additional name spaces.

Note TACCFG now creates a DEFAULT.CFG file in the \SYSTEM\CD_ROM directory. This default file contains a default owner, group, and set name. DEFAULT.CFG is created the first time any CD is converted, and the values contained within the DEFAULT.CFG file change based on the last CD converted.

5. Press Esc to exit this screen.

6. If you want to proceed with the configuration process, answer YES to the `Configure?` prompt. If not, answer NO, and the NLM returns you to the drive listing window. If multiple CD-ROM drives are selected, the NLM proceeds to the next CD-ROM.

7. If you elected to configure the CD-ROM disk, a status window appears showing the progress of the conversion.

Note Depending on the size of the CD, several seconds might pass before the status display begins updating. During this delay, however, the activity LED on the drive (if one is available) indicates that the CD is being read. After a disk has been successfully analyzed, you are asked if you want to mount the CD-ROM.

Now that the CD-ROM is configured, if you return to the main menu and select Manage Volumes, the configured CD-ROM appears on the list of configured CD-ROMs.

After a CD-ROM has been configured, the volume name, owner name, group name, and set name can be edited through TACCFG as long as the volume is not currently mounted. To edit the volume's information, complete the following steps:

1. Highlight Manage Volumes, then press Enter.

2. Select the volume you want to edit, then press Enter.

3. Edit the data, then press Esc when finished.

4. Answer the verification prompt to verify the data you just edited.

   The new information is now recorded.

If the message `This volume is mounted. Data cannot be edited.` appears, dismount the volume first, then re-edit.

You also can delete a volume. To delete a previously configured volume from the network, complete the following steps:

1. From the Volumes Configured window, use the arrow keys to highlight the volume to be deleted, and press Del. The volume to be deleted cannot be mounted when you delete it. If it is mounted when you try to delete it, you will see an error message. If an error message appears, dismount the volume and try once again to delete it.

2. Confirm your desire to delete by answering either YES or NO to the `OK to Delete?` confirmation box.

CHILAGA
NORVMBEGA
MOCOSA
AVACAL
APALCHEN
CALICVAS
MARATA
CVLIACAN
ASTATLAN
TERLICHICHIMECHI
CAPASCHI
LA FLORIDA
HISPANIA NOVA
TOVA
XALISCO
TOPIRA
MEXICO
MECHVACAN
CVBA
HISPANIOLA
C. Camaron
MAR DEL SVR, quod
Circulus Æquinoctialis
240
250
260
270
280
290
In Peru
et PACIFICUM
Las farallones
CHARCAS
PARANA
CHILI
PATAGONES vel REGIO GIGANTVM
FRETVM MAGELLANICVM
Archipelago del C. delleado
Caribana
Paguana
Picora
ICAE SIVE
ORBIS, NO
SCRIPTIO.

19 CHAPTER

TRITICOM

The TRITICOM directory on the CD contains the MASTERMON subdirectory, which contains software called *MasteRMON,* Triticom's distributed LAN monitoring system. The version of MasteRMON on the CD includes built-in simulated Ethernet and Token-Ring RMON Probes. With this demo, you can experiment with all of MasteRMON's features, even if your PC is not connected to a network.

The DEMOPAK subdirectory in the TRITICOM directory contains demonstration software for additional Triticom programs. Instructions for installing and using the DOS-based demos of these programs follows the instructions for using the Windows MasteRMON demo.

Note Much of the information in this chapter is taken from the help and text files included on the CD. Some minor editing and format changes were made to keep the format of this chapter consistent with that of the other chapters in this book, and to enable you to read and follow the text more easily. The figures in this chapter and some of its text were provided by the author.

This chapter explains how to install the MasteRMON demonstration software. If you want more information about MasteRMON or to purchase the software, contact Triticom as follows:

Phone: (612) 937-0772 between 8:30 a.m. and 5:30 p.m. CST

FAX: (612) 937-1998

BBS: (612) 829-0135 (N-8-1, up to 14.4 Kbps baud)

CompuServe: GO TRITICOM or e-mail to account 74774,630

Internet: support@triticom.com
WWW: http://www.triticom.com

Installing MasteRMON

To install the MasteRMON software, change the default drive on your PC to the TRITICOM\MASTERMON directory on the CD. Then, complete the following steps:

1. Start Windows, and choose Run from the File menu.
2. Choose Browse, then search for the TRITICOM\MASTERMON directory on the CD.
3. From the TRITICOM\MASTERMON directory, choose INSTALL.EXE.
4. Choose Continue to start the installation process.
5. When prompted, provide the name of the directory into which you want the MasteRMON software installed, then choose Continue. You can accept the default directory by simply choosing Continue.
6. During installation of the files, a screen shows the progress of the installation process. Choose Cancel here if you need to stop the installation.
7. After all the files have been copied, you are prompted to enable the installation to create a set of icons and the program group into which they are placed (see fig. 19.1). Choose Create to continue, or change the name of the program group and then choose Create to continue.

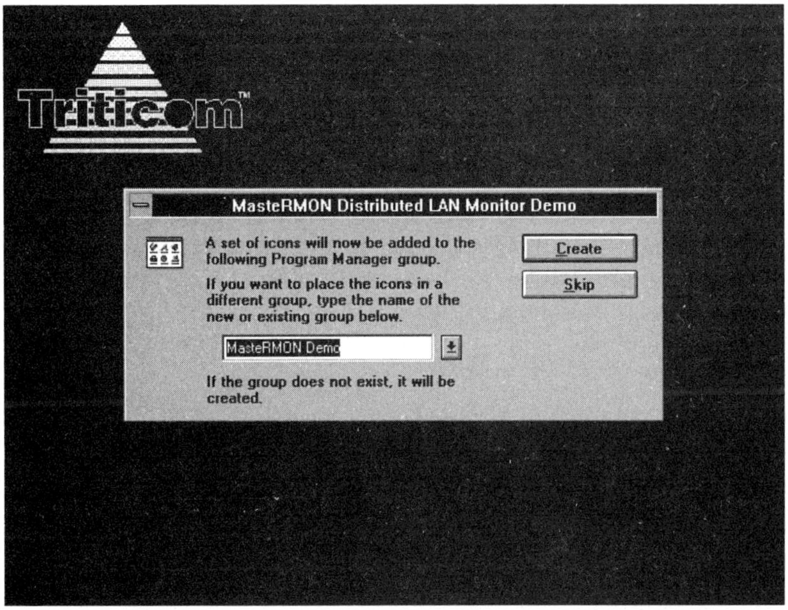

Figure 19.1
The MasteRMON Distributed LAN Monitor Demo window.

8. When `The installation is complete and the application has been properly setup.` message appears, choose OK to finish the installation process.

No changes are made to any INI files when the MasteRMON files are installed, and demo files are installed into a single directory that you can remove at any time. A single file may be copied to your WINDOWS\SYSTEM directory (CTL3DV2.DLL). This file is copied only if the file is not already present on your system, however, or if an older version is found.

To remove the demo, use Windows File Manager to delete the directory into which you installed the demo and remove the MasteRMON Demo program group.

Running the MasteRMON Demo

You can run the MasteRMON demo from your workstation. To run the demo, choose the MasteRMON Demo icon from the MasteRMON program group.

In its opening screen, Triticom provides the following information about running the demo:

> When you run the Demo, you should begin by opening a New network (File, New) from the Main Menu. The IP Address which you specify is unimportant—since no real LAN communications are taking place, any address will do (you don't even really have to specify an address at all—just clicking the OK button

will yield a perfectly reasonable demo). The only significance of the IP Address is its last digit—an odd number means that your simulated LAN is an Ethernet, an even number means it is a Token-Ring (thus, the address 2.3.4.5 is an Ethernet, while 2.3.4.4 is a Token-Ring).

Once you have "connected" to a simulated RMON Probe, you can experiment with MasteRMON's various display windows and features. Note that, when you exit MasteRMON, all of your current Monitoring Windows and Settings are saved in a .NET file—you may open this file again later and restore all settings and windows to the way you last left them. The one exception to this is "Names"—logical station names are built into the demo, and any changes you make to Names using "Settings, Names, Edit" are not saved when you exit the demo, as they would be with the "real" MasteRMON.

Note that the Demo has a fully operational help system, which also functions as an on-line manual. Be sure to consult it with any questions you may have, or simply browse through it to learn more about MasteRMON and its features.

The Demo allows for 3 simultaneous invocations of MasteRMON—thus you can monitor 3 simulated networks simultaneously from a single Windows station.

The MasteRMON window is then displayed. To start the demo, choose **O**pen from the **F**ile menu to open the Network Definition dialog box (see fig. 19.2). Then choose OK to continue past the information screen.

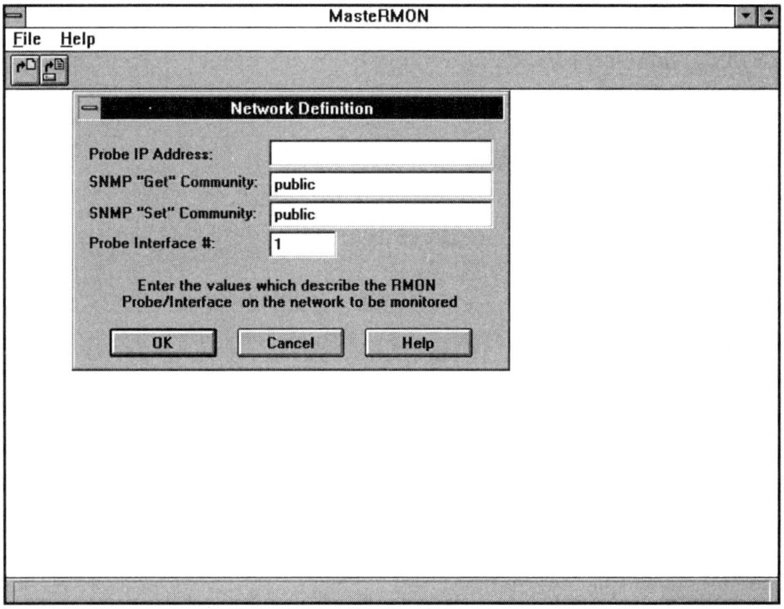

Figure 19.2
The Network Definition dialog box.

Enter a network number in the Network Definition dialog box (or leave it blank; because this is a demo, it does not matter). Choose OK to continue. The Probe Info dialog box opens.

In the Probe Info dialog box, you can choose a variety of options from any of the menus in the menu bar. Choose Graph from the Monitor menu, for example, to open the Graph Definition dialog box (see fig. 19.3). In this box you choose a statistic to graph, the time scale of the graph, and the type of graph lines.

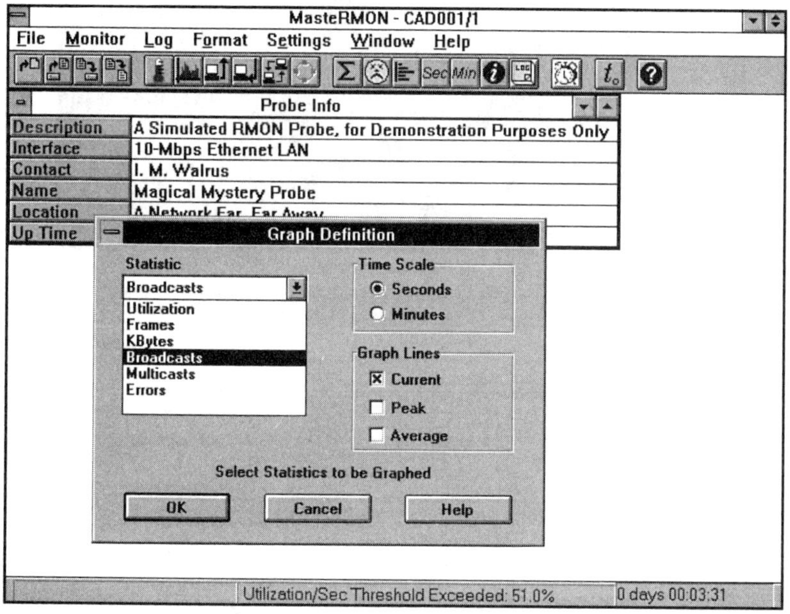

Figure 19.3
The Graph Definition dialog box.

In figure 19.3, Broadcasts is the choice of information to be graphed.

Next, make your choices of time scale (seconds or minutes) and graph lines (current, peak, or average). Then choose OK to display the graph. If you choose Utilization from the Graph Definition window, for example, a graph similar to that shown in figure 19.4 appears.

You can choose from many other options in the menu bar. If you choose Alarms from the Settings menu, for example, the General Alarms dialog box opens (see fig. 19.5), from which you can enable or disable alarms to sound when either of two conditions occur:

- ✔ Intruder Station
- ✔ Source=Broadcast Frames

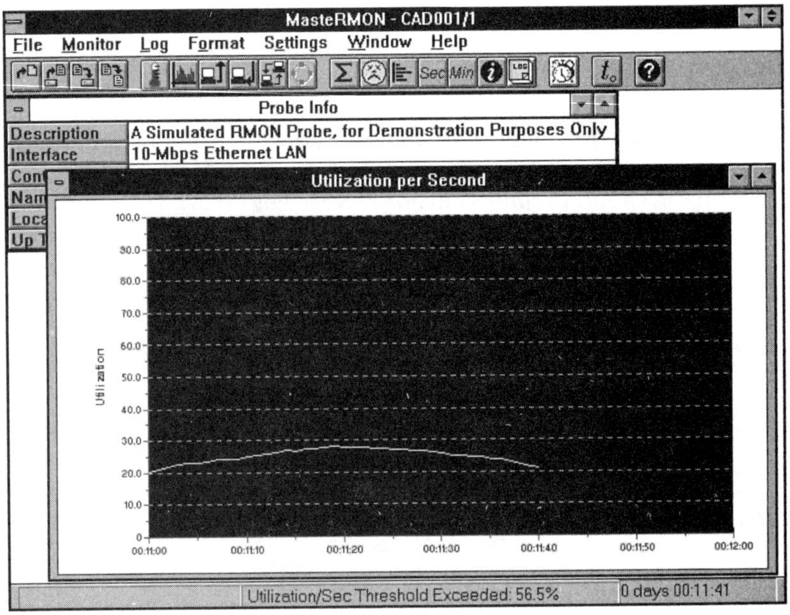

Figure 19.4 A Utilization graph.

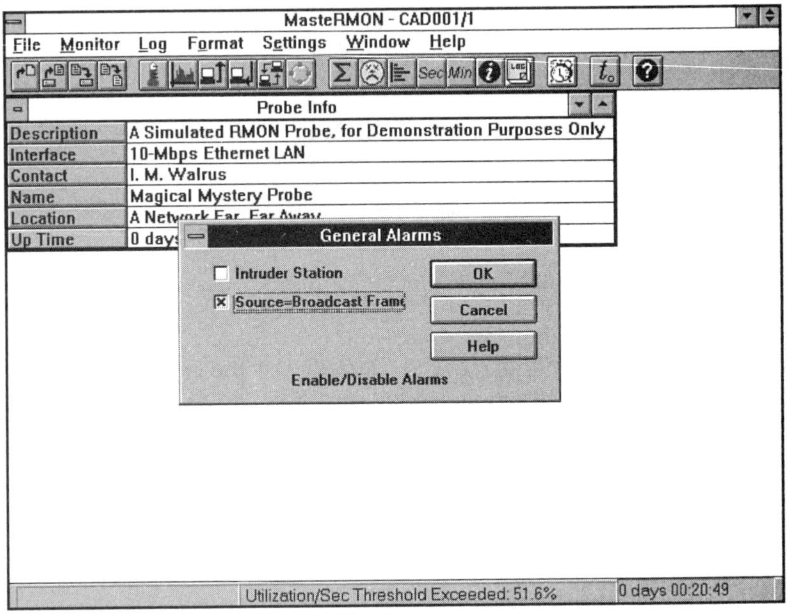

Figure 19.5 The General Alarms dialog box.

The best way to learn about the options in the MasteRMON utility is to experiment with them using the demo. This chapter has only provided brief discussions of what is available when using the MasteRMON software by Triticom.

Triticom also offers online help that explains each of the available options, as well as the features of this software. Press Shift+F1 to activate the mouse pointer for online help. Point the mouse toward a menu item and choose it to open the related Help screen. You also can choose the Help menu option to obtain more information. In addition, the windows that open when you choose the Help option often have Help options of their own.

Installing and Using the DEMOPAK Directory Demos

The DEMOPAK directory contains DOS-based demonstration versions of some of Triticom's products, including the DOS-based version of MasteRMON. To install these demos, change your default DOS directory to the TRITICOM\DEMOPAK directory on the CD, then type **DEMO** and press Enter. This procedure installs the software and walks you through the use of the demos. You also can choose to view information screens as you work through each demo.

The best way to learn about the demos is to work with them. Figures 19.6, 19.7, and 19.8, however, should give you an idea of the types of information and screens you can expect to see when you run these DOS-based demos.

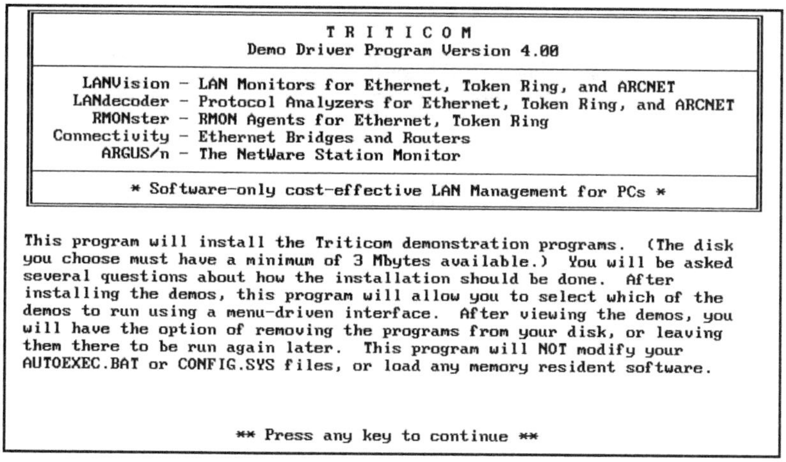

Figure 19.6
The Triticom main window listing available demos.

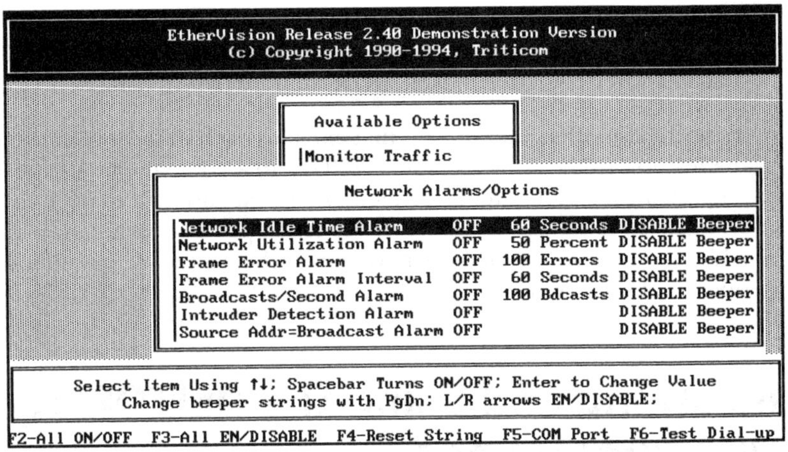

Figure 19.7 The Network Alarms/Options screen.

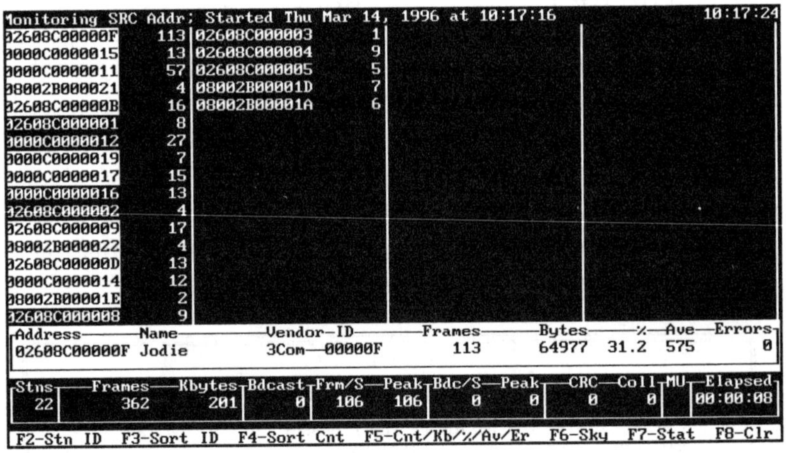

Figure 19.8 The Traffic Monitoring screen.

Tip

Run TDEMO.EXE from the installed directory to re-run the demos.

CHILAGA
NORVMBEGA
MOCOSA
TEAC
MARATA
CVLIACAN
AVACAL
CALICVAS
CAPASCHI
TERLICHICHI MECHI
HISPANIA NOVA
TOVA
LA FLORIDA
CVBA
MAR DEL SVR, quod
Circulus Aequinoctialis
240
250
260
270
280
290
PACIFICVM
CHARCAS
CHILI
PATAGONES, vel REGIO GIGANTVM
ICAE SIVE
ORBIS, NO
SCRIPTIO.
Archipelago del C. delleado

20

CHAPTER

VFX_TECH

The VFX_TECH directory contains the CNE Endeavor software. CNE Endeavor from VFX Technologies, Inc., is an interactive learning management system designed to provide users with complete control over their individual learning process.

CNE Endeavor's standard features include thousands of questions and answers organized into tests and categories, the capability to flag questions to ask often or never, tracking testing time, and reporting testing results. CNE Endeavor enhances these features by adding a unique and powerful feature called the *FocusArea*, which allows users to select questions based on a *QuestionHistory*. CNE Endeavor also offers the capability to facilitate research by providing cross references to many popular study guide textbooks.

Note Some of the information in this chapter has been adapted from the online documentation provided with this software on the CD.

This chapter provides a brief overview of CNE Endeavor. First, it explains how to run the installation software, then it provides a brief overview of the software.

VFX Technologies, Inc., is committed to providing quality software with reliable support. They provide several communication channels (e-mail, help lines, and so on), and they offer technical support through online and traditional avenues that provide users with an inexpensive and prompt way to answer questions quickly.

VFX Technologies doesn't charge for support, other than when normal user connection/time charges apply. Registered users receive priority and can expect immediate results. CNE Endeavor shareware users can use the following means to contact VFX Technologies for technical support or additional ordering information:

US Mail: VFX Technologies, Inc.
P.O. Box 80222
Valley Forge, PA 19484-0222

(610) 265-9222 ext. 3 (phone, registered users only)

Internet: vfxtech@ix.netcom.com
CompuServe: 70543,366 (VFX Technologies, Inc.)

If you contact VFX, you can request a fax response. Be sure to include your fax number, name, and CNE Endeavor serial number when you call.

Installing CNE Endeavor

Before you can install CNE Endeavor, you might need to unzip the VFXSETUP.EX_ file and related files. The VFXSETUP.EXE file must be located in the Windows directory before you can install CNE Endeavor, so if you have to unzip VFXSETUP.EX_, be sure to unzip it into the Windows directory.

You can use WinZip v5.6 to unzip these files, or you can try other versions of software to unzip these files if you do not have WinZip v5.6.

To install the CNE Endeavor software, complete the following steps:

1. Load Windows and choose **F**ile, **R**un from the Windows Program Manager. Then choose **B**rowse to find and select SETUP.EXE from the VFX_TECH\CNENDVOR directory on the CD. Then run this setup program.

2. When the CNE Endeavor Setup screen appears (see fig. 20.1), choose the directory where you want to install the software.

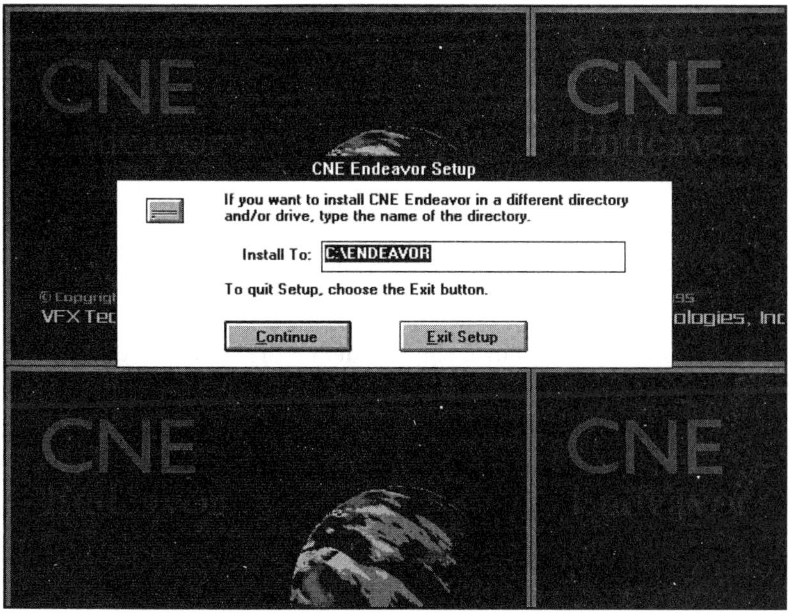

Figure 20.1
CNE Endeavor Setup screen.

3. Now, follow the prompts to install the CNE Endeavor software.

Understanding CNE Endeavor

CNE Endeavor is easy and intuitive. The Guide Maps provided should give you a good understanding of each component of the program and its basic operations. This verbal guide also serves as a guide to optimal results. Upon execution, the first screen to appear is the Control Panel.

Tip If installation of CNE Endeavor Windows properties are improper, a message appears regarding the missing ENDEAVOR.INI file. (Refer to the INIREAD.ME file for help.)

To use CNE Endeavor, complete the following steps:

1. From the Control Panel, select a test using the pull-down menu. After you select a test, all categories will be listed.

2. Select any number of categories, from one to all.

3. Check off the number of questions to ask.

4. Select both previously attempted and previously unattempted questions. First-time users cannot select Only Previously Attempted Questions.
5. Select all check boxes in the FocusArea.
6. Click on OK to exit the Control Panel.
7. When the Testing Screen appears, click on the Play button to start the test.

Refer to the Information Box for basic help, or the Help System for detailed information.

Testing can begin after you use the Control Panel to define the *criteria.* The Testing Screen contains all the menus and icons that give access to the entire CNE Endeavor environment.

QVIVIRA
TOLM.
TOTO
TEAC
MARATA.
CVLIACAN
ASTATLAN
HISPANIA NOVA
TERLICHICHI
MECHVACAN
LAZARO.
Los Volcanes
La Farfana
Los Mongos
MAR DEL SVR, quod
Circulus Æquinoctialis
210
220
230
240
250
260
270
PACIFICVM
Insulae Salomonis
Isabella
S. Nicolas
VINEA. Andre
A AVSTRA
S. SIVE
AGELLA
ICA HAC
TENVS IN
COGNITA
AMERICAE SIVE
NOVI ORBIS, NO
VA DESCRIPTIO.

Part 2

Appendixes

Part 2 is the last section in Volume 3 of this three-volume set. It consists of three appendixes which provide basic information about companies and vendors in the PC industry. It also provides a list of vendor NCI identification codes. The three appendixes included in Part 2, Volume 3, are as follows:

CHILAGA
NORVMBEGA
MOCOSA
TEAC.
MARATA.
CVLIACAN.
CALICVAS.
CAPASCHI.
TERLICHICHI MECHI.
HISPANIA NOVA
TOVA
CVBA
MAR DEL SVR, quod
et PACIFICVM
CHILE.
PATAGONES vel REGIO GIGANTVM
ICAE SIVE
ORBIS, NO
SCRIPTIO.

A

APPENDIX

Industry Directory

Following is a listing of several industry related companies and their contact information. Although this is by no means a listing of every company, it should prove to be a valuable reference on which you can build.

3COM
5400 Bayfront Plaza
Santa Clara, CA 95052
Phone: (800)638-3266
Phone: (408)764-5000
FAX: (408)764-5001
Products: Ethernet cards, bridges, routers, token ring cards

3M Data Storage Products Division
3M Center Building #223-5N-01
St. Paul, MN 55144
Phone: (612)736-1866
Products: Magnetic tape and disk media

Accton Technology
46750 Fremont Blvd. #104
Fremont, CA 94538
Phone: (800)926-9288
Phone: (510)226-9800
FAX: (510)226-9833
Products: Bridges, NICs, Hubs, management software

Accurite Technologies, Inc.
231 Charcot Ave.
San Jose, CA 95131
Phone: (408)433-1980
Products: Floppy disk diagnostic tests

Acer Technologies Corporation
401 Charcot Ave.
San Jose, CA 95131
Phone: (408)922-0333
Phone: (800)538-1542
BBS: (800)833-8241
Products: PC compatible systems

Acme Electric/Safe Power
20 Water Street
Cuba, NY 14727
Phone: (716)968-2400
Phone: (800)325-5848
Products: UPS and power conditioners

Adaptec
691 S. Milpitas Boulevard
Milpitas, CA 95035
Phone: (408)945-8600
Technical Support: (800)959-7274
Technical Support: (408)945-2550
Literature: (800)934-2766
BBS: (408)945-7727
Products: Disk controllers and SCSI HBAs

Addison-Wesley Publishing Co., Inc.
Route 128
Reading, MA 01867
Phone: (617)944-3700
Products: Books and technical publications

Adobe Systems, Inc.
1585 Charleston Road
Box 7900
Mountain View, CA 94039
Phone: (415)961-0911
Phone: (800)447-3577
Products: Graphics software

Advanced Digital Information Corporation
14737 NE 87th Street
Box 2996
Redmond, WA 98073-2966
Phone: (206)881-8004
Phone: (800)336-1233
FAX: (206)881-2296
BBS: (714)894-0893
Products: Tape backup systems

Advanced Logic Research (ALR)
9401 Jeronimo Street
Irvine, CA 92718
Phone: (800)444-4257
Phone: (714)581-6770
FAX: (714)581-9240
Technical Support: (714)458-1952
BBS: (714)458-6834
Products: PC compatible systems

Advanced Micro Devices (AMD)
901 Thompson Place
Box 3453
Sunnyvale, CA 94088
Phone: (408)732-2400
Products: CPU and math coprocessors

Aeronics, Inc.
12741 Research Blvd.
Suite #500
Austin, TX 78759
Phone: (512)258-2303
FAX: (512)258-4392
Products: SCSI terminators

Aldus Corporation
411 1st Avenue South
Seattle, WA 98104
Phone: (206)622-5500
Phone: (800)333-2538
Products: Desktop publishing and graphics software

AllMicro, Inc.
1250 Rogers Street
Suite D
Clearwater, FL 34616
Phone: (813)446-6660
Products: Data recovery software and diagnostics utils

Alloy Computer Products
165 Forest Street
Malborough, MA 01752
Phone: (800)544-7551
Phone: (508)481-8500
Technical Support: (508)486-0001
FAX: (508)481-7711
BBS: (508)460-8140
Products: Tape backup systems

Alpha Research Corporation
8200 Mopac Expressway North
Park North Building, #120
Austin, TX 78759
Phone: (512)345-6465
FAX: (512)345-6496
Products: Video/Disk controllers and motherboards

Altex Electronics, Inc.
300 Breesport
San Antonio, TX 78216
Phone: (800)531-5369
Phone: (512)349-8795
Products: Mail order electronics devices

Ambra Computer Corporation
3200 Beechleaf Court
Raleigh, NC 27604-1063
Phone: (919)713-1550
Phone: (800)25-AMBRA
FAX: (919)713-1599
Products: PC Compatible systems

Amdek Corporation
3471 N. First Street
San Jose, CA 95134
Phone: (800)722-6335
Phone: (408)473-1200
Technical Support: (408)435-2770
FAX: (408)922-5729
BBS: (408)922-4400
Products: Monitors

American Megatrends, Inc. (AMI)
6145-F Northbelt Parkway
Norcross, GA 30071
Phone: (800)828-9264
Phone: (404)263-8181
BBS: (404)246-8780
Products: BIOS and diagnostic software

American National Standards Institute
11 West 42nd Street
13th Floor
New York, NY 10036
Phone: (212)642-4900
Products: Standards committee

American Power Conversion
132 Fairgrounds Rd.
West Kingston, RI 02880
Phone: (800)800-4272
Phone: (401)789-5735
FAX: (401)789-3710
Products: Power protection equipment

AMP, Inc.
AMP Building
Harrisburg, PA 17105
Phone: (800)522-6752
Phone: (717)564-0100
FAX: (717)986-7575
Products: Computer cables, connectors, hubs, concentrators

Annabooks
11848 Bernardo Plaza Court
Suite 110
San Diego, CA 92128-2417
Phone: (800)642-1042
Phone: (619)673-0870
FAX: (619)673-1432
Products: Books and technical publications

Anthem Technology Systems (ATS)
1160 Ridder Park Drive
San Jose, CA 95131
Phone: (800)359-3580
Phone: (408)441-7177
FAX: (800)359-9877
Products: DAT drives and hard disks

Anvil Cases
15650 Salt Lake Avenue
Industry, CA 91745
Phone: (800)359-2684
Phone: (818)968-4100
Products: Equipment cases

AOX, Inc.
486 Totten Pond Road
Waltham, MA 02154
Phone: (800)726-0269
Phone: (617)890-4402
Products: Processor upgrade boards

Apple Computer, Inc.
20525 Mariani Avenue
Cupertino, CA 95014
Phone: (800)538-9696
Phone: (408)996-1010
Products: Macintosh computer systems

Archive Technology/Ardat, Inc.
1650 Sunflower Avenue
Costa Mesa, CA 92626
Phone: (800)537-2724
Phone: (714)641-1230
Products: Tape drives

Arco Electronics, Inc.
2750 N. 29th Ave.
Suite 316
Hollywood, CA 33020
Phone: (305)925-2688
FAX: (305)925-2889
BBS: (305)925-2791
Products: MCA IDE adapters

Areal Technology, Inc.
2075 Zanker Road
San Jose, CA 95131
Phone: (408)436-6800
Products: 3 1/2 hard drives

Arrow Electronics, Inc.
25 Hub Drive
Melville, NY 11747
Phone: (516)391-1300
Phone: (800)447-5270
Products: Peripherals distributor

Arrowfield International, Inc.
2822-C Walnut Ave.
Tustin, CA 92680
Phone: (714)669-0101
FAX: (714)669-0526
Products: Cabinets, drive brackets, rails, cable adapters

Artisoft
691 East River Road
Tucson, AZ 85704
Phone: (800)846-9726
Phone: (602)293-4000
Products: NICS, Com servers, print servers, hubs, and concentrators

Asante
404 Tasman Dr.
Sunnyvale, CA 94089
Phone: (800)662-9686
Phone: (408)752-8388
Fax: (408)734-4864
Products: NICs, hubs, concentrators, email software

AST Research, Inc.
16215 Alton Parkway
Irvine, CA 92713-9658
Phone: (800)876-4278
Phone: (714)727-4141
BBS: (714)727-4723
Products: PC compatible systems

Astec Standard Power
Division of Astec America, Inc.
401 Jones Road
Oceanside, CA 92054-1216
Phone: (619)757-1880
FAX: (619)439-4243
Products: Power supplies

AT&T
55 Corporate Drive
Bridgewater, NJ 08807
Phone: (800)247-1212
Phone: (404)446-4734
BBS: (201)769-6397
Products: PC compatible systems

AT&T National Parts Sales Center
2551 E. 40th Avenue
Denver, CO 80205
Phone: (800)222-7278
Products: Parts distribution

Attachmate
13231 S.E. 36th St.
Bellevue, CA 98006
Phone: (800)426-6283
Phone: (206)644-4010
FAX: (206)747-9924
Products: Mainframe gateway software

ATI Technologies, Inc.
33 Commerce Valley Drive East
Thornhill, ONT L3T7N6
Phone: (416)882-2600
Technical Support: (416)882-2626
FAX: (416)882-2620
BBS: (416)764-9404
Products: Video controllers and chips

Autodesk, Inc.
2320 Marinship Way
Sausalito, CA 94965
Phone: (800)445-5415
Phone: (415)332-2344
Products: AutoCAD software

Banyan Systems
120 Flanders Rd.
Westboro, MA 01581
Phone: (800)828-2404
Phone: (508)898-1000
Fax: (508)898-1755
Products: NOS, bridges, comm/print servers, routers, misc software

Beame & Whiteside Software
3883 Ruffin Rd.
P.O. Box 8130
Dundas, Ont. L9H3E7
Phone: (905)765-0822
FAX: (416)765-0815
Products: TCP/IP Software

Beckman Industrial
3883 Ruffin Road
San Diego, CA 92123
Phone: (619)495-3200
Phone: (800)854-2708
Products: Diagnostic test equipment

Belden Wire and Cable
P.O. Box 1980
Richmond, IN 47375
Phone: (317)983-5200
Phone: (800)235-3361
Products: Cabling and wire products

Berkshire Products, Inc.
2180 Pleasant Hill Road
Suite A-5185
Duluth, GA 30136-4663
Phone: (404)271-0088
FAX: (404)932-0082
Products: Diagnostic equipment

Best Power Technology, Inc.
P.O. Box 280
Necedah, WI 54646
Phone: (608)565-7200
Phone: (800)356-5794
FAX: (608)565-2221
Products: Power protection equipment

Bitstream, Inc.
215 1st Street
Cambridge, MA 02142
Phone: (800)522-3668
Phone: (617)497-6222
Products: Font software and fonts

Black Box Corporation
P.O. Box 12800
Pittsburgh, PA 15241
Phone: (412)746-5530
Products: Wide variety of cables, connectors, and custom switch boxes

Boca Research, Inc.
6413 Congress Avenue
Boca Raton, FL 33487-2841
Phone: (407)997-6227
Technical Support: (407)241-8088
FAX: (407)997-0918
BBS: (407)241-1601
Products: Modems and adapters

Bondwell Industrial Company, Inc.
47485 Seabridge Drive
Fremont, CA 94538
Phone: (415)490-4300
Products: Laptops

Borland International
1800 Green Hills Road
Scotts Valley, CA 95066
Phone: (800)331-0877
Phone: (408)439-1411
Technical Support: (408)438-8400
FAX: (408)439-9344
BBS: (408)431-5096
Products: Quattro Pro, dBASE, and Paradox

Boston Computer Exchange
55 Temple Place
Boston, MA 02111
Phone: (617)542-4414
Products: PC compatible systems broker

Bureau of Electronic Publishing
141 New Road
Parsippany, NJ 07054
Phone: (800)828-4766
Phone: (201)808-2700
Products: Distribute and produce CD-ROMs

Bytex
Four Technology Dr.
Westborough, MA 01581-1760
Phone: (800)227-1145
Phone: (508)366-8000
Fax: (508) 366-0344
Products: Hubs, concentrators, testing equipment

C. Itoh Electronics, Inc.
19300 S. Hamilton Avenue
Box 9116
Torrance, CA 90508
Phone: (213)327-9100
Products: Printers and peripherals

Cable Connection
557 Salmar Avenue
Suite B
Campbell, CA 95008
Phone: (408)379-9224
Products: Cables, connectors, and switch boxes

Cables To Go
26 W. Nottingham
Suite 200
Dayton, OH 45405
Phone: (800)826-7904
Phone: (513)275-0886
Products: Cables, connectors, and switch boxes

Cabletron Systems
35 Industrial Way, P.O. Box 5005
Rochester, NH 03878-0505
Phone: (603)332-9400
Fax: (603)332-4616
Products: NICs, bridges, hubs, concentrators

Cache Computers, Inc.
46600 Landing Parkway
Fremont, CA 94538
Phone: (510)266-9922
Products: Motherboards

Cal-Abco
6041 Variel Avenue
Woodland Hills, CA 91367
Phone: (800)669-2226
Phone: (818)704-7733
Products: Computer systems and peripherals

Canon USA, Inc.
One Canon Plaza
Lake Success, NY 11042
Phone: (800)221-3333
Phone: (516)488-6700
FAX: (516)354-5805
BBS: (516)488-6528
Products: Printers, drives, and video equipment

Castelle
3255-3 Scott Blvd.
Santa Clara, CA 95054
Phone: (800)359-7654
Phone: (408)496-0474
Fax: (408)496-0502
Products: fax servers, print servers

Central Point Software, Inc.
15220 NW Greenbrier Parkway
Beaverton, OR 97006-9937
Phone: (800)445-4208
Phone: (503)690-8090
FAX: (503)690-8083
BBS: (503)690-6650
Products: Tape backup, remote access, and virus software

Cherry Electrical Products
3600 Sunset Avenue
Waukegan, IL 60087
Phone: (708)662-9200
Products: IBM compatible keyboards

Cheyenne Software
55 Bryant Ave.
Roslyn, NY 11576
Phone: (800)243-9462
Phone: (516)484-5110
Fax: (516)484-3446
Products: Tape backup, fax, security and management software

Chicago Case Company
4446 S. Ashland Avenue
Chicago, IL 60609
Phone: (312)927-1600
Products: Equipment travel cases

Chinon America, Inc.
660 Maple Avenue
Torrance, CA 90503
Phone: (800)441-0222
Phone: (213)533-0274
Products: Floppy and CD-ROM devices

Chips & Technologies, Inc.
3050 Zanker Road
San Jose, CA 95134
Phone: (800)944-6284
Phone: (408)434-0600
Products: Motherboard chips

Ci Design Company
1711 Langley Avenue
Irvine, CA 92714
Phone: (714)261-5524
Products: Drive mounting kits

Cipher Data Products, Inc.
10101 Old Grove Road
San Diego, CA 92131
Phone: (800)424-7437
Phone: (619)578-9100
Products: Tape backup products

Ciprico, Inc.
2955 Xenium Lane
Minneapolis, MN 55441
Phone: (800)727-4669
Phone: (612)559-2034
Products: SCSI HBAs

Citizen America Corporation
2450 Broadway
Suite 600
Santa Monica, CA 90404
Phone: (800)556-1234
Phone: (310)453-0614
FAX: (310)453-2814
BBS: (310)453-7564
Products: Printers and floppy disk drives

CMD Technology, Inc.
1 Vanderbilt
Irvine, CA 92718
Phone: (800)426-3832
Phone: (714)454-0800
FAX: (714)455-1656
Products: Various disk drive adapters

CMS Enhancements, Inc.
2722 Michelson Drive
Irvine, CA 92715
Phone: (714)222-6000
Products: Hard drives and peripherals

Colorado Memory Systems, Inc.
800 S. Taft Avenue
Loveland, CO 80537
Phone: (800)346-9881
Phone: (303)669-8000
FAX: (303)667-0997
BBS: (303)635-0650
Products: Tape backup systems

Columbia Data Products
1070B Rainer Drive
Altamonte Springs, FL 32714
Phone: (407)869-6700
FAX: (407)862-4725
BBS: (407)862-4724
Products: SCSI drivers

Comb
720 Anderson Avenue
Street Cloud, MN 56372
Phone: (800)328-0609
Phone: (612)654-4800
Products: Distributes discontinued products

Compaq Computer Corporation
20555 State Hwy.
Suite 249
Houston, TX 77070
Phone: (800)231-0900
Phone: (713)370-0670
Technical Support: (800)345-1518
BBS: (713)374-1518
Products: PC compatible systems

CompuServe Information Service (CIS)
5000 Arlington Centre Boulevard
Columbus, OH 43220
Phone: (800)848-8199
Phone: (614)457-8600
Products: Online information service

Computer Reseller News Magazine
CMP Publications, Inc.
600 Community Drive
Manhasset, NY 11030-3875
Phone: (516)562-5000
Phone: (516)562-5468
Products: Magazine intended for resellers

Computer Retail Week Magazine
CMP Publications, Inc.
600 Community Drive
Manhasset, NY 11030-3875
Phone: (516)562-5000
Phone: (516)562-5468
Products: Industry news trade magazine

Connector Resources Unlimited (CRU)
1005 Ames Avenue
Milpitas, CA 95035
Phone: (408)942-9077
Products: A wide variety of mounting kits and disk enclosures

Conner Peripherals, Inc.
3081 Zanker Road
San Jose, CA 95134
Phone: (800)275-4642
Phone: (408)456-4500
Technical Support: (408)456-3388
FAX: (408)456-4501
FAXback : (800)4CONNER(426-6637)
BBS: (408)456-4415
Products: Hard disks

Core International, Inc.
7171 North Federal Hwy.
Boca Raton, FL 33487
Phone: (407)997-6055
BBS: (407)241-2929
Products: Hard disk distributor

Corel Systems, Inc.
1600 Carling Avenue
Ottawa, ONT. K1Z8R7
Phone: (613)728-8200
Phone: (800)836-7874
FAX: (613)728-9790
BBS: (613)728-4752
Products: CorelDRAW

Creative Labs, Inc.
2050 Duane Avenue
Santa Clara, CA 95054
Phone: (408)428-6600
Phone: (800)544-6146
Technical Support: (408)428-6622
FAX: (408)428-6011
BBS: (408)428-6660
Products: Sound Blaster sound card

CS Electronics
1342 Bell Avenue
Tustin, CA 92680
Phone: (714)259-9100
FAX: (714)259-0911
Products: High quality disk cabling

Cumulus Corporation
23500 Mercantile Road
Cleveland, OH 44120
Phone: (216)464-2211
BBS: (216)464-3019
Products: Clone processor upgrades

Curtis Manufacturing Co., Inc.
30 Fitzgerald Drive
Jaffrey, NH 03452
Phone: (603)532-4123
Phone: (800)548-4900
Products: Miscellaneous computer accessories

Cyrix Corporation
2703 N. Central Expressway
Richardson, TX 75080
Phone: (800)327-6284
Phone: (214)234-8387
FAX: (214)699-9857
Products: Processors

Dak Industries, Inc.
8200 Remmet Avenue
Canoga Park, CA 91304
Phone: (800)325-0800
Phone: (818)888-8220
BBS: (818)715-7153
Products: Distribute discontinued products

Damark International, Inc.
7101 Winnetka Avenue North
Minneapolis, MN 55429
Phone: (800)729-9000
Products: Distribute discontinued products

Data Spec
20120 Plummer Street
Chatsworth, CA 91311
Phone: (800)431-8124
Phone: (818)993-1202
Products: Printer and video switch boxes

Data Technology Corporation (DTC)
1515 Centre Pointe Drive
Milpitas, CA 95035-8010
Phone: (408)942-4000
FAX: (408)942-4027
BBS: (408)942-4197
Products: Disk controllers

Datastorm Technologies, Inc.
3212 Lemone Boulevard
Columbia, MO 65205
Phone: (314)443-3282
BBS: (314)443-3282
Products: ProCOMM Software

Dell Computer Corporation
9505 Arboretum Boulevard
Austin, TX 78759
Phone: (800)426-5150
Phone: (512)338-4400
BBS: (512)338-8528
Products: PC compatible systems

DiagSoft, Inc.
5615 Scotts Valley Drive
Suite 140
Scotts Valley, CA 95066
Phone: (800)342-4763
Phone: (408)438-8247
FAX: (408)438-7113
Products: Diagnostic Software

Digi-Key Corporation
701 Brooks Ave. South
P.O. Box 677
Thief River Falls, MN 56701-0677
Phone: (800)344-4539
FAX: (218)681-3380
Products: Computer and electrical components and tools

Direct Drives
1107 Euclid Lane
Richton Park, IL 60471
Phone: (708)481-1111
Products: Hard disk drives and controllers

Distributed Processing Tech. (DPT)
140 Candace Drive
Maitland, FL 32751
Phone: (407)830-5522
BBS: (407)831-6432
Products: High performance SCSI controllers

Diversified Technology
112 E. State Street
Ridgeland, MS 39158
Phone: (800)443-2667
Phone: (201)891-8718
Products: Rack mount computer systems

DTK Computer, Inc.
17700 Castleton Street
Industry, CA 91748
Phone: (818)810-8880
BBS: (818)333-6548
Products: PC compatible systems

Dukane Corporation
2900 Dukane Drive
St. Charles, IL 60174
Phone: (708)584-2300
FAX: (708)584-5156
Products: Audio visual equipment

Dynatech Computer Power, Inc.
5800 Butler Lane
Scotts Valley, CA 95066
Phone: (408)438-5760
Phone: (800)638-9098
Products: Power protection equipment

Emerson Computer Power
15041 Bake Parkway #L
Irvine, CA 92718
Phone: (800)222-5877
Phone: (714)380-1005
Products: Power protection devices

Epson America, Inc. OEM Division
20770 Madrona Avenue
Torrance, CA 90509-2842
Phone: (213)782-0770
FAX: (213)782-5220
FAXback:(800)922-8911
BBS: (408)946-8777
Products: Printers, floppy drives, and PC compatibles

Exabyte Corporation
1685 38th Street
Boulder, CO 80301
Phone: (303)447-7359
Products: Tape backup hardware

Fedco Electronics, Inc.
184 W. 2nd Street
Fond du Lac, WI 54936
Phone: (800)542-9761
Phone: (414)922-6490
Products: Computer batteries

Fessenden Technologies
116 N. 3rd Street
Ozark, MO 65721
Phone: (417)485-2501
Products: Hard disk and monitor repairs

Fluke, John Manufacturing Company, Inc.
P.O.Box 9090
Everett, WA 98206-9090
Phone: (206)347-6100
Phone: (800)443-5853
FAX: (206)356-5116
Products: Troubleshooting tools

Forbin Project
P.O.Box 702
Cedar Falls, IA 50613
Phone: (319)266-0543
Products: QMODEM software

Fujitsu America, Inc.
3055 Orchard Drive
San Jose, CA 95134
Phone: (800)626-4686
Phone: (408)432-1300
BBS: (408)944-9899
Products: Hard drives

Future Domain Corporation
2801 McGaw Avenue
Irvine, CA 92714
Phone: (714)253-0400
FAX: (714)253-0913
BBS: (714)253-0432
Products: SCSI HBAs

Gateway 2000
610 Gateway Drive
North Sioux City, SD 57049
Phone: (605)232-2000
Phone: (800)523-2000
BBS: (605)232-2109
Products: PC compatible systems

Gazelle
305 North 500 West
Provo, UT 84601
Phone: (801)377-1288
Phone: (800)RUN-FAST
FAX: (801)373-6933
Products: Disk defragmenter

GigaTrend, Inc.
2234 Rutherford Road
Carlsbad, CA 92008
Phone: (619)931-9122
Products: Tape backup hardware

Globe Manufacturing, Inc.
1159 Route 22
Mountainside, NJ 07092
Phone: (908)232-7301
Phone: (800)227-3258
Products: PC adapters and brackets

Golden Bow Systems
842 N. Washington Street
San Diego, CA 92103
Phone: (800)284-3269
Phone: (619)298-9349
Products: VOPT disk optimizer

GoldStar Technology, Inc.
3003 N. First Street
San Jose, CA 95134
Phone: (408)432-1331
BBS: (408)432-0236
Products: Monitors and FAX machines

Harbor Electronics
650 Danbury Road
Ridgefield, CT 06877
Phone: (203)438-9625
FAX: (203)431-3001
Products: SCSI cabling

Hauppauge Computer Works, Inc.
91 Cabot Court
Hauppauge, NY 11788
Phone: (800) 443-6284
Phone: (516) 434-1600
Products: Motherboards

Hayes Microcomputer Products
P.O.Box 105203
Atlanta, GA 30348
Phone: (800) 874-2937
Phone: (404) 840-9200
BBS: (404) 446-6336
Products: Modems

Hewlett-Packard
16399 W. Bernardo Drive
San Diego, CA 92127
Phone: (619) 592-4522
FAXback: (800) 333-1917 HP FIRST
FAXback: (208) 344-4809 HP FIRST
Products: Printers and PC compatible systems

Hewlett-Packard, Disk Memory Division
11413 Chinden Boulevard
Boise, ID 83714
Phone: (208) 323-6000
Products: Disk drives

Hitatchi America, Ltd.
50 Prospect Avenue
Tarrytown, NY 94005
Phone: (914) 332-5800
Products: Disk drives and peripherals

Honeywell, Inc.
4171 North Mesa
Building D
El Paso, TX 79902
Phone: (800) 445-6939
Phone: (915) 543-5146
Products: Keyboards

Hyundai Electronics America
166 Baypointe Parkway
San Jose, CA 95134
Phone: (408)473-9200
Phone: (800)544-7808
Products: PC compatible systems

IBM National Distribution Division (NDD)
101 Paragon Drive
Montvale, NJ 07645
Phone: (800)426-9397
Products: DOS and OS/2

IBM OEM Division
1133 Westchester Avenue
White Plains, NY 10604
Phone: (914)288-3000
Products: Manufacture and distribute IBM products

IBM Parts Order Center
P.O. Box 9022
Boulder, CO 80301
Phone: (303)924-4100 Orders
Phone: (303)924-4015 Part Number ID and Lookup
Products: Parts and service center

IBM PC Direct
3039 Cornwallis Road
Building 203
Research Triangle Park, NC 27709-9766
Phone: (800)IBM-2YOU
Phone: (800)465-7999 Canada
FAX: (919)517-2050
Products: Direct mail order and sales

IBM Technical Directory
P.O. Box 2009
Racine, WI 53404
Phone: (414)633-8108
Phone: (800)426-7282
Products: Reference material and documentation

Illinois Lock
301 West Hintz Road
Wheeling, IL 60090-5754
Phone: (708)537-1800
FAX: (708)537-1881
Products: Computer keylocks

InfoChip Systems, Inc.
2840 San Tomas Expressway
Santa Clara, CA 95051
Phone: (800)447-0200
Phone: (408)727-0514
BBS: (408)727-2496
Products: Data compression products

Inline, Inc.
625 S. Palm Street
La Habra, CA 90631
Phone: (213)690-6767
Phone: (800)882-7117
Products: Video connection accessories

Integrated Information Technology (IIT)
2445 Mission College Boulevard
Santa Clara, CA 95054
Phone: (800)832-0770
Phone: (408)727-1885
Products: Match coprocessors

Intel Corporation
3065 Bowers Avenue
Santa Clara, CA 95051
Phone: (800)548-4725
Phone: (408)765-8080
Products: Processors and accelerator cards

Intel PC Enhancement Operations
5200 NE Elam Young Parkway
Hillsboro, OR 97124
Phone: (800)538-3373
Phone: (503)629-7354
BBS: (503)645-6275
Products: Miscellaneous upgrade products

Iomega Corporation
1821 West 4000 South
Roy, UT 84067
Phone: (800)456-5522
Phone: (801)778-1000
BBS: (801)778-4400
Products: Bernoulli drives

Irwin Magnetic Systems, Inc.
2101 Commonwealth Boulevard
Ann Arbor, MI 48105
Phone: (800)421-1879
Phone: (313)930-9000
BBS: (313)930-9380
Products: Tape backup equipment

Kingston Technology Corporation
17600 Newhope Street
Fountain Valley, CA 92708
Phone: (800)835-6575
Phone: (714)435-2600
FAX: (714)435-2699
Products: Processor upgrades and RAM

Laser Magnetic Storage
4425 Arrowswest Drive
Colorado Springs, CO 80907
Phone: (800)777-5764
Phone: (719)593-7900
Products: Optical disk products

Lexmark
740 New Circle Road
Lexington, KY 40511
Phone: (606)232-6814
BBS: (606)232-5653
Products: IBM printers and keyboards

Liuski International, Inc.
10 Hub Drive
Melville, NY 11747
Phone: (516)454-8220
Phone: (800)347-5454
Products: Miscellaneous peripherals

Longshire Computer, Inc.
2013 N. Capitol Avenue
San Jose, CA 95132
Phone: (408)942-1746
Products: Miscellaneous adapters

Lotus Development Corporation
55 Cambridge Parkway
Cambridge, MA 02142
Phone: (800)343-5414
Phone: (617)577-8500
Products: Notes, 123, Symphony, and other software

LSI Logic, Inc.
1551 McCarthy Boulevard
Milpitas, CA 95035
Phone: (408)433-8000
Products: Motherboard chipsets

Manzana Microsystems, Inc.
P.O. Box 2117
Goleta, CA 93118
Phone: (805)968-1387
Products: Floppy disk upgrades and controllers

Maxell Corporation of America
22-08 Route 208
Fair Lawn, NJ 07410
Phone: (800)533-2836
Phone: (201)795-5900
Products: Storage media

Maxi Switch, Inc.
2901 East Elvira Road
Tuscon, AZ 85706
Phone: (602)294-5450
FAX: (602)294-6890
Products: Industrial keyboards

Maxoptix
2520 Junction Avenue
San Jose, CA 95134
Phone: (800)848-3092
Phone: (408)954-9700
Products: WORM and magneto devices

Maxtor Corporation
211 River Oaks Parkway
San Jose, CA 95134
Phone: (800)262-9867
Phone: (408)432-1700
BBS: (303)678-2222 (2400bps)
BBS: (303)678-2020 (9600+bps)
Products: Hard disks

Maynard Electronics, Inc.
36 Skyline Drive
Lake Mary, FL 32746
Phone: (800)821-8782
Phone: (407)263-3500
BBS: (407)263-3502
Products: Tape backup equipment

McAfee Associates
4423 Cheeney Street
Santa Clara, CA 95054
Phone: (408)988-3832
BBS: (408)988-4044
Products: Virus protection and Brightwork software

McGraw-Hill, Inc.
Princeton Road N-1
Highstown, NJ 08520
Phone: (619)426-5000
Phone: (800)822-8158
Products: Publishing company

Megahertz Corporation
4505 S. Wasatch Boulevard
Salt Lake City, UT 84124
Phone: (800)527-8677
Phone: (801)272-6000
Products: Laptop network adapters and modems

Memorex Computer Supplies
1200 Memorex Drive
Santa Clara, CA 95050
Phone: (408)957-1000
Products: Disk media and miscellaneous supplies

Meritec
1359 West Jackson Street
P.O. Box 8003
Painesville, OH 44077
Phone: (216)354-3148
FAX: (216)354-0509
Products: SCSI adapters

Merritt Computer Products, Inc.
5565 Red Bird Center Drive #150
Dallas, TX 75237
Phone: (214)339-0753
Products: Keyboard Safeskin protector

Methode Electronics, Inc.
DataMate Division
7444 W. Wilson Ave.
Chicago, IL 60656
Phone: (708)867-9600
FAX: (708)867-3149
Products: SCSI terminators

Micro 2000, Inc.
1100 E. Broadway
Third Floor
Glendale, CA 91205
Phone: (818)547-0125
Products: Diagnostic equipment

Micro Accessories, Inc.
2012 Hartog Drive
San Jose, CA 95131
Phone: (800)777-6687
Phone: (408)441-1242
Products: Cables and disk mounting equipment

Micro House International
4900 Pearl East Circle
Suite 101
Boulder, CO 80301
Phone: (800)926-8299
Phone: (303)443-3389
FAX: (303)443-3323
BBS: (303)443-9957
Products: Publishes valuable technical resource CD

Microcom, Inc.
500 River Ridge Drive
Norwood, MA 02062
Phone: (800)822-8224
Phone: (617)551-1000
Products: Modems

Micron Technologies
2805 E. Columbia Road
Boise, ID 83706
Phone: (800)642-7661
Phone: (208)368-3900
BBS: (208)368-4530
Products: Memory related products

Micronics Computers, Inc.
232 E. Warren Avenue
Fremont, CA 94539
Phone: (510)651-2300
BBS: (510)651-6837
Products: PC compatible systems, laptops, and motherboards

Micropolis Corporation
21211 Nordhoff Street
Chatsworth, CA 91311
Phone: (800)395-3000
Phone: (818)709-3300
BBS: (818)709-3310
Products: Hard Disks

Microprocessors Unlimited, Inc.
24000 S. Peoria Avenue
Beggs, OK 74421
Phone: (918)267-4961
Products: Memory chips, SIMMS, and coprocessors

Microscience International Corporation
90 Headquarters Drive
San Jose, CA 95134
Phone: (800)334-3595
Phone: (408)433-9898
Products: Hard disks

Microsoft Corporation
One Microsoft Way
Redmond, WA 98052-6399
Phone: (800)426-9400
Phone: (206)882-8080
BBS: (206)936-6735
Products: DOS, Windows, NT, and miscellaneous software

MicroWay, Inc.
Research Park
Box 79
Kingston, MA 02364
Phone: (508)746-7341
Products: Accelerator products

Mitsubishi Electronics America, Inc.
991 Knox Street
Torrence, CA 90502
Phone: (800)843-2515
Phone: (213)217-5732
BBS: (213)324-3092
Products: printers, monitors, hard disks, and storage systems

Motorola, Inc.
6501 William Cannon Drive West
Austin, TX 78735
Phone: (512)891-2000
Products: Processors and components

Mountain Network Solutions, Inc.
240 Hacienda Avenue
Campbell, CA 95008
Phone: (800)458-0300
Phone: (408)379-4300
BBS: (408)438-2665
Products: Tape backup systems

Mylex Corporation
34551 Ardenwood Boulevard
Fremont, CA 94555
Phone: (800)446-9539
Phone: (510)796-6100
Products: Motherboards and disk controllers

NCL America, Inc.
1221 Innsbruck Drive
Sunnyvale, CA 94086
Phone: (408)734-1006
Products: SCSI adapters

NEC Technologies, Inc.
1414 Massachusetts Avenue
Boxborough, MA 01719
Phone: (800)632-4636
Phone: (508)264-8000
BBS: (708)860-2602
Products: Monitors, CD-ROMs, video adapters

Northgate Computer Systems, Inc.
7075 Flying Cloud Drive
Eden Prairie, MN 55344
Phone: (800)548-1993
Products: PC compatible systems

NovaStor Corporation
30961 Agoura Rd.
Suite 109
Westlake Village, CA 91361
Phone: (818)707-9900
FAX: (818)707-9902
Products: Tape backup equipment

Okidata
532 Fellowship Road
Mount Laurel, NJ 08054
Phone: (609)235-2600
Phone: (800)654-3282
BBS: (800)283-5474
Products: Printers

Olivetti
765 US Hwy. 202
Somerville, NJ 08876
Phone: (201)526-8200
Products: PC compatible systems

Ontrack Computer Systems, Inc.
6321 Bury Drive
Suites 15-19
Eden Prairie, MN 55346
Phone: (612)937-1107
Phone: (800)752-1333
Technical Support: (612)937-2121
Data Recovery Service: (800)872-2599
Data Recovery Service: (612)937-5161
FAX: (612)937-5750
BBS: (612)937-0860 (2400bps)
BBS: (612)937-8567 (9600+bps)
Products: Data recovery products and services

Orchid Technology
45365 Northport Loop West
Fremont, CA 94538
Phone: (800)767-2443
Phone: (510)683-0300
BBS: (510)683-0329
Products: Video and memory board products

Osborne/McGraw Hill
2600 10th Street
Berkeley, CA 94710
Phone: (800)227-0900
Phone: (415)549-6618
Products: Publishing company

Pacific Magtron, Inc.
568-8 Weddell Drive
Sunnyvale, CA 94089
Phone: (408)774-1188
Products: Hard disks

Packard Bell
9425 Canoga Avenue
Chatsworth, CA 91311
Phone: (800)733-4411
Phone: (818)886-4600
BBS: (818)773-7207
Products: PC compatible systems

Panasonic Communications & Systems
2 Panasonic Way
Secaucus, NJ 07094
Phone: (800)233-8182
Phone: (201)348-7000
BBS: (201)863-7845
Products: FAX systems, optical drives, monitors, and laptops

Philips Consumer Electronics
One Philips Drive
Knoxville, TN 37914
Phone: (615)521-4366
Products: Monitors, CD-ROM devices, and PCs

Phoenix Technologies, Ltd.
846 University Avenue
Norwood, MA 02062
Phone: (617)551-4000
Products: BIOS

Pivar Computing Services, Inc.
165 Arlington Heights Road
Buffalo Grove, IL 60089
Phone: (800)266-8378
Phone: (708)459-6010
Products: Media conversion services

PKWare, Inc.
9025 N. Deerwood Drive
Brown Deer, WI 53223
Phone: (414)354-8699
FAX: (414)354-8559
BBS: (414)354-8670
Products: Compression utilities such as PKZIP

PTI Industries
269 Mount Hermon Road
Scott Valley, CA 95066
Phone: (408)438-3900
Products: Power protection equipment

Public Brand Software
P.O. Box 51315
Indianapolis, IN 46251
Phone: (800)426-3475
Phone: (317)856-7571
Products: Public domain and shareware libraries

Quantum Corporation
500 McCarthy Boulevard
Milpitas, CA 95035
Phone: (408)894-4000
BBS: (408)434-1664
Products: Hard disk drives

Quarterdeck Office Systems
150 Pico Boulevard
Santa Monica, CA 90405
Phone: (213)392-9851
BBS: (213)396-3904
Products: QEMM memory manager, Desqview

Seagate Technology
920 Disc Drive
Scotts Valley, CA 95066
Phone: (408)438-6550
FAX: (408)429-6356
Sales: (408)438-8111
Service: (800)468-3472
Service: (405)491-6260
Service FAX: (405)491-6261
FAXback: (408)438-2620
BBS: (408)438-8771
Products: Hard disks

Sharp Electronics Corporation
Sharp Plaza
Mahwah, NJ 07430-2135
Phone: (201)529-8200
Sales: (201)529-8731
FAX: (201)529-9636
Products: Monitors, laptops, overheads

Shugart Corporation
9292 Jeronimo Road
Irvine, CA 92714
Phone: (714)770-1100
Products: Floppy and hard disk drives

Sigma Data
Scytheville Row
P.O. Box 1790
New London, NH 03257
Phone: (800)446-4525
Phone: (603)526-6909
FAX: (603)526-6915
Products: Memory related

Silicon Valley Computer
441 N. Whisman Road
Building 13
Mountain View, CA 94043
Phone: (415)967-1100
FAX: (415)967-0700
BBS: (415)967-8081
Products: Hard disk adapters and interfaces

Sola Electric
1717 Busse Road
Elk Grove, IL 60007
Phone: (800)289-7652
Phone: (708)439-2800
Products: Power protection equipment

Sony Corporation of America
Sony Drive
Park Ridge, NJ 07656
Phone: (201)930-1000
Products: Storage media

Stac Electronics
5993 Avenida Encinas
Carlsbad, CA 92008
Phone: (800)522-7822
Phone: (619)431-7474
BBS: (619)431-5956
Products: Disk compression utilities

Standard Microsystems Corporation
35 Marcus Boulevard
Hauppauge, NY 11788
Phone: (800)992-4762
Phone: (516)273-3100
Products: Network adapters

Star Micronics America, Inc.
200 Park Avenue
Pan Am Building
#3510
New York, NY 10166
Phone: (800)447-4700
Phone: (212)986-6770
Products: Printers

Storage Dimensions, Inc.
2145 Hamilton Avenue
San Jose, CA 95125
Phone: (408)879-0300
Phone: (800)765-7895
BBS: (408)944-1220
Products: Hard disks and related utilities

Symantec Corporation
10201 Torre Avenue
Cupertino, CA 95014
Phone: (800)441-7234
Phone: (408)253-9600
BBS: (408)973-9598
Products: Miscellaneous utilities such as Norton Utilities

SyQuest Technology
47071 Bayside Parkway
Fremont, CA 94538
Phone: (800)245-2278
Phone: (415)226-4000
BBS: (415)656-0470
Products: Removable hard disks

Sysgen, Inc.
556 Gibraltar Drive
Milpitas, CA 95035
Phone: (800)821-2151
Phone: (408)263-4411
BBS: (408)946-5032
Products: Tape backup devices

Sytron
134 Flanders Road
P.O. Box 5025
Westboro, MA 01581-5025
Phone: (800)877-0016
Phone: (508)898-0100
FAX: (508)898-2677
Products: Tape backup equipment

Tadiran
2975 Bowers Avenue
Santa Clara, CA 95051
Phone: (408)727-0300
Products: Computer batteries

Tandon Corporation
405 Science Drive
Moorpark, CA 93021
Phone: (805)523-0340
Products: PC compatible systems

Tandy Corporation/Radio Shack
1800 One Tandy Center
Fort Worth, TX 76102
Phone: (817)390-3700
Products: PC compatible systems

Tatung Company of America, Inc.
2850 El Presidio Street
Long Beach, CA 90810
Phone: (800)827-2850
Phone: (213)979-7055
Products: Monitors

TDK Electronics Corporation
12 Harbor Park Drive
Port Washington, NY 11050
Phone: (516)625-0100
Products: Miscellaneous storage media

Teac America, Inc.
7733 Telegraph Road
Montebello, CA 90640
Phone: (213)726-0303
Products: Floppy and tape drives

Tecmar, Inc.
6225 Cochran Road
Solon, OH 44139
Phone: (800)344-4463
Phone: (216)349-0600
BBS: (216)349-0853
Products: Miscellaneous adapter boards

Thermalloy, Inc.
2021 W. Valley View Lane
P.O. Box 810839
Dallas, TX 75381-0839
Phone: (214)243-4321
FAX: (214)241-4656
Products: CPU heatsinks and cooling devices

Toshiba America, Inc.
9740 Irvine Boulevard
Irvine, CA 92718
Phone: (800)999-4823
Phone: (714)583-3000
BBS: (714)837-2116
Products: Floppy and hard disks, printers, laptops

TouchStone Software Corporation
2130 Main Street
Suite 250
Huntington Beach, CA 92648
Phone: (800)531-0450
Phone: (714)969-7746
FAX: (714)960-1886
Products: CheckIT diagnostic software

Trantor Systems, Ltd.
5415 Randall Place
Fremont, CA 94538
Phone: (510)770-1400
BBS: (415)656-5159
Products: Parallel port SCSI adapters

Tripp Lite Manufacturing
500 N. Orleans
Chicago, IL 60610
Phone: (312)329-1777
Products: Power protection equipment

U.S. Robotics, Inc.
8100 N. McCormick Boulevard
Skokie, IL 60076
Phone: (800)982-5151
Phone: (708)982-5010
BBS: (708)982-5092
Products: Modems

Ultrastor Corporation
15 Hammond Street
#310
Irvine, CA 92718
Phone: (714)581-4100
Products: Hard disks systems

UNISYS
Township Line and Union Meeting Roads
Blue Bell, PA 19424
Phone: (800)448-1424
Phone: (215)542-2691
Products: PC compatible systems

Universal Memory Products
1378 Logan Avenue #F
Costa Mesa, CA 92626
Phone: (800)678-8648
Phone: (714)751-9445
Products: Miscellaneous memory related products

Varta Batteries, Inc.
300 Executive Boulevard
Elmsford, NY 10523
Phone: (914)592-2500
Products: Computer batteries

Verbatim Corporation
1200 WT Harris Boulevard
Charlotte, NC 28262
Phone: (704)547-6500
Products: Miscellaneous storage media

Visiflex Seels
16 E. Lafayette Street
Hackensack, NJ 07601
Phone: (201)487-8080
Products: Keyboard covers

Wang Labratories, Inc.
One Industrial Avenue
Lowell, MA 01851
Phone: (800)225-0654
Phone: (508)656-1550
Products: PC compatible systems

Wangtek, Inc.
41 Moreland Road
Simi Valley, CA 93065
Phone: (800)992-9916
Phone: (805)583-5525
BBS: (805)582-3370
Products: Tape backup devices

Western Digital Corporation
8105 Irvine Center Drive
Irvine, CA 92718
Phone: (800)832-4778
Phone: (714)932-5000
BBS: (714)753-1234 (2400bps)
BBS: (714)753-1068 (9600+bps)
Products: Hard disks and miscellaneous other products

Wyse Technology
3471 N. First Street
San Jose, CA 95134
Phone: (800)438-9973
Phone: (408)473-1200
BBS: (408)922-4400
Products: PC compatible systems and monitors

Xircom
26025 Mureau Road
Calbasas, CA 91302
Phone: (800)874-7875
Phone: (818)878-7600
BBS: (818)878-7618
Products: Parallel port network adapters and modems

Zeos International, Ltd.
530 5th Avenue NW
St. Paul, MN 55112
Phone: (800)423-5891
Phone: (612)633-4591
Products: PC compatible systems

NOVA
CHILAGA
NORVMBEGA
FRANCIA
MOCOSA
AVACAL
APALCHEN
WINGANDEKOA
LA FLORIDA
CALICVAS
CAPASCHI
TEAC
MARATA
CVLIACAN
ASTATLAN
HISPANIA NOVA
TOTIRA
MECHVACAN
CVBA
HISPANIOLA
MAR DEL SVR, quod
Circulus Aequinoctialis
240
250
260
270
280
290
PACIFICVM
CHARCAS
CHILI
PATAGONES, vel REGIO GIGANTVM
PARANA
Cari
ICAE SIVE
ORBIS, NO
SCRIPTIO.
FRETVM MAGELLANICVM
Archipelago del C. delleado

B

APPENDIX

Vendor Profiles

When we first started working on this book, we had one clear-cut goal, to provide the reader with the information necessary to get certification, and to provide a valuable reference of information for use even after you complete your certification.

To enhance the material included within this book, we decided that, although information is very valuable, so are tools! With that in mind, we searched for vendors that we felt produced products that you, the candidate or Network Administrator, would find valuable in your day to day work. The result of this search is the CD-ROM in this book. On this CD-ROM, you will find numerous demonstration and evaluation copies of software offered by some of the top software developing companies around, such as Microsoft, Novell, Avanti, Citadel, ON Track, and many more. In this appendix, we provide a listing of some of the companies that have participated in providing products for this book.

As an added bonus, many of these companies have decided to offer discounts on their products for the readers of this book. Where applicable, the discounted rate has been included in their profile.

A.N.D. Technologies

Contact Name	NA
Address	P.O. Box 64811 Los Angeles, CA 90064
Phone Number	(213)782-6923
Fax Number	(213)782-6923
Online E-mail Addresses	CompuServe: 71011,3570 Internet: andtech@netcom.com
Online Support Areas	ftp://ftp.netcom.com/pub/an/andtech
Company Description	A.N.D. Technologies specializes in programming for Novell networks.
Name of Product	PCOUNTER
Terms	45-day unlimited usage trial period, 2-hour time limit after that
Description	PCOUNTER V3.11a is a totally automated solution for print accounting. It comes in EXE (dedicated print server) or NLM format, and it counts pages on PCL (LaserJet compatible) and PostScript printers, whether serial, parallel, networked, or remote. It includes many other enhancements to the standard Netware printing mechanism that will ease the administration of your printing setup
Cost	$125 for 1 file server, $75 for each additional file server
Discount	NA
Ordering	By phone or e-mail

Avanti Technology, Inc.

Contact Name	NA
Address	13492 Research Blvd., #120-271 Austin, TX 78750

Phone Number	(800)638-1168 (512)335-1168
Fax Number	(512)335-7838
Online E-mail Addresses	Internet: avanti@avanti-tech.com Internet: prodinfo@avanti-tech.com
Online Support Areas	CompuServe: GO LANUTILS Internet: tech@avanti-tech.com http://www.avanti-tech.com/~prodinfo/
Company Description	Avanti has been a leader in the development of NetWare management software since releasing one of the first network monitoring utilities and the first baseline sampling/trend tracking utility back in 1990. Some of that technology was later licensed to XTree Company as the foundation for their Tools for Networks product. They also created network technology which has used by 3Com, Central Point, and Command Software. While other companies have recently entered the network management market, they have long been active behind the scenes and are considered a technological leader. Their objective is developing network management solutions for NetWare administrators.
Name of Product	NConsole v2 for Windows
Terms	30-day evaluation
Description	NLM with DOS and Windows clients for NW v3.1*x*/v4.0*x*/v4.1*x* which collects, averages, accumulates, and tracks key Server performance statistics. NLM displays 100+ active statistics plus a sliding bargraph of the last 74 seconds of CPU Utilization while doubling as a scrolling screen saver with Console keyboard lock. Expands upon MONITOR and STAT features by logging statistics over configurable periods with ASCII and comma delimited output options. Windows client displays exportable 2D/3D graphs on 60+ practical trends/ratios from 100+ statistics. DOS Client accesses the NLM w/o RCONSOLE. Optional SNMP MIB Agent. Extensive online help.

Cost	$295 first server (w/o SNMP MIB Agent) $395 first server (w/ SNMP MIB Agent) discounts for additional Servers
Discount	25%
Ordering	By phone, e-mail or Fax
Name of Product	TaskMaster v1
Terms	30-day evaluation
Description	Server task scheduler NLM for NW v3.1*x*/v4.*x* (bindery emulation required) with script processor combining DOS batch and Login script simplicity with extended commands and system vars, plus IF/ELSE, WHILE/LOOP, CALL/GOTO directives and NOT/AND/OR, ==, >, <, >=, and <= conditionals. Dynamic variables can be read from a file, incremented, and decremented. Schedules .NCF and enhanced .TSK scripts by date, day of month, weekday, time, time after the hour, and interval. Adds 20+ DOS commands (CHOWN, COPY, DIR, DEL, FLAG, REN, TYPE, XCOPY, and so on) to server console with most supporting files on the DOS partition.
Cost	$395 first server, discounts for additional servers
Discount	25%
Ordering	By phone, e-mail, or Fax

Citadel Computer Systems, Inc.

Contact Name	USA & Canada Sales: Sales Department (any sales representative) Dealer Inquiries and International Sales: Larry Hurwitz, Marketing Director Technical Inquiries and Customer Support: Dr. Paul Harder, Chief Technical Officer
Address	2950 North Loop West Suite 1080 Houston, TX 77092

Phone Number

(800)962-0701 (sales)
(713)686-6400 (technical support and international Sales)

Fax Number

(713) 686-6495

Online E-mail Addresses

CompuServe: 73541,2014
America Online: CitadelCS
Internet: contact@citadel.com

Online Support Areas

http://www.citadel.com/~pharder/citadel/home.htm

Company Description

Citadel Computer Systems, Inc., was incorporated in July of 1992 to develop and market computer software products. Our first product was NetOFF, a computer network security program that logs off unattended computers. We have subsequently added products directed toward network administration and financial management needs, so that our current product base may be characterized very broadly as administration and management tools, with a strong security emphasis. Most of the company's products are oriented toward administration of networks running under Novell's NetWare and other popular network operating systems. We provide comprehensive technical support and database conversion services for all of our products.

Name of Product

NetOFF System IV

Terms

Fully functional

Description

Network security software that runs on DOS and Windows workstation PCs in NetWare 3.*x* or 4.*x* networks. Password-protected screen blanker that activates in response to a hot key or after a configurable period of workstation inactivity, from 1 minute to 24 hours; uses NetWare password, shared group password, or no password. Automatic logoff after workstation inactivity and/or at specified clock time. Logoff can gracefully exit Windows applications, saving unsaved work. Can be configured to clear network connection, exit Windows, and/or

	reboot PC. NetOFF Administrator is a Windows application with GUI and full online help, for easy configuration of NetOFF.
Cost	$995/license: 1–5 servers, up to 500 workstations. Upgrade pricing available for users of earlier versions. Price subject to change; call for current pricing.
Discount	10%
Ordering	By phone, e-mail, Fax, or snail mail
Name of Product	NetOFF NLM
Terms	Fully functional
Description	NetWare Loadable Module that logs off users at a specified clock time, helping you get a clean backup. May be configured to send warning of imminent logoff, and can prevent further logins during a specified time interval. Administrator can specify NetWare groups to be logged off and/or exempted from logoff. Optionally logs off only those users who have a specified file open or exempts users who have a specified file open.
Cost	$995/license: 1–5 servers. Price subject to change; call for current pricing.
Discount	10%
Ordering	By phone, e-mail, Fax, or snail mail
Name of Product	NetOFF OS/2
Terms	Fully functional
Description	Network security program that runs in OS/2 workstations on Novell networks. Logs the user off after a specified period (1 to 999 minutes) of workstation inactivity. Can execute user-configurable command file prior to logoff.
Cost	$995/license: 1–5 servers, up to 500 workstations. Price subject to change; call for current pricing.

Discount	10% off price current when you order.
Ordering	By phone, e-mail, Fax, or snail mail
Name of Product	NetPURGE
Terms	Fully functional
Description	NetWare Loadable Module that deletes old files from server drives to free up space for current work. At administrator option, file age may be measured as days since last file update or days since last file access. Can optionally copy files to a backup directory before deleting them; or it can merely prepare an inventory of old files, without actually deleting them.
Cost	$995/license: 1–5 servers. Price subject to change; call for current pricing.
Discount	10%
Ordering	By phone, e-mail, Fax, or snail mail
Name of Product	NetCONSOLE
Terms	Fully functional
Description	A NetWare Loadable Module that provides a timed execution facility for the server's console screen. Any command that you can type into the console screen may be programmed into NetCONSOLE's initialization file, where you also enter the time and days of the week when the command is to be executed. When the specified day and time occurs, the NLM executes the command. No longer do you have to be present in your network control center at 3 a.m. to unload database NLMs prior to routine backups.
Cost	$995/license: 1–5 servers; price subject to change; call for current pricing
Discount	10%
Ordering	By phone, e-mail, Fax, or snail mail

Name of Product	NetWATCH
Terms	Fully functional
Description	NetWare Loadable Module that watches your network for unowned files. Whenever you delete a user from your network, all of the user's files become unowned. If others on your network continue to use these files, everything may appear to work for awhile. But when a user tries to make the file grow beyond its final segment, NetWare will return a spurious "Disk Full" error. NetWATCH overcomes this difficulty by scanning your network for unowned files and changing their ownership to a valid account of your choice.
Cost	$995/license: 1–5 servers; price subject to change; call for current pricing
Discount	10%
Ordering	By phone, e-mail, Fax, or snail mail.
Name of Product	NetCLEAR
Terms	Fully functional
Description	NetWare Loadable Module that periodically scans your network looking for unlogged users and clearing those connections. If you have a 10-user NetWare license on a network of 15 workstations, this utility can be indispensable.
Cost	$995/license: 1–5 servers; price subject to change; call for current pricing
Discount	10%
Ordering	By phone, e-mail, Fax, or snail mail
Name of Product	NetQ
Terms	Fully functional
Description	A DOS program that runs on one of your workstations to let you more effectively manage your network's queues.

Cost	$995/license: 1–5 servers; Price subject to change; call for current pricing
Discount	10%
Ordering	By phone, e-mail, Fax, or snail mail

Classic Software

Contact Name	Chip Cox
Address	4746 Spottswood Ave., Suite 107 Memphis, TN 38117
Phone Number	(901)726-5328
Fax Number	(901)726-5328
Online E-mail Addresses	CompuServe: 72460,33 Internet: support@classic.com
Online Support Areas	support via e-mail
Company Description	Classic Software is a software development company specializing in NetWare utilities and contracts involving NetWare aware applications.
Name of Product	NOVCRON
Terms	Full-blown shareware
Description	NOVCRON.NLM provides scheduled execution of any NLM, NCF, or NetWare console command. Commands can be scheduled by any combination of Month, Day of Month, Day of Week, Hour, and Minute. Keystrokes can also be sent to any NLM screen to aid in loading or unloading NLMs. Compatiable with Netware 3.*x* and 4.1.
Cost	$50 U.S.
Discount	NA
Ordering	Mail or Fax registration form to above address or phone number. Purchase orders accepted. Quantity discounts available. Foreign registrations should include $5 U.S. shipping and handling fee.

Name of Product	CLRUSR
Terms	Full-blown shareware
Description	Clear Unauthorized users off of the network and keep them off. CLRUSR.NLM will clear all users not appearing in an exception file from the network while running. Users are validated based on Userid or Network address. Compatiable with NetWare 3.*x* and 4.1.
Cost	$50 U.S.
Discount	NA
Ordering	Mail or Fax registration form to company address or phone number. Purchase orders accepted. Quantity discounts available. Foreign registrations should include $5 U.S. shipping and handling fee.
Name of Product	CKUSERS
Terms	Full-blown shareware
Description	Monitor network bindery for inactive accounts, disabled accounts or accounts with intruder detection set. Configurable options include inactivity period, servers to monitor, and accounts to ignore. Inactive accounts may be either reported or automatically disabled on all monitored servers. Compatiable with NetWare 3.*x* and 4.1.
Cost	$50 U.S.
Discount	NA
Ordering	Mail or Fax registration form to company address or phone number. Purchase orders accepted. Quantity discounts available. Foreign registrations should include $5 U.S. shipping and handling fee.

Computer Automation Systems, Inc.

Contact Name	Thomas Neuman
Address	3950 Riverlook Parkway Marietta, GA 30067
Phone Number	(770)956-0580
FAX Number	(770)956-0580
Online E-mail Addresses	CompuServe: 70571,1373
Online Support Areas	NA
Company Description	Computer Automation Systems, Inc., is a consulting company that offers custom software for a variety of customers. We have CNE on staff who also provides network installation, maintenance, and design for LAN and WAN systems.
Name of Product	Flashcards for DOS/Windows
Terms	Fully functional working copy, limited only by database creation functionality. Users are requested to register the product within 30 days. Product registration is required for the purchase of additional knowledge databases.
Description	This study aid provides a memory drill by posing questions randomly chosen from a database, then checking the responses against the answers stored in the database. This program has proven to be very valuable in preparing for the CNE, CNI, and ECNE exams. The NetWare 3.1*x* System Manager database is included. Other knowledge databases are available for elective courses including TCP/IP, NFS, SAA, and many more. Registered users can create and modify knowledge databases. Free version upgrades to registered users of Flashcards software. DOS and Windows version included.
Cost	Flashcards program only $20. CNE bundles approximately $100.
Discount	NA

Ordering	When ordering, please specify the Flashcards for DOS program. This will entitle you to the DOS and Windows program at no additional charge.

Computer Tyme, Inc.

Contact Name	Marc Perkel
Address	411 North Sherman, Suite 300 Springfield, MO 65802 USA
Phone Number	(417)866-1222 (800)548-5353
FAX Number	(417)866-1665
Online E-mail Addresses	Internet: MARC@CTYME.MHS.COMPUSERVE.COM
Online Support Areas	CompusServe: GO NVENA
Company Description	Computer Tyme is a network software utilities company founded in 1984.
Name of Product	Network Survival Kit
Terms	NA
Description	50 killer network utilities and menu system
Cost	$495/Server
Discount	Save $100 with coupon enclosed in this book
Ordering	Via Faxed PO

Cyber Pass, Inc.

Contact Name	Rene Caron
Address	417 Bay St., Suite 3 Ottawa, ON K1R 6A5
Phone Number	(800)255-3763 (613)237-4991

FAX Number	(613)230-5279
Online E-mail Addresses	CompuServe: 72603,1004
Online Support Areas	BBS: (613)237-6820
Company Description	Cyber Pass is a software development company specializing in Certification Examination Preparation software. Most notably since 1991 Cyber Pass has been producing CNEQUIZR.
Name of Product	CNEQUIZR
Terms	Fully functional software, questions databases partially locked
Description	Monster collection of 20 CNEQUIZR tests. These tests prepare you for CNA, CNE, CNI, ECNE, or Master CNE. CNEQUIZR tests have been the most popular study aid used for Novell certification since their introduction in 1991.
Cost	U.S. $12 per test
Discount	NA
Ordering	Registrant must supply Registration Code from within software

Dvorak Development & Publishing

Contact Name	NA
Address	385 S. Pierce Ave. Louisville, CO 80027 USA
Phone Number	(303)661-0345
FAX Number	(303)661-0635
Online E-mail Addresses	NA
Online Support Areas	CompuServe: GO DVORAK Internet: sales@dvorak.com
Company Description	Windows software developer and publisher specializing in navigation tools for commercial and Internet information services.

Name of Product	NavCIS Pro TE for Windows
Terms	30-day Timed Edition, countdown begins from first day you log on to CompuServe using it.
Description	A Windows-based offline navigator designed to greatly decrease CompuServe online charges while increasing information flow, and making CompuServe easier to understand, use, and navigate.
Cost	$69
Discount	NA
Ordering	Complete ordering screen is built into NavCIS TE demo provided on CD-ROM. The order is then sent via secure e-mail directly to Dvorak Development, where it is processed and shipped.
Name of Product	OUI TE for Windows
Terms	30-day Timed Edition, countdown begins from first successful login to Usenet via PPP, SLIP or TCP/IP connection.
Description	OUI is an offline navigator that allows the user to follow and participate in Usenet newsgroups easily and efficiently while reducing the amount of connect time dramatically. OUI has advanced features such as auto-UUdecoding and encoding, graphical thread structures, and a built-in spell checker. OUI is fully Winsock compliant and can be used by any PPP, SLIP, or TCP/IP Internet or CompuServe user.
Cost	$39
Discount	NA
Ordering	OUI will provide the user with complete ordering information.

Horizons Technology, Inc.

Contact Name	Eric Hjalmarson (USA) Jim Agenant (Europe)
Address	U.S. Office: 3990 Ruffin Road San Diego, CA 92123 European Office: Transpolis Commerce Centre Polarisavenue 87 2132 JH Hoofddorp The Netherlands
Phone Number	(800)828-3808 (619)292-8860 +31-2503-85558
Fax Number	(619)292-9439 +31-2503-85554
Online E-mail Addresses	jagenant@horizons.com
Online Support Areas	31-2503-85558 Compuserve: LANVEN Internet: techsup@horizons.com BBS: (619)268-0380
Company Description	The firm was founded in 1977 with three employees and one contract, and now employs over 450 scientists, engineers, technicians, and support personnel. The company is employee-owned, with shares held by a cadre of key employees. The company is headquartered in San Diego, with other offices in Alexandria, VA, and Boston, MA, and a European headquarters located in The Netherlands.
Name of product	LANauditor
Terms	Test Kit that works for 30 days
Description	LANauditor is a comprehensive network management tool that includes both DOS and Windows interface, inventories the hardware

and software installed on DOS, Windows, OS/2, Windows NT client, and Macintosh workstations and file servers. It supports every network operating system (NetWare, Vines, Pathworks, LAN Manager, 3+Open, StarLAN, Windows for Workgroups, etc.). LANauditor helps network administrators concerned with software licence compliance, planning system upgrades, and managing network inventories.

Cost	$545 for a 50-user base license
Discount	NA
Ordering	By phone or Fax
Name of Product	LANshadow
Terms	Needs only one server; works for three days after installation
Description	LANshadow is an easy-to-use, cost-effective network mirroring tool that provides fast recovery from server failures and assures constant availability of critical network data. LANshadow runs as an NLM and can be configured to mirror entire servers, volumes, directories, or even individual files, including open files, to a designated backup server. LANshadow doesn't require a dedicated backup platform physically connected to and configured exactly like a production server. Nor does it require any dedicated hardware or tape drive. LANshadow can even mirror data to a backup server (servers) at another physical site using existing WAN links. It will also do software distribution for file servers. It supports NW 3.*x* and 4.*x* servers.
Cost	$1095 for a base license
Discount	NA
Ordering	By phone or Fax

Infinite Technologies

Contact Name	Patty Lummis
Address	11433 Cronridge Drive Owings Mills, MD 21117
Phone Number	(410)363-1097 (800)678-1097
Fax Number	(410)363-0846
Online E-mail Addresses	Internet: Sales@Infinite.ihub.com Sales@Infinite (through CompuServe or NHUB)
Online Support Areas	CompuServe: GO INFINITE
Company Description	Infinite Technologies provides enterprise messaging solutions to customers. We offer e-mail, message routing, message exchange between different e-mail systems, and a variety of utilities and gateways to improve and expand message systems. These include Internet connectivity, alphanumeric pagers, Fax, and more. Our products are available domestically through our authorized resellers, and internationally through our distributor partners.
Name of Product	Connect^2
Terms	30 day evaluation version
Description	Connect^2 is a high-performance message switch that provides message transport and exchange within and between a variety of e-mail systems including Microsoft Mail, cc:Mail, Da Vinci e-mail, BeyondMail, ExpressIT!, and Notework. It runs in both NetWare and non-NetWare environments. Connect^2 moves mail rapidly and provides enhanced security features. Message tunneling lets you maintain message formatting even when sending messages through alternate service providers such as the Internet. With Connect^2 you can also specify backup routes to the same host to build fault tolerance intro your system, and customize your host connection schedules to reduce your long distance expenses.

Cost	$149 (10 users) – $6,999 (1000 users)
Discount	NA
Ordering	Available through your local Infinite Technologies reseller; call 800-678-1097 for the name of a reseller near you.
Name of Product	Connect^2 Remote
Terms	30-day evaluation version
Description	Connect^2 Remote is a high-performance message switch for traveling users and telecommuters. It reduces message exchange costs by supporting high-speed modems, and offers automatic compression of attachments when communicating with a Connect^2 network host. Connect^2 Remote also lets users execute gateways to other systems, such as facsimile or MCI Mail. Users work from the same inbox whether they are connected to or dialing into the network. Connect^2 Remote allows users to preview waiting messages before downloading them. Users may tag messages to download or delete after reviewing the message subject, sender or size.
Cost	$89
Discount	NA
Ordering	Available through your local Infinite Technologies reseller; call 800-678-1097 for the name of a reseller near you.
Name of Product	Connect^{2}SMTP
Terms	30-day evaluation version
Description	Connect^{2}SMTP is an integrated solution for connecting e-mail products such as BeyondMail, Da Vinci e-mail, ExpressIT!, and Notework with the Internet and SMTP-based electronic mail. The product runs as a gateway on a Connect^2, MHS, or Global MHS messaging server. It also provides users with access to today's popular Internet tools such as Mosaic, Netscape, FTP,

	Telnet, and Gopher. It supports MIME, SLIP, and PPP, and it can handle unlimited dial-in or dial-out accounts. It's easy to administer, provides error detection in the form of e-mail messages to the e-mail administrator, and includes extensive debugging tools for trouble-shooting problems.
Cost	$1,899 (single workgroup)
Discount	NA
Ordering	Available through your local Infinite Technologies reseller; call 800-678-1097 for the name of a reseller near you.
Name of Product	ExpressIT!
Terms	30-day evaluation version
Description	ExpressIT! is a full-featured e-mail product for DOS and Windows. It's easy to use and accessible. The DOS product runs as a TSR requiring less than 2 KB of RAM! Manage your e-mail with mail folders, ASCII import and export, message search based on sender and message text, registered mail, and TO/CC/BCC addressing. Customize ExpressIT! with Personal Address Books to remember common e-mail addresses. ExpressIT! can automatically launch applications to view file attachments. A Directory Assistant is included to provide directory synchronization between multiple sites. Wide area network communication through Connect^2, NetWare MHS, or NetWare Global MHS.
Cost	$299 (5 users)– $9,999 (1000 users)
Discount	NA
Ordering	Available through your local Infinite Technologies reseller; call 800-678-1097 for the name of a reseller near you.
Name of Product	Mach^2 TCP/IP Router
Terms	30-day evaluation version

Description	The Mach^2 TCP/IP Router is for LAN administrators who need Internet access. It's a software-only router that operates from a DOS-based PC, unlike other routers that require additional hardware and Unix. It is a cost-effective way for smaller LANs to connect directly to the Internet and gain immediate benefits using tools such as Mosaic, Netscape, FTP, Telnet, and Gopher. Mach^2 supports multiple SLIP and PPP connections to an Internet Service Provider. The router supports remote access so that remote users, or other networked sites, can access the Internet through you with a dial-in connection into the Mach^2 Router.
Cost	$599
Discount	NA
Ordering	Available through your local Infinite Technologies reseller; call 800-678-1097 for the name of a reseller near you.

Intrusion Detection

Contact	Daniel Dorr
Address	217 E 86th St., Suite 213 New York, NY 10028
Phone Number	(800)408-6104 (212)348-8900
Fax Number	(212)427-9185
Online E-mail Addresses	CompuServe: 75162,452
Online Support Areas	NA
Company Description	Intrusion Detection specializes in network security consulting and custom software development. The expert knowledge base used in the Kane Security Analyst is derived from years of evaluating Novell NetWare security for a wide variety of Fortune 500 clients.

Name of Product	The Kane Security Analyst v. 2.0
Terms	Evaluation copy for NDS will only assess up to 250 objects. If user's tree is larger than this it will allow the user to register a particular context for assessment, i.e., container or business unit. The 3.*x* assessment will assess any one 3.*x* file server.
Description	The Kane Security Analyst (KSA) is a Novell security assessment product that works with NetWare 3.*x*, 4.*x* (NDS), and Windows NT. The KSA will run a complete security assessment in minutes, and provide information across six crucial security areas: user account restrictions, password strength, access control, system monitoring, data integrity, and data confidentiality. It also identifies easily guessed passwords, packet hijacking, effective rights, inactive user Ids, and so on.
Cost	$495/server; Traveling license and Enterprise-wide license available
Discount	NA
Ordering	By phone or e-mail

Klos Technologies, Inc.

Contact Name	Patrick Klos
Address	604 Daniel Webster Highway Merrimack, NH 03054
Phone Number	(603)424-8300
FAX Number	(603)424-9300
Online E-mail Addresses	Internet: support@klos.com Internet: sales@klos.com
Online Support Areas	http://www.klos.com/ ftp://ftp.klos.com/

Company Description	Klos Technologies, Inc., was established in 1989 to provide networking software development services to local companies and has done work for Cabletron, Banyan Systems, Phoenix Technologies, Racal-Datacom, BBN, and others. In recent years, Klos Technologies, Inc., has made available several PC-based software products, including LAN and WAN protocol analysis tools and a DOS PPP client package with support for both IP and IPX.
Name of Product	PacketView
Terms	Reduced-functionality live demo
Description	PacketView is a low-cost PC-based protocol analyzer for Ethernet, token-ring, ARCNET, and FDDI networks. PacketView uses either a packet driver or ODI driver in promiscuous mode to collect packets from the network, supporting expanded memory to store packets. PacketView can decode many standard protcols, including TCP/UDP/IP, SNMP, IPX/SPX/NCP/RIP/SAP, NetBIOS, Vines IP, and more. Custom protocol decoders can easily be added to PacketView.
Cost	$299
Discount	NA
Ordering	We accept company purchase order, VISA, MasterCard, Discover, and American Express
Name of Product	SerialView
Terms	Reduced-functionality live demo
Description	SerialView is a low-cost PC-based asynchronous protocol analyzer for use in async PPP, SLIP, NRN (NetWare Connect), and Vines Block Async (PC-Dialin) environments. SerialView requires a PC with two standard async ports and a SerialView cable to capture packets between two async devices, supporting expanded memory to store packets. SerialView can decode many low-level protocols, including LCP, PAP, CHAP, IPCP, IPXCP, ATCP, NBFCP, VJ

Compression (both PPP and CSLIP), and CIPX (IPX Header Compression), as well as TCP/UDP/IP, SNMP, IPX/SPX/NCP/RIP/SAP, NetBIOS, Vines IP, and more. Custom protocol decoders can easily be added to SerialView.

Cost	$399
Discount	NA
Ordering	We accept company purchase order, VISA, MasterCard, Discover, and American Express.
Name of Product	PPP Remote Client
Terms	Time-limited live demo
Description	PPP is a fully standard PPP ODI driver for DOS PCs using standard async ports. PPP supports LCP, PAP, CHAP, IPCP, and IPXCP. PPP comes with an easy-to-use dial/configuration program, as well as several utilities, including a program to allow Ethernet packet driver-based IP stacks to utilize the PPP driver. PPP has been tested and works with Cisco, Cayman Systems, Livingston, Shiva, Xylogics, and Xyplex terminal servers.
Cost	$29.95 for single user, $129.95 for five user. Higher quantities and per-port site licenses available.
Discount	NA
Ordering	We accept company purchase order, VISA, MasterCard, Discover, and American Express.

Microsoft

Contact Name	Teresa Fagan
Address	Microsoft TechNet One Microsoft Way Redmond, WA 98052-6399
Phone Number	(800) 344-2121
Fax Number	(206) 936-7329

Online E-mail Addresses	Internet: technet@microsoft.com
Online Support Areas	CompuServe: GO TECHNET
Company Description	Microsoft TechNet is the frontline resource for fast, complete answers to technical questions on Microsoft desktop and system products. When you subscribe to Microsoft TechNet, you'll receive two CDs every month with over 100,000 pages of up-to-date technical information. The first disc is packed with current technical notes and backgrounders, Microsoft Resource Kits, the entire Microsoft Knowledge Base, and much more. The second disc contains the latest drivers and patches to keep your systems running smoothly. With these two CDs, you'll have the most complete collection of Microsoft technical information available anywhere, right at your fingertips.
Name of Product	Microsoft TechNet
Terms	Sample TechNet content
Description	see above
Cost	Single one year subscription: $299 U.S. $399 CDN Single server-unlimited users license: $699 U.S. $999 CDN
Discount	NA
Ordering	To subscribe to Microsoft TechNet, see your local authorized reseller, or call (800) 344-2121, weekdays between 6:30 a.m. and 5:30 p.m. (pacific time)

Off-Site Labs

Contact Name	Rodney Copeland
Address	P.O. Box 536 Barker, TX 77413

Phone Number	(800)242-4775 (credit card orders only) (713)524-6394 (credit card orders only)
Fax Number	(713)524-6398
Online E-mail Addresses	Internet: rodney.copeland@bbs.hal-pc.org
Company Description	Consulting firm providing software development, hardware integration, evaluations, and networking solutions.
Name of Product	WorkStation Clone
Terms	Full working system. Requires registration after 30 days. Each registered copy is licensed for 10 servers.
Description	Network client installation utility. Windows application maintains model configurations. Install disk allows configuration duplication.
Cost	$25.00
Discount	NA
Ordering	Use telephone numbers for ordering only. Support calls should be directed to the company's e-mail address.

OnDemand Software, Inc.

Contact Name	Jack Palmer
Address	1100 Fifth Avenue South Suite 208 Naples, FL 33940
Phone Number	(800)368-5207 (941)261-6678
FAX Number	(941)261-6549
Online E-mail Addresses	Internet: sales@ondemand.com
Online Support Areas	Internet: support@ondemand.com CompuServe: GO ONDEMAND

Company Description	OnDemand Software, Inc., is a software development and marketing company specializing in products that assist in network management.
Name of Product	WinINSTALL
Terms	Full Working Copy with time out option 15 days after it is installed. The evaluation can be brought back up for an additional 15 days with a telephone call to OnDemand.
Description	WinINSTALL is best way to install/uninstall software on any network. WinINSTALL eliminates the need for complicated scripting languages with the DISCOVER feature that monitors all the changes made during an installation including all changes to .INI files, all ASCII files, automatically builds icons and program groups and automatically updates the registration database or the registry in a Windows 95 client or NT client. WinINSTALL offers three delivery methods for packages including automatic, interactive, or via electronic mail attachments. WinINSTALL provides full integration with network management systems such as Microsoft Systems Management Server, Novell NMS, Tally Systems NetCensus and CentaMeter, Bindview NCS, and many others and is truly a best of class software distribution product supporting Novell 3.*x* and 4.*x*, NT, Banyan, LAN Manager, LAN Server, as well as NFS.
Cost	$495/license (50 user) $695/license (100 user) $1,295/license (250 user)
Discount	10%
Ordering	By phone, Fax, e-mail or snail mail

ON Technology Corporation

Contact Name	NA
Address	One Cambridge Center Cambridge, MA 02142
Phone Number	(800)406-5828 (617)374-1400
Fax Number	(617)374-1433
Online E-mail Addresses	NA
Online Support Areas	http://www.on.com
Company Description	ON Technology is a leading provider of networking products that connect and manage DOS, Windows, Macintosh, and Unix workstations on networks. In addition to SofTrack software metering ON Technology DaVinci e-MAIL, Notework E-mail, AuditTrack, Meeting Maker XP, and Common Knowledge. ON Technology now has more than 4 million users world-wide.
Name of Product	SofTrack
Term	30-day trial of SofTrack. Full working copy that times out 30 days after installation.
Description	By limiting the number of people using an application to the number of licenses that you own, SofTrack keeps you legal. If a user requests an application and all the licenses are in use, the user is put into a queue and notified immediately when a license becomes available.
Cost	Prices start from $495 and vary with size of server license.

Peripheral Technology Group

Contact Name	David Mastbaum
Address	7625 Golden Triangle Drive Suite T Eden Prairie, MN 55344
Phone Number	(800)875-0068 (612)942-7474
Fax Number	(612)942-7586
Online E-mail Addresses	Internet: sales@ptgs.com
Online Support Areas	Internet: sales@ptgs.com ftp.netinst.com
Company Description	Peripheral Technology Group, Inc. is a domestic and international distributor of PC/MAC to UNIX/INTERNET InterConnectivity Products representing Network Instruments.
Name of Product	Observer
Terms	Demo software only, call for full working demo
Description	A powerful Microsoft Windows-based network monitor and LAN analyzation tool. With Observer, a LAN user or network administrator can view their LAN more clearly, see network traffic in real time and with this new information, make network decisions based on facts not guesswork. Once you use Observer, you will wonder how you ever got along without this effective tool. Observer removes the mystery of what is being sent or received by anyone on your LAN.
Cost	$295 for 1-25 user LAN $495 for 25+ user LAN
Discount	20%
Ordering	all
Name of Product	Analyst/Probe

Terms	Demo software only, call for full working demo
Description	Analyst/Probe is a network protocol analyzer and LAN monitoring tool for multi-segment LANs and WANs. With Analyst/Probe you can improve network performance, monitor bandwidth utilization, collect statistics by user, packet size, or protocol, and capture, view, and decode LAN traffic. More importantly, Analyst/Probe lets you to perform these functions from a single location for any LAN or WAN segment in your network.
Cost	$795 $195 for additional PROBES
Discount	20%
Ordering	all
Name of Product	NIPrint
Terms	21-day full working evaluation
Description	NIPrint is a leader in a new generation of high-performance print servers based on Windows sockets. NIPrint employs the industry standard LPD/LPR protocol to transfer print jobs to and from remote Unix hosts and Windows PCs. Using LPD/LPR protocol makes NIPrint inherently compatible with the vast majority of Unix and other systems that implement LPD services.
Cost	$29 Site Licensing available
Discount	20%
Ordering	all
Name of Product	FarPRINT and FarPRINT/264
Terms	21-day full working evaluation

Description	LPD/LPR NLM for the Netware Server FarPRINT allows direct cross-mapping of Unix and NetWare print queues. FarPRINT enriches any Unix/NetWare installation, providing immediate, high-speed, reliable, bi-directional server-to-server printing. FarPRINT employs the industry standard LPD/LPR protocol to transfer print jobs to and from remote Unix hosts and NetWare Servers. Using LPD/LPR protocol makes FarPRINT inherently compatible with the vast majority of Unix and other systems that implement LPD services. With FarPRINT you no longer need to use an intermediate PC when printing from Novell to Unix or Unix to Novell. Server-to-server print queue mapping enhances both end user usability and overall reliability when printing from one environment to another.
Cost	A single Netware Server license for FarPRINT is $395 U.S. / £395 UK A single Netware Server license for FarPRINT/264 is $795 U.S. / £795 UK
Discount	20%
Ordering	all
Name of Product	LANdecoder/e
Terms	Demo only or call for full version with 30-day money-back guarantee.
Description	Troubleshooting and learning tool for anyone whose job includes Ethernet LAN support and maintenance. LANdecoder/e performs the following three major functions: ✔ monitors and captures traffic from an Ethernet LAN ✔ performs protocol analysis of the captured traffic ✔ generates LAN traffic

LANdecoder/e lets you see what is really happening on your LAN. It includes decode suites for all major LAN operating systems. It is an affordable, software only solution. You provide a LAN adapter card and a computer to make your own protocol analysis station. Choose a machine: 286, 386, 486, or PCMCIA-equipped sub-notebook, to meet your performance and portability requirements.

Cost A single copy of LANdecoder/e is $945 U.S.

Discount 20%

Ordering all

Name of Product LANdecoder/tr

Terms Demo only or call for full version with 30-day money-back guarantee.

Description Troubleshooting and diagnostic tool that is designed to capture, analyze, and interpret data on your Token Ring LAN. LANdecoder/tr performs the following three major functions:

- ✔ monitors and captures traffic from an IBM Token Ring/IEEE 802.5 4 or 16 MBS LAN
- ✔ performs protocol analysis of the captured traffic
- ✔ generates LAN traffic

Some of the many capabilities that LANdecoder/tr uses to assist you include full seven-layer decode of the captured frames, monitors network activity of all communicating station pairs, shows overall network utilization, excellent filtering and triggering capabilities, and a capacity for planning.

LANdecoder/tr is an affordable, software-only solution. All you provide is a supported Token Ring adapter card and a computer. Since LANdecoder/tr is software-based, it is portable

	and can turn most any DOS-based PC workstation on your network into a powerful protocol analysis.
Cost	A single copy is $1,195 U.S.
Discount	20%
Ordering	all
Name of Product	EtherVision & TokenVision
Terms	Demo Only or call for full version with 30-day money-back guarantee.
Description	Both EtherVision and TokenVision are low-cost real time Ethernet and Token Ring LAN Monitors that monitor and display the activity of an Ethernet or Token Ring LAN respectively. A single workstation can monitor all the traffic present on the Ethernet or Token Ring that it is attached to. Both EtherVision and TokenVision are DOS-based programs that take advantage of a site's exisiting PC and network cards and works with all Ethernet and Token Ring media types. Therefore no other hardware is necessary.
Cost	A single copy of EtherVision is $395 U.S. A single copy of TokenVision is $495 U.S.
Discount	20%
Ordering	all

Podell Systems, Inc.

Contact Name	Thomas McLamore
Address	2001 Union Street, Suite 450 San Francisco, CA 94123
Phone Number	(800)350-0001 (415)292-1634
Fax Number	(415)292-6938

Online E-mail Address	CompuServe: 74777,3134
Online Support Areas	CompuServe: GO PODELL
Company Description	Podell Systems develops graphical network management utilities that work directly from the Novell server console. Podells tools are NLMs that are loaded and run at the server console and display on the file server console screen. Although Podell's server-based tools are often run through RCONSOLE from a client, they are designed to be fully functional without a client. The tools and utilities that are developed by Podell Systems are thoroughly tested on all current versions of NetWare and are fully certified by Novell Labs as Tested and Approved NLM applications.
Name of Product	Console Manager for NetWare V1.01b
Terms	Fully functional demo copy expires on October 31, 1996
Description	Console Manager for NetWare is a graphical and easy-to-use network management utility that works directly from the Novell server console. Console Manager for NetWare greatly enhances the limited command-line utilities supplied by Novell and provides the NetWare system administrator with a combination of client-based utilities with server functions in a single package. Console Manager for NetWare provides users with a Microsoft-Windows like DOS interface with hot key strokes, pull-down menus, and function keys.
Cost	1 server license $795 5 server license $2,750 10 server license $5,000
Discount	60%
Ordering	By phone, e-mail, or Fax
Name of Product	Print Manager for NetWare V1.10
Terms	Fully functional 30 day-demonstration

Description	Print Manager for NetWare provides all of the features of Novell's PCONSOLE, but is an NLM that loads and works directly on the Novell file server console. Print Manager for NetWare is a Windows-like print queue management utility that has been enhanced with the ability to view the contents of text files in the queue. Any file on any queue can be examined, held, reprioritized, or deleted. The queue status is updated in real time. This product is especially useful as a queue monitor when run on a server near a printer. Print Manager for NetWare runs on and is certified Tested and Approved by Novell Labs for NetWare 3.11 through 4.10, including SFT III and SMP. Print Manager for NetWare also has a screen for setting up, monitoring, and configuring bindery mode Print Queues, Print Servers, and attached printers. Great efforts have been made to simplify and increase ease of use of this occasionally used, but important area of NetWare. Each step necessary for the connection of a printer to the server and associating it with a queue is logically laid out with additional descriptive detail being provided in the online help and user manual.
Cost	$450
Discount	$180
Ordering	By phone, e-mail, or Fax

Safetynet, Inc.

Contact Name	NA
Address	140 Mountain Ave. Springfield, NJ 07081 USA
Phone Number	(800)OS2-SAFE (908)276-9641
FAX Number	(201)467-1611

Online E-mail Addresses	Internet: safety@safe.net
Online Support Areas	CompuServe: GO SAFE http://www.safe.net/safety/ ftp://ftp.safe.net/pub/safetynet/
Company Description	Safetynet, Inc., develops leading antivirus, security, and network management software. Our products support all major networks running DOS, Windows, and OS/2 clients. Our cross-platform approach and low memory overhead designs are ideal for heterogeneous environments.
Name of Product	Drive-In LAN
Terms	Full-blown evaluation version
Description	Drive-In LAN provides instant access to programs and DOS commands. Menu choices can be logically grouped, with up to twenty choices per menu and eight menu levels. Drive-In LAN provides shared and private menus, dynamic menu display, and no memory overhead. By changing a user's network privileges, menus will automatically change to reflect the new user rights. There are no scripts or compiler commands to learn. Password protection is available for each menu choice, including Exit to DOS and Program Setup. When a menu choice is selected, you can prompt the user for additional information. File and directory windows assist the user's selection.
Cost	$495/server for unlimited workstations
Discount	25%
Ordering	Specify the number of servers that will run Drive-In LAN for additional quantity discounts.
Name of Product	StopLight LAN
Terms	Full-blown evaluation version
Description	StopLight LAN provides centrally installed and controlled security for network workstations. It was recently given a 4-node review by *LAN Times.*

	Protection is available on bootup, controlling access to the workstation hard disk. Security is managed from the server by an elegant Windows security console. Full drag and drop capability along with pop-up menus make security management effortless. On the workstation, StopLight LAN provides hard disk access control, pass-thru login, audit log, keyboard lock/screen saver and secure files, directories, floppy drives, and I/O ports. 13 KB of total memory overhead on the client is required.
Cost	$1495/10 workstations
Discount	25%
Ordering	Contact Safetynet for substantial quantity discounts.
Name of Product	VirusNet LAN
Terms	Full-blown evaluation version
Description	VirusNet LAN is an NCSA-certified antivirus and disaster system. It protects against existing and unknown viruses by dual signature, checksum, and heuristic scanning. VirusNet LAN combines the antivirus protection of VirusNet with the powerful central managment found in our LAN Scheduler and Distribution system. The result is fully automatic anti-virus protection for several or hundreds of workstations. VirusNet LAN is preconfigured to maintain workstation files, monitor for virus infections and update workstations with the latest files. It can also distribute your own software and schedule your own events, making it an unbeatable value. 3.5 KB of total memory overhead on the client is required for real-time protection.
Cost	$995/server for up to 50 workstations
Discount	25%
Ordering	Contact Safetynet for substantial quantity discounts.

Scott Wertz

Contact Name	Scott Wertz
Address	19099 Brookfield Road Aurora, OH 44202
Phone Number	NA
FAX Number	NA
Online E-mail Addresses	CompuServe: 71541,3051
Online Support Areas	CompuServe e-mail
Company Description	Independent developer
Name of Product	ZZNotify
Terms	Fully working, timed demo
Description	ZZNotify is a program that uses native NetWare broadcast (SEND) messages to notify users when they have unread mail waiting. No TSR or Windows program is required. The notification interval is set by the network administrator. An excellent addition to FirstMail in NetWare 3.12, but runs with any version of MHS.
Cost	$25
Discount	NA
Ordering	By mail, check, or money order in U.S. funds only
Name of Product	ZZPeg
Terms	Fully working, timed demo
Description	ZZPeg is a program that uses native NetWare broadcast (SEND) messages to notify users when they have unread Pegasus mail. No TSR or Windows program is required. The notification interval is set by the network administrator.
Cost	$25
Discount	NA

Ordering	By mail, check or money order in U.S. funds only
Name of Product	ZZClear
Terms	Fully working
Description	ZZClear works just like Novell's NLICLEAR.NLM to clear NOT-LOGGED-IN connections, but ZZClear only does so when you need more free connection slots, and will NOT clear stations that you specify in a config file.
Cost	Freeware
Discount	NA
Ordering	NA

Secure Design

Contact Name	NA
Address	PO Box 475 Corvallis, OR 97339 USA
Phone Number	(541)752-5988
FAX Number	(541)752-5990
Online E-mail Addresses	Internet : support@sdesign.com
Online Support Areas	http://www.peak.org/~sdesign
Company Description	Secure Design is a software company committed to writing quality applications for network management.
Name of Product	SDLP v1.12
Terms	60-day full demo
Description	SDLP is a NetWare Loadable Module (NLM) that provides the ability to transfer print jobs between NetWare print queues, and Unix print queues. SDLP acts as a print server/client that

	implements the LPR/LPD protocol as described in RFC 1179. Supports NetWare 3.*x* and 4.*x* with bindery emulation.
Cost	$80/fileserver
Discount	NA
Ordering	By phone, e-mail, or Fax
Name of Product	QView Pro v2.24
Terms	60-day full demo
Description	QView Pro is a print queue management tool for Novell networks. QView Pro is a utility designed to allow complete control of multiple print queues. Most of the functions provided in Novell's pconsole are available in QView Pro. QView Pro also allows the operator to view the contents of more than one print queue at a time, move jobs between queues, view the job contents, and other queue management functions. QView Pro can also monitor print queues and make changes automatically. Supports NetWare v2.*x*, 3.*x* and 4.*x*.
Cost	$80/fileserver
Discount	NA
Ordering	By phone, e-mail, or Fax

Support Group, Inc.

Contact Name	NA
Address	Lake Technology Park P.O. Box 130 McHenry, MD 21541 USA
Phone Number	(800)872-4768 (301)387-4500
Fax Number	(301)387-7322
Online E-mail Addresses	Compuserve: 74020,10

Online Support Areas	CompuServe: GO TAPCIS
Company Description	Publisher of TAPCIS; The Access Program for the CompuServe Information Service (since 1986)
Name of Product	TAPCIS Version 6.0 for DOS
Terms	30-day "trial" period
Description	TAPCIS Version 6.0 is the program that makes CompuServe fit both your pocketbook and your busy schedule. The Version 6.0 interface includes mouse support, pull-down menus, and intuitive keystrokes. It has unsurpassed message "threading," user-definable message "Views" (allowing messages to be displayed in virtually any combination and order), fully automated file uploading and downloading, and much more. Version 6.0 is all the software you need to connect to CompuServe, send and receive Mail and transfer files, participate in Forum messages and Conferences, capture weather forecasts, stock quotes, and much more.
Cost	$79.00 U.S. + $3.50 shipping and handling
Discount	NA
Ordering	By phone, Fax, e-mail, or online via CompuServe — GO SWREG

TAC Systems

Contact Name	Larry Katz
Address	1035 Putman Drive, Suite A Huntsville, AL 35816
Phone Number	(205) 721-1976
FAX Number	(205) 721-0242
Online E-mail Addresses	Internet: sales@tacsys.com

Online Support Areas	Internet: support@tacsys.com,www.tacsys.com
Company Description	TAC Systems, Inc., is an Alabama-based corporation that designs and builds data storage peripherals for computer networks. Founded in 1991 by Luis Ayala, the company has realized steady growth in sales since the introduction of the CD-ROM TowerDrive and SCSI Shuttle NLM.
Name of Product	SCSI Shuttle for NetWare
Terms	Will allow only 2 CD-ROM drives per server
Description	SCSI Shuttle in an NLM that extends the functionality of the existing file server by enhancing its ability to manage and share CD-ROM resources. No TSRs or additional software need be added to client workstations and no additional user training is necessary. Supports up to 63 drives.
Cost	$1,295
Discount	10%
Ordering	By phone, e-mail, or Fax
Name of Product	SCSI Shuttle for NetWare Lite
Terms	Will allow only 2 CD-ROM drives per server
Description	SCSI Shuttle in an NLM that extends the functionality of the existing file server by enhancing its ability to manage and share CD-ROM resources. No TSRs or additional software need be added to client workstations and no additional user training is necessary. Supports up to 7 drives.
Cost	$695
Discount	10%
Ordering	By phone, e-mail, or Fax

VFX Technologies

Contact Name	Michael Herrick
Address	PO Box 80222 Valley Forge, PA 19484-0222
Phone Number	(610)265-9222
FAX Number	(610)265-6007
Online E-mail Addresses	Internet: vfxtech@ix.netcom.com CompuServe: 70543,366 America Online: VFX

Company Description	VFX Technologies, Inc., is a young software development company. We specialize in creating powerful, low-cost self-evaluation tools to help those preparing for certification testing. Our applications deliver the necessary means to both identify and intelligently manage personal learning needs. Our expert team utilizes extensive experience to develop products that will significantly impact and leverage the user's time and material investments. It is our goal to meet the challenges of the future by continually developing progressive products and providing unequaled customer service.
Name of Product	CNE Endeavor
Terms	Evaluation
Description	CNE Endeavor for Windows is a new, unique, and powerful CNE test preparation application. As you will discover, the Endeavor interface tests your knowledge of NetWare through a series of comprehensive questions and answers. By recording an extensive performance history, the program can quickly help you identify your areas of consistent strength and weakness. Through the "control panel," it's easy to define the necessary criteria to construct personalized tests from the extensive database. Unlike multiple choice products, CNE Endeavor challenges you to correctly answer questions,

not simply identify a valid response. This version contains the complete interface, plus over 500 of the more than 5,000 available questions.

Cost $99.95

Discount 15%

Ordering Please note that some of the tests contained in this evaluation software are sold separately.

CHILAGA
NORVMBEGA
FRANCIA
MOCOSA
AVACAL
APALCHEN
CALICVAS
CAPASCHI
TERLICHICHIMECHI
LA FLORIDA
TEAC.
MARATA.
CVLIACAN
ASTATLAN
HISPANIA NOVA
TOPIRA
MECHVACAN
CVBA
HISPANIOLA
MAR DEL SVR, quod
Circulus Æquinoctialis
PACIFICVM
CAE SIVE
ORBIS NO
SCRIPTIO.
CHARCAS
PARANA
CHILE
PATAGONES
Archipelago del C. deseado

C

APPENDIX

Vendor NIC Identifier Codes

The IEEE assigns the first six bytes of the physical layer addresses of your NICs to the manufacturer. You might sometimes find yourself with a card and need to determine what it is, but have no idea where to look.

This appendix includes a basic listing of many of the currently assigned IDs. Owing to the nature of networking, however, the IEEE regularly assigns new IDs. If you would like to receive an up-to-date master lising of all company-assigned IDs, use one of the following three methods:

- ✔ Send e-mail to info.stds.oui@ieee.org to receive a full listing via e-mail.
- ✔ If you have Internet access, you can retrieve the master listing via anonymous FTP from ftp.ieee.org as /info/stds/info.stds.oui.
- ✔ If you do not have Internet access, but do have dial-up access, you can contact the IEEE and retrieve the file using the following information:

Phone (2400bps):	908-981-0290
Phone (>2400bps):	908-981-0035
Emulation Mode:	VT100
COM Settings:	E71

Other:	Login as "guest" and retrieve the file OUILIST.TXT from the LOBBY/IEEEstds directory

Hex	Manufacturer
00-00-0C	CISCO
00-00-0E	FUJITSU
00-00-0F	NEXT
00-00-0E	FUJITSU LIMITED
00-00-1B	NOVELL, INC.
00-00-23	ABB AUTOMATION AB, DEPT.
00-00-31	QPSX COMMUNICATIONS
00-00-37	OXFORD METRICS
00-00-3C	AUSPEX SYSTEMS
00-00-3F	SYNTREX, INC.
00-00-46	OLIVETTI NORTH AMERICA
00-00-49	APRICOT COMPUTERS
00-00-4C	NEC CORPORATION
00-00-50	RADISYS CORPORATION
00-00-51	HOB ELECTRONIC
00-00-52	OPTICAL DATA SYSTEMS
00-00-58	RACORE COMPUTER PRODUCTS
00-00-5E	USC INFORMATION SCIENCES
00-00-61	GATEWAY COMMUNICATIONS
00-00-65	NETWORK GENERAL CORPORATION
00-00-68	ROSEMOUNT CONTROLS
00-00-6D	CRAY COMMUNICATIONS, LTD.

Hex	Manufacturer
00-00-6E	ARTISOFT, INC.
00-00-6F	MADGE NETWORKS, LTD.
00-00-74	RICOH COMPANY
00-00-79	NETWORTH INCORPORATED
00-00-7D	CRAY RESEARCH SUPERSERVERS, INC.
00-00-8A	DATAHOUSE INFORMATION SYSTEMS
00-00-93	PROTEON
00-00-94	ASANTE TECHNOLOGIES
00-00-98	CROSSCOMM CORPORATION
00-00-99	MEMOREX TELEX CORPORATION
00-00-94	ASANTE TECHNOLOGIES
00-00-A2	WELLFLEET
00-00-A3	NETWORK APPLICATION TECHNOLOGY
00-00-A4	ACORN COMPUTERS, LTD
00-00-A5	COMPATIBLE SYSTEM CORP
00-00-A7	NETWORK COMPUTING DEVICES, INC.
00-00-A8	STRATUS COMPUTER, INC.
00-00-A9	NETWORK SYSTEMS CORP.
00-00-AA	XEROX CORPORATION
00-00-B1	ALPHA MICROSYSTEMS, INC.
00-00-B6	MICRO-MATIC RESEARCH
00-00-B7	DOVE COMPUTER CORPORATION
00-00-C1	OLICOM A/S
00-00-E3	INTEGRATED MICRO PRODUCTS, LTD.

Hex	Manufacturer
00-00-E7	STAR GATE TECHNOLOGIES
00-00-E8	ACCTON TECHNOLOGY CORP.
00-00-E9	ISICAD, INC.
00-00-F4	ALLIED TELESIS
00-00-F8	DIGITAL EQUIPMENT CORPORATION
00-02-67	NODE RUNNER
00-07-01	RACAL DATACOM
00-20-00	LEXMARK INTERNATIONAL
00-20-02	SERITECH ENTERPRISE CO.
00-20-03	PIXEL POWER
00-20-04	YAMATAKE-HONEYWELL
00-20-05	SIMPLE TECHNOLOGY
00-20-08	CABLE AND COMPUTER TECHNOLOGY
00-20-09	PACKARD BELL ELEC., INC.
00-20-0A	SOURCE-COMM
00-20-0B	OCTAGON SYSTEMS CORP.
00-20-0C	ADASTRA SYSTEMS CORP.
00-20-0E	SATELLITE TECHNOLOGY MANAGEMENT
00-20-0F	TANBAC CO.
00-20-10	JEOL SYSTEM TECHNOLOGY
00-20-11	CANOPUS CO.
00-20-12	CAMTRONICS MEDICAL SYSTEMS
00-20-14	GLOBAL VIEW CO., LTD.
00-20-18	CIS TECHNOLOGY, INC.

Hex	Manufacturer
00-20-1B	NORTHERN TELECOM
00-20-1C	EXCEL, INC.
00-20-1D	KATANA PRODUCTS
00-20-1E	NETQUEST CORPORATION
00-20-1F	BEST POWER TECHNOLOGY
00-20-20	MEGATRON COMPUTER INDUSTRIES
00-20-21	ALGORITHMS SOFTWARE
00-20-22	TEKNIQUE, INC.
00-20-23	T.C. TECHNOLOGIES
00-20-24	PACIFIC COMMUNICATION SCIENCES
00-20-25	CONTROL TECHNOLOGY
00-20-26	AMKLY SYSTEMS
00-20-27	MING FORTUNE INDUSTRY
00-20-28	WEST EGG SYSTEMS, INC.
00-20-29	TELEPROCESSING PRODUCTS
00-20-2B	ADVANCED TELECOMMUNICATIONS
00-20-2C	WELLTRONIX CO., LTD.
00-20-2D	TAIYO CORPORATION
00-20-2E	DAYSTAR DIGITAL
00-20-2F	ZETA COMMUNICATIONS, LTD.
00-20-30	ANALOG AND DIGITAL SYSTEMS
00-20-31	ERTEC
00-20-32	ALCATEL TAISEL
00-20-33	SYNAPSE TECHNOLOGIES

Hex	Manufacturer
00-20-34	ROTEC
00-20-35	CPN ARCHITECTURES/IBM CORP.
00-20-36	BMC SOFTWARE
00-20-37	SEAGATE TECHNOLOGY
00-20-38	VME MICROSYSTEMS INTERNATIONAL
00-20-39	SCINETS
00-20-3A	DIGITAL BIOMETRICS
00-20-3B	WISDM, LTD
00-20-3C	EUROTIME
00-20-3D	NOVAR ELECTRONICS
00-20-3E	LOGICAN TECHNOLOGIES
00-20-3F	JUKI CORP.
00-20-42	DATAMETRICS
00-20-43	NEURON COMPANY
00-20-44	GENITECH
00-20-45	SOLCOM SYSTEMS
00-20-46	CIPRICO
00-20-48	FORE SYSTEMS
00-20-49	COMTRON, INC.
00-20-4A	PRONET
00-20-4B	AUTOCOMPUTER CO.
00-20-4C	MITRON COMPUTER
00-20-4D	INOVIS
00-20-4E	NETWORK SECURITY SYSTEMS, INC.

Hex	Manufacturer
00-20-4F	DEUTSCHE AEROSPACE
00-20-50	KOREA COMPUTER, INC.
00-20-51	PHOENIX DATA COMMUNICATIONS
00-20-52	RAGULA SYSTEMS
00-20-53	HUNTSVILLE MICROSYSTEMS
00-20-54	EASTERN RESEARCH
00-20-55	ALTECH CO.
00-20-56	NEOPRODUCTS
00-20-57	TITZE DATENTECHNIK
00-20-58	ALLIED SIGNAL, INC.
00-20-59	MIRO COMPUTER PRODUCTS
00-20-5A	COMPUTER IDENTICS
00-20-5B	SKYLINE TECHNOLOGY
00-20-5C	INTERNET SYSTEMS
00-20-64	PROTEC MICROSYSTEMS, INC.
00-20-69	ISDN SYSTEMS CORPORATION
00-20-6C	EVERGREEN TECHNOLOGY CORP.
00-20-6D	DATA RACE, INC.
00-20-80	SYNERGY (UK), LTD.
00-20-82	ONEAC CORPORATION
00-20-89	T3PLUS NETWORKING, INC.
00-20-8C	GALAXY NETWORKS, INC.
00-20-90	ADVANCED COMPRESSION
00-20-94	CUBIX CORPORATION

Hex	Manufacturer
00-20-95	RIVA ELECTRONICS
00-20-A2	GALCOM NETWORKING, LTD.
00-20-A3	DIVICOM, INC.
00-20-A4	MULTIPOINT NETWORKS
00-20-AA	NTL
00-20-AF	3COM CORPORATION
00-20-B0	GATEWAY DEVICES, INC.
00-20-B1	COMTECH RESEARCH, INC.
00-20-BE	LAN ACCESS CORP.
00-20-C5	EAGLE TECHNOLOGY
00-20-C6	NECTEC
00-20-CA	DIGITAL OCEAN
00-20-CC	DIGITAL SERVICES, LTD.
00-20-CD	HYBRID NETWORKS, INC.
00-20-DB	XNET TECHNOLOGY, INC.
00-20-EA	EFFICIENT NETWORKS, INC.
00-20-EC	TECHWARE SYSTEMS CORP.
00-20-ED	GIGA-BYTE TECHNOLOGY CO., LTD.
00-20-FB	OCTEL COMMUNICATIONS CORP.
00-40-0D	LANNET DATA COMMUNICATIONS, LTD.
00-40-27	SMC MASSACHUSETTS, INC.
00-40-32	DIGITAL COMMUNICATIONS
00-40-48	SMD INFORMATICA S.A.
00-40-50	IRONICS, INC.

Hex	Manufacturer
00-40-52	STAR TECHNOLOGIES, INC.
00-40-57	LOCKHEED - SANDERS
00-40-76	AMP, INC.
00-40-82	LABORATORY EQUIPMENT CORP.
00-40-91	PROCOMP INDUSTRIA ELECTRONICA
00-40-92	ASP COMPUTER PRODUCTS, INC.
00-40-9A	NETWORK EXPRESS, INC.
00-40-9C	TRANSWARE
00-40-9D	DIGIBOARD, INC.
00-40-9F	LANCAST/CASAT TECHNOLOGY, INC.
00-40-A6	CRAY RESEARCH, INC.
00-40-B4	3COM K.K.
00-40-BD	STARLIGHT NETWORKS, INC.
00-40-E9	ACCORD SYSTEMS, INC.
00-40-ED	NETWORK CONTROLS INTNATL, INC.
00-40-F0	MICRO SYSTEMS, INC.
00-40-FF	TELEBIT CORPORATION
00-60-8C	3COM CORPORATION
00-80-16	WANDEL AND GOLTERMANN
00-80-23	INTEGRATED BUSINESS NETWORKS
00-80-26	NETWORK PRODUCTS CORPORATION
00-80-2D	XYLOGICS, INC.
00-80-5B	CONDOR SYSTEMS, INC.
00-80-69	COMPUTONE SYSTEMS

Hex	Manufacturer
00-80-8E	RADSTONE TECHNOLOGY
00-80-90	MICROTEK INTERNATIONAL, INC.
00-80-93	XYRON CORPORATION
00-80-98	TDK CORPORATION
00-80-9A	NOVUS NETWORKS, LTD.
00-80-9F	ALCATEL BUSINESS SYSTEMS
00-80-A1	MICROTEST
00-80-A3	LANTRONIX
00-80-AD	CNET TECHNOLOGY, INC.
00-80-F3	SUN ELECTRONICS CORP.
00-C0-00	LANOPTICS, LTD.
00-C0-0D	ADVANCED LOGIC RESEARCH, INC.
00-C0-13	NETRIX
00-C0-19	LEAP TECHNOLOGY, INC.
00-C0-1D	GRAND JUNCTION NETWORKS, INC.
00-C0-21	NETEXPRESS
00-C0-27	CIPHER SYSTEMS, INC.
00-C0-33	TELEBIT COMMUNICATIONS APS
00-C0-51	ADVANCED INTEGRATION RESEARCH
00-C0-58	DATAEXPERT CORP.
00-C0-5B	NETWORKS NORTHWEST, INC.
00-C0-64	GENERAL DATACOMM IND., INC.
00-C0-6D	BOCA RESEARCH, INC.
00-C0-7D	RISC DEVELOPMENTS, LTD.

Hex	Manufacturer
00-C0-84	DATA LINK CORP., LTD.
00-C0-87	UUNET TECHNOLOGIES, INC.
00-C0-8F	MATSUSHITA ELECTRIC WORKS, LTD.
00-C0-93	ALTA RESEARCH CORP.
00-C0-A0	ADVANCE MICRO RESEARCH, INC.
00-C0-A8	GVC CORPORATION
00-C0-AC	GAMBIT COMPUTER COMMUNICATIONS
00-C0-AF	TEKLOGIX, INC.
00-C0-B5	CORPORATE NETWORK SYSTEMS, INC.
00-C0-B7	AMERICAN POWER CONVERSION CORP.
00-C0-C2	INFINITE NETWORKS, LTD.
00-C0-D1	COMTREE TECHNOLOGY CORPORATION
00-C0-DB	IPC CORPORATION (PTE), LTD.
00-C0-DE	ZCOMM, INC.
00-C0-EF	ABIT CORPORATION
00-C0-FB	ADVANCED TECHNOLOGY LABS
02-07-01	INTERLAN
02-60-8C	3COM
08-00-02	3COM
08-00-07	APPLE COMPUTER, INC.
08-00-09	HEWLETT-PACKARD
08-00-0D	INTERNATIONAL COMPUTERS, LTD.
08-00-1F	SHARP CORPORATION
08-00-28	TEXAS INSTRUMENTS

Hex	Manufacturer
08-00-2B	DIGITAL EQUIPMENT CORPORATION
08-00-30	CERN
08-00-5A	INTL BUSINESS MACHINES CORP.
08-00-8F	CHIPCOM CORPORATION
10-00-5A	IBM CORPORATION
10-02-41	DCA
AA-00-00	DIGITAL EQUIPMENT CORPORATION
AA-00-03	DIGITAL EQUIPMENT CORPORATION
AA-00-04	DIGITAL EQUIPMENT CORPORATION

NOVA
CHILAGA
NORVMBEGA
MOCOSA
AVACAL
APALCHEN
CALICVAS
CAPASCHI
TERLICHICHIMECHI
LA FLORIDA
TEAC
MARATA
CVLIACAN
ASTATLAN
HISPANIA NOVA
TOVA
CVBA
HISPANIOLA
MECHVACAN
MAR DEL SVR, quod
Circulus Æquinoctialis
CHILI
PATAGONES
CHARCAS
ICAE SIVE
ORBIS NO
SCRIPTIO.
Archipelago del C.
deseado

I
INDEX

A

D

E

F

G-H

I

J-K

N

O

S

T

U

V

W

CD-ROM Quick Start Instructions

1. Insert the CD-ROM into your CD-ROM drive.

2. From File Manager or Program Manager, choose **R**un from the **F**ile menu. (If you are running Windows 95, press the Start Button, select Run, and then Run again.)

3. Type ***<drive>*:\INSTALL** and press Enter (where *<drive>* is the drive letter of your CD-ROM). If your CD-ROM is drive D, for example, type **D:\INSTALL** and press Enter.

4. The Install program opens a Windows write file (.WRI) that provides an overview of the CD-ROM, along with contact information for New Riders Publishing. Install does not copy files to your hard drive. Instead, we invite you to browse Volume 3 of the *Novell 3 CNE Resource Library* to identify the programs you want to install. Volume 3 is devoted entirely to the contents of the CD-ROM. It provides comprehensive coverage of the software on the CD-ROM.

Technical Support:

If your CD-ROM is damaged, please contact our support department.

E-mail: support@mcp.com

World Wide Web: http://www.mcp.com/newriders

Telephone: (317) 381-3833

Fax: (317) 581-4773

Mail: Macmillan Computer Publishing
Attention: Support Department
201 West 103rd Street
Indianapolis, IN 46290-1093